Dynamics at Boardroom Level

How can boards and members of boards reach their full potential? The Tavistock Institute of Human Relations (TIHR) has been at the forefront of thinking about organizations since its inception in 1947. Today, as then, the corporate world is undergoing increasing pressure to demonstrate a sustainable, generative and meaningful impact on society and employees whilst delivering improved services and products. These tensions and others are explored in this important new book, *Dynamics at Boardroom Level: A Tavistock Primer for Leaders, Coaches and Consultants*.

In this book, the reader gets a useful framework of theory and practice that broadens vision and deepens thinking about what is happening in boardrooms. The book opens the door to the reader to a new world of board dynamics, edited by those who really understand the deeper workings of the complex human system and its work at board level. This edited volume brings together insights and contemporary case studies from participants on the Tavistock Institute Dynamics @ Board Level programme that draws on the thinking of Tavistock scholars and practitioners and their work on the dynamics of task, role, authority and power.

Edited by programme co-directors Dr Mannie Sher and Dr Leslie Brissett and their fellow Tavistock Associate Tazi Lorraine Smith, and with contributions from senior leadership practitioners and board evaluators from the government, international consultancy firms, FTSE 100 and global UN institutions, this book speaks directly to issues of our time. It represents essential reading for leaders of organizations and businesses, as well as leadership coaches and mental health professionals.

Leslie Brissett, JP, PhD, is Company Secretary, Principal Consultant/Researcher and Director of the Group Relations Programme at the Tavistock Institute of Human Relations.

Mannie Sher, PhD, is Principal Researcher and Consultant in organizational development and change and an executive coach at the Tavistock Institute of Human Relations.

Tazi Lorraine Smith, BSc, DipPFS, is a management consultant in healthcare.

"The approach of boards vary for obvious reasons – the character of a company's business, the need for public or democratic involvement, a role in supervising wider membership organizations. Yet they need strong, common attributes as well. They should represent and sustain a strong, positive culture, be transparent and as accountable as possible and capable of holding executives to account. For all this complexity too few boards are effectively guided about their internal dynamics or dynamic relationships with others. It is a gap of considerable importance, a source of risk. This book, and The Tavistock Institute approach, are an essential addition to board capabilities."

Lord David Triesman, *Chairman, a Merchant and Investment Bank, Former Chairman of a PLC, The Football Association, and Government Minister*

"The world is at a tipping point and this book is a timely and welcome reminder of the vital need for leaders, in both the organizational and political spheres, to have an understanding of the powerful unconscious forces that can derail any board. It comes at a time too when governance codes are demanding increasingly, and rightly imposing, behavioural requirements for board members. This book should be on the reading list for all leaders who want a deeper awareness of what happens below the surface when group members interact."

Mitzi Wyman, *LLM, MSc, Founder of FulcrumLeaders.com, Ambassador, International Integrated Reporting Council*

"The governance of organizations has never been more important as the demands of an increasingly complex world draw us into considering role, group dynamics, systems, values and outcomes. Boards and how they operate are at the centre of the complex mix of interactions, and how boards function – what makes them 'tick' – has never been more important. This book is a valuable contribution to understanding board functioning and thus the making of better organizations."

Lord Victor Olufemi Adebowale, *Chair, Social Enterprise UK, Board Member, Co-op Group CEO, Turning Point*

Dynamics at Boardroom Level

A Tavistock Primer for Leaders, Coaches and Consultants

**Edited by
Leslie Brissett, Mannie Sher
and Tazi Lorraine Smith**

Foreword by Susan Long

Routledge
Taylor & Francis Group

LONDON AND NEW YORK

First published 2020
by Routledge
2 Park Square, Milton Park, Abingdon, Oxon OX14 4RN

and by Routledge
52 Vanderbilt Avenue, New York, NY 10017

*Routledge is an imprint of the Taylor & Francis Group, an informa
business*

British Library Cataloguing-in-Publication Data
A catalogue record for this book is available from the British Library

Library of Congress Cataloging-in-Publication Data
A catalog record for this book has been requested

ISBN: 978-0-367-41943-1 (hbk)
ISBN: 978-0-367-42087-1 (pbk)
ISBN: 978-0-367-82170-8 (ebk)

Typeset in Times New Roman
by Apex CoVantage, LLC

Contents

PART II
Process, growth and performance 55

PART III
Introduction: States of mind 107

Table and figures

Table

Figures

Foreword

Boards at all levels are increasingly important in today's societies. They have responsibilities for not only the fortune of the companies, associations, groups and community organizations that they govern but hold an important place in decision-making about bigger societal issues such as poverty, climate change, violence, the environment, social equality, health and well-being because our organizations can no longer hold themselves apart from such issues for ethical, social, financial and risk reasons. Because they have such a massive influence, we need to know more about the ways in which they operate and about how they are affected by a vast number of influences from within their own structures and processes as well as from external sources. This book provides a step towards that deeper knowledge.

Go to that ubiquitous 21st century search engine *Google* and you will find multiple entries about political and personal in-fighting in corporates, companies, not-for-profits, schools and community boards. The dysfunction in boards it seems, is primarily attributed to its own internal politics and to individual interests, including the interests of powerful stakeholders.

Not that *Google* itself is free from such dynamics, as noted in its own accounts of the recent dismissal of an external artificial intelligence ethics advisory body to the company.[1] Before even its first meeting, this external council was replaced by a group of internal executives, raising questions of accountability. Bloomberg's Joshua Brustein and Mark Bergen write, "The short life of the external council was a case study in the company's vitriolic internal politics".

It is generally agreed that boards should pay attention to the problems facing the organization from its culture and context – take for example the warning to banks by a senior banking lawyer: "A board needs to plan for both how to recognize discrimination and how to respond forcefully".[2] But what of the culture of the board itself?

There are many stories of power and shifting interests, but do we ever get behind what are seen simply as the political interests of powerful individuals? A board is a human system and the fortunes and risks associated with the purposes, values and tasks of the organization it governs affect the ways in which board members think and feel. What happens when accountabilities weigh so heavily that they create tensions and anxieties; sleeplessness and irritability: all calling, at least at some level, for solutions that dismiss such uncomfortable experiences? Or, alternatively, when already busy people lose sight of purpose and task as they are inundated with voluminous board papers and have to make quick decisions about where to focus their energies. And what of cultural issues within the board itself: unconscious bias; fears of failure; arrogance or complacency following successes?

This book, edited by Mannie Sher, Leslie Brissett and Tazi Lorraine Smith from Britain's Tavistock Institute of Human Relations, looks at these and other associated questions from the perspective of systems psychodynamics (Gould et al., 2004) or socioanalysis (Bain, 1999; Long, 2017). The chapters come from participants and staff of a Tavistock Institute programme: Dynamics @ Board Level. This programme engages participants in learning from experience and provides rigorous theoretical education as well. Participants become part of a temporary board having real effects in the here-and-now of the programme, as well as examining their real-life experiences of the boards they work on or with. The focus is not simply on the individual consciously and deliberately making self-interested decisions but instead on the dynamics of unthinking adherence to peer-pressured cultures; to unconscious collective defences against anxieties in the workplace and in human communication; to inherent biases in cultural assumptions and such dynamics as scapegoating, bullying and envious attacks. Understanding such dynamics enables board members to guard against these destructive influences and work towards creative, collaborative processes.

Boards are charged as caretakers of an organization's purpose, values and future. They must weigh the risks associated with organizational ambitions and face the realities of complex contexts. In so doing they discuss, decide, negotiate, and make alliances – all of which, while seeming rational and consciously deliberated, reflect the social and emotional dynamics present in the social system that is the board. The chapters assembled in this book explore how these social and emotional dynamics lie at the basis of boardroom behaviours and influence those decisions that can be either life-giving to, or destructive of, the organization, its work and its culture.

My own study of organizational dysfunction has led me to see many collusive dynamics between boards, management and a variety of stakeholders. For example, when some board members feel unable to express their views and a culture of dependency dominates, as happened with the Australian insurance company Heath International Holdings; or when the tasks and accountabilities of the board become 'too difficult' to face and a fight/flight dynamic is present; or when pride or greed override prudent decision-making as evidenced in the hedge company Long Term Capital Management or as operated in the case of Italian dairy giant Parmalat's CEO, Calisto Tanzi (Long, 2008).

In my studies, I uncovered what I understand as "perverse dynamics". These are notable at an organizational level and can be seen through five major indices many of which are explored in this book:

1   A narcissistic culture, where self-interest predominates;
2   A culture where denial is a major defence – executives and board members believing "A" and "not A" at the same time – such as seen in the denials given

during cover-up stories when large corporate mistakes are made and hidden yet managers and directors also believe they just need time to rectify such issues, not considering those as mistakes but dips in fortunes. The organizational leaders know they are doing the wrong thing and at the same time think they are doing the right thing in the long run, despite being mistaken – perhaps through pride or ineptness or at times sheer greed (Long, 2012);

3   A culture that draws in accomplices to the denial or cover-up – such as other corporations, banks or regulators. Armstrong and Frances (2008), for instance, describe how greed in one organization corrupted the morals of other organizations with whom they had dealings. This was strongly evident in many cases during the sub-prime crisis leading to global economy collapses in 2008–2009;

4   A culture of instrumentalism where people are used as objects towards an end rather than as persons with their own thoughts, feelings and needs; where bullying or scapegoating may occur;

5   A self-perpetuating culture where facing the issues noted above does not happen.

Most individuals in organizations are not themselves perverse and enter their work with good intentions, wishing to progress the fortunes and purposes of their groups or companies. But organizations are more than just a collection of individuals. They act as a system or entity outside the conscious volition of individuals or small groups, and are in fact treated in the law in many countries as if they are a person (Bakan, 2004) separate from their major players. Just as the editors of this book say about their programme, my interest has never been about "the individual in isolation, not the board in isolation, not the organization in isolation, not the organization's context in isolation, but the dynamic inter-relationships between them all, happening at the same time and in complex ways". An organizational culture, a property of the whole or of sub-groupings in the whole, is something that grows in the fertile fields of many pushes and pulls, all of which add to the dynamics to which board directors are often unwittingly subjected.

It is mind boggling to attend to all these influences simultaneously and to be aware of one's own reactions in the here-and-now of decision-making. Such influences are often deeply embedded in our social structures (Hopper, 2003; Vince, 2018). The programme Dynamics @ Board Level helps participants to be more aware of board dynamics, external influences and their own reactions. The chapters here reflect that awareness and should also aid the reader to do so. Many concepts are introduced, explained and applied to boardroom dynamics that help this process of awareness and learning. Learning from experience is highly valued and there is case study material here that demonstrates how board members, consultants and managers can learn from their own experience in the boards where they work. Unconscious dynamics including basic assumptions, social defences, anxieties, collusion and narcissistic propensities are explored as well as approaches and methods that help board members guard against the negative influences of these, such as the development of negative capability, the recognition of unconscious collusion and the development of collective collaboration.

I believe that we will hear more "good stories" about effective, ethical and accountable boards should their psychodynamics be more fully understood and should their members attend more to reflecting on their own practices. The chapters here will aid in that process.

Susan Long

April 2019

Director of Research and Scholarship

National Institute of Organisation Dynamics Australia

Notes

1 See www.bloomberg.com/news/articles/2019-04-06/the-google-ai-ethics-board-with-actual-power-is-still-around
2 See https://bankingjournal.aba.com/2018/08/challenges-facing-bank-boards/

References

Armstrong, A., & Frances, R. (2008). An ethical climate is a duty of care. *Journal of Business Systems Governance and Ethics*, 3(3): 15–20.

Bain, A. (1999). On socioanalysis. *Socio-Analysis*, 1(1).

Bakan, J. (2004). *The Corporation: The Pathological Pursuit of Profit and Power*. London: Constable.

Gould, L., Stapley, L., & Stein, M. (2004). *Systems Psychodynamics*. London: Karnac.

Hopper, E. (2003). *The Social Unconscious: Selected Papers*. London: Jessica Kingsley Publications.

Long, S.D. (2008). *The Perverse Organisation and Its Deadly Sins*. London: Karnac.

Long, S.D. (2012). Greed. In: Long, S., & Sievers, B. (Eds.), *Towards a Socioanalysis of Money, Finance and Capitalism: Beneath the Surface of the Financial Industry*. London: Routledge.

Long, S.D. (2017). The socioanalytic approach to organisations. *Socioanalysis*, 19.

Vince, R. (2018, May). Institutional illogics: The unconscious and institutional analysis. *Organization Studies*. Thousand Oaks: Sage Journals Online.

Contributors

Maria Claudia Benassi, PhD, is an independent consultant and executive coach in leadership and team development and cross-border career transition. She works with senior leaders and boards to uncover blockers lurking in the group's dynamics. As Executive Education Director at INSEAD, she created a niche to support women's leadership development. Claudia designs spaces for reflection, networking, and empowerment that encourage women to undertake bold steps towards reshaping their professional identity. A Brown University alumna, Claudia has lived in ten countries, coaches in four languages and is now based in Berlin.

Joe Binnion, BSc (Econ.), MSc (Econ.), is Managing Director of BiG Innovation and holds several board roles in high growth digital businesses. As a practitioner, Joe is a leader and facilitator of design-led transformation, working alongside some of the world's leading brands and public sector organizations when they need to make transformation breakthroughs. His professional work tends to be focused on board level applied strategy – the point at which organizations need to transition from strategic thinking to delivery and execution.

Beatriz Boza, MBA, LLM, is a partner at EY Peru and a regional leader for corporate governance, family enterprise and growth markets in northern Latin American countries. She has worked with boards and board members and families in Bolivia, Chile, Colombia, Ecuador and Peru and she leads the corporate governance survey project launched by EY together with the Lima Stock Exchange and other stock exchanges in the Pacific Alliance. She is also the Academic Director of the Board Member programme at Pacifico Business School. Boza was a member of Tavistock Institute's Dynamics @ Board Level 2016 cohort.

Leslie Brissett JP, FRSA, BSc (Hons), MSc, PhD, is Company Secretary, Principal Consultant/Researcher and Director of the Group Relations Programme at the Tavistock Institute of Human Relations. He oversees a global practice since joining the Institute in 2012 after 30 years in institutional partnership development. He has been a charity chief executive and has chaired boards and committees in the community and voluntary sector, Further Education and

National Health Service in the UK. The nature of experience and the ways that people bring their experience into a knowingness that can inform future action are central to his approach to leadership and followership. The encounter with boundaries of self and other and the relationship between internal and external realities are pre-occupations that have taken him deep into the question of human existence. He is a seeker of meaning in the human condition and profoundly impacted by the intersection of science, spirituality, nature, the built environment and culture on human relations. He spends his time between the UK and the USA.

Thomas Brull, BA (Bus. Admin), MSc, MBA, is a non-executive board member in family-owned businesses and public companies. He holds a degree in business administration from Getulio Vargas University, São Paulo, Brazil, and an MBA from Indiana University, Bloomington, USA. Thomas attended the Tavistock Institute's Leicester Conference, UK, in 2015 and earned a certificate in Dynamics @ Board Level in 2016. Thomas is also a certified mediator. He is a lecturer at Fundação Dom Cabral, a high-level executive education school in Brazil, and also at the Brazilian Institute of Corporate Governance on its Directors Training Programme. He has co-authored two books on finance.

Vincent H. Dominé, MSc, is Adjunct Professor of Leadership at INSEAD and founding partner of Dominé & Partners, a Swiss-based international consultancy firm specialized in strategic leadership development. Prof. Dominé consults with senior executive teams and boards and delivers leadership development programmes to leading organizations. He is also Director of Leadership Development in the INSEAD Global Executive MBA degree programmes and regularly contributes to INSEAD's International Directors programme. He has co-authored the book *The Coaching Kaleidoscope* with Prof. Manfred Kets de Vries and is a member of the International Society for the Psychoanalytic Study of Organisations and the Singapore Institute of Directors.

Paul Duggan, BE (Mechanical), MBA, MSc, currently lives in Dublin with his wife and children. A mechanical engineer, he has worked in a wide range of industries ranging from semi-conductors to industrial supplies. He was CEO of an engineering group quoted on the Dublin and London Stock Exchanges and is an experienced executive and non-executive director in the for-profit and voluntary sectors. He is currently CEO and a shareholder in a group of distribution businesses. He has an MBA from University College Dublin, professional certificate in coaching and has recently completed an MSc in behavioural change both from Henley Business School as well as the Tavistock Institute's Certificate in board dynamics.

Rachael Etebar, BA (Hons), PGDip, chartered FCIPD, spent 20 years in various HR roles in a number of FTSE 100 and FTSE 250 retail organizations. She joined the civil service in 2007 as HR Director for the newly created UK Border Agency. She subsequently held roles in the Home Office, Insolvency

Service and was lately Group HR Director for the department for transport and its executive agencies. Rachael recently joined the British Transport Police in the newly created role as Director of People and Culture.

George Th. Fischer-Varvitsiotis, MD, FRSM, Psychoanalyst and Group Analyst, is an organizational and leadership development consultant with long-standing experience in supporting top level executives and executive teams in developing their leadership cultures for values and innovation. George was born and raised in Athens, and he studied medicine (ophthalmology and ophthalmic surgery) and music. He lectures regularly on the psychology of organizational leadership. George is a training coach at the Institute for Psychodynamic Organisation Development and People Management, Düsseldorf. He has also trained in systemic theory and attended the Dynamics @ Board Level programme and the Leicester conference of the Tavistock Institute of Human Relations, London.

Ashley Harshak, BSc (Jt Hons), MA, MBA, is an economist by training and a management consultant for nearly 20 years. A Partner at PA Consulting, a transformation and innovation consultancy, where he focuses on organisational change and people capability development. Ashley works with management boards and executive teams to build the dynamics and behaviours that support their organizational purpose. Recent and previous clients include: Central England Co-op, the DWP, English Heritage, IMI, Nokia, and npower. Ashley is currently undertaking a doctorate in organizational change with Ashridge Business School, researching board dynamics and effectiveness.

Toya Lorch, BSc, PGDip, MA, began her career as an occupational therapist, then moved to human resources at Ryder International and Unilever International Training Center in London. In 2003 she was a founding partner of Kampas Coaching & Consultoria in São Paulo, Brazil, specializing in organizational consultancy and coaching. Toya holds a degree in the programme Consultation and the Organization: Psychoanalytical Approaches (Tavistock Clinic, London, 2002), an executive master's in Consulting and Coaching for Change (INSEAD, France, 2013) and attended the Dynamics @ Board Level programme (Tavistock Institute, London, 2017). Toya is part of the executive coaching team at the INSEAD Business School.

Janette McCrae, BA, was a development advisor and an executive coach at senior leadership levels within policing in the UK for ten years. Her work focused on facilitating development activities for force executive teams, chief officers, senior staff and board members of the Scottish Police Authority. Her participation in the Tavistock Institute's Dynamics @ Board Level programme synchronized with her board development activities. She has participated in several Tavistock group relations conferences. From her private consultancy, Janette's work focuses on improving board effectiveness, particularly within the public sector.

Wayne Mullen, MSc, DProf, is the Senior Director of HR Services for a global technology company. Previously, Wayne held roles managing leadership development globally in emerging markets, investment banking and gaming. He served as consultant both internally and externally to a number of companies including: The Bank of Tokyo-Mitsubishi, National Australia Bank, Ericsson, Vodafone, The Home Office, Siemens Business Services, Standard Bank, Schlumberger Sema and King. His work has been featured in *The Independent, Coaching at Work* and *Finance Week*. He holds an MSc in organizational behaviour and is currently writing his doctoral thesis in leadership and organizational development.

Anand Narasimhan, PhD, is the Dean of Faculty and Research and Shell Professor of Global Leadership at IMD, Lausanne. Anand advises organizations on transforming their leadership capability. Anand's research on institutional change, organizational design and social networks has been published in journals such as *Harvard Business Review*, *Academy of Management Journal*, and *Organization Science*. Anand is part of the Governance and Board Education faculty at IMD, and serves as a non-executive director for the Case Center. Anand has previously been on the faculty of London Business School and Imperial College Business School.

Tammy Noel, MSc, is an internal organizational development consultant practitioner, working within the UK civil service and public sector for over 15 years. She works with clients to support the transformation of public sector organizations at cross-system and team level. Tammy has a particular interest in group process consultation and human systems dynamics; two very different disciplines which help to surface patterns at play within a team or organization. Her development in the area of unconscious group behaviour has helped deepen her expertise in supporting senior boards in improving organizational performance.

Toy Odiakosa, LLB, MSc, MBPsS, is the Leadership Director at ELA Consulting Ltd. She has a special interest in teams and groups and holds a master's degree in applied psychology. This informs her approach to evaluating and co-creating objectives, communication flows and the role of dynamics. As an organizational role and management consultant, Toy has spoken at conferences and symposia about perception, creativity, negotiation and performance in senior teams and boards. She is a member of the British Psychological Society, and an accredited member of the Association of Professional Executive Coaches and Supervision.

Martin Palethorpe, BSc Hons, is the founder Director of The Pragma Group, a UK-based performance consultancy. He coaches CEOs and executive teams to help them improve in all aspects of human, leadership and organizational performance. His transformational approach working with the human mind is at the core of much of his work with clients. Martin has a pragmatic bold approach, employs wide business and sporting experience and perspectives, and his knowledge of human and organizational development. Martin has significant experience with clients in the technology, retail and agency sectors. During his first career, he worked at a senior level inside large and small technology businesses. He is also a regularly published writer and an inspirational conference speaker on high performance, having raced to the magnetic north pole and run across three of the world's most remote deserts.

Steven Phillips, CIPD (Assoc), FRSA, consults with major organizations to develop innovative approaches to leadership and organizational development. He works with senior executives, directors and their teams on their leadership of their businesses through times of tough and turbulent change and renewal. Steven's career to date has included working on entrepreneurship for the UK government and international development with the UN before his current focus on corporate leadership, building on his own experience as a leadership team member. As Director of Ideas Unlimited for 15 years, Steven's clients included John Lewis, Tesco, HSBC, Camelot, RBS, Sky, PepisCo, Unilever, ATS-Euromaster, BT, EY, NHS, RWE, Standard Life and Wolff-Olins.

Anja Salmi, MD, psychiatrist and psychoanalyst, is a graduate of the Dynamics @ Board Level programme of the Tavistock Institute. She is the chief editor of the web magazine *National Dynamics*. Anja is the Founder and CEO of Ego-funktio Ltd., a clinic specializing in psychiatric and psychotherapeutic clinical practice, providing supervision, creating new knowledge and consulting to health care systems in management and organizational development. Anja is a board member of the AGSLO Foundation and a member of ISPSO; she has long-standing experience of working with large group dynamics based on Kleinian psychoanalytic thinking and has a special interest in collective loss.

Paul Schanzer, BEd, Chartered FCIPD, joined NHS Wales during the 90s focusing on senior leadership development. In 2013 he joined Academi Wales, leading on governance, executive and board level development with public and 3rd sectors in Wales. Paul is currently leading the development of a team-assessment framework for senior teams and boards to identify the characteristics, approaches and strategies required to implement and sustain organizational high performance. Paul has a particular interest in concepts around individual, group and system dynamics and their impact on effective decision-making at board level, having recently completed the certificate in Dynamics @ Board Level programme with the Tavistock Institute.

Mannie Sher, BA (Hons), AAPSW, TQAPsych, FBAP, PhD, is Principal Researcher and Consultant in organizational development and change and an executive coach at the Tavistock Institute of Human Relations. In these roles, he works with top teams on their leadership functions in effecting strategic change. Mannie's research and consultancy work focuses on the impact of thought on the dialectic relationship between social constructivism, the unconscious and liberal democracy. Mannie is the former Director of the Group Relations Programme of the Tavistock Institute of Human Relations, London, which involved developing and directing group relations conferences in the UK and in many other countries. Mannie has held senior management positions in local government, the National Health Service and voluntary organizations, before moving to the Tavistock Institute in 1997. Mannie is married to a teacher trainer and consultant in primary school education and a soul-mate in group relations. They live in London, have three grown children and a great bunch of grandchildren with whom he loves spending his summers.

Tazi Lorraine Smith, BSc, DipPFS, is a management consultant in healthcare. She is a former independent financial planning consultant and she is a member of the Chartered Insurance Institute and holds the Personal Finance Society's diploma in financial planning. She is currently undertaking her master's degree in the programme Management Consulting and Organizational Change at Birkbeck College, University of London. Her special interests include organizational change, social justice and the contribution that psychoanalytic theory offers to our understanding of groups and organizations. In 2018, Tazi completed a six-month internship at the Tavistock Institute of Human Relations.

David Strudley, CBE MBA MA FCMI FRSA, is CEO Acorns Children's Hospice and Chairman of the UK Transition Taskforce. During ten years with Acorns, the charity has developed a growth strategy that by the end of the decade will see care being provided annually to 1,000 children with life shortening conditions and support to their families, including those who are bereaved. In 2012, David was also appointed Chair of the UK Transition Taskforce to support older children, moving from children's to adult services. The taskforce brings together organizations from health and social care, education, housing and employment, to enable these young people to live as independently as possible, while receiving essential health and social care.

Grant Taylor, BA, FRSA, is Founder and Managing Director of Peridot Partners Ltd., and has over 20 years of experience of working with boards to recruit executive and non-executive leadership and over eight years of trustee experience on the boards of the Evelina Children's Heart Organisation and Working Families. At Peridot Partners, Grant leads on Board Development Services including diagnostic reviews, skills audits and recruiting board members for a range of organizations from social enterprises, charities and educational institutions, including colleges and universities. Grant is currently a Fellow of the RSA and an advisor to the Young Trustees Project run by the Social Change Agency, funded by the Blagrave Trust and supported by the Charity Commission.

Paula Wilson, BA Hon, FCIPD, AC Master, TTT Certified, is the Founder and Director of Wilson Sloan Consulting Ltd, which specializes in the provision of executive and board coaching, team coaching, executive assessment and coach supervision in Ireland and the UK. An AC accredited and qualified master executive coach (FCIPD, BPS, NLP), team coach and psychometrician, Paula is also qualified with Nancy Kline as a Time to Think coach and practitioner. She is also an accredited coach supervisor.

Homage
Edward Craft of Wedlake Bell LLP

Genesis

We came up with the idea of extending board breakfasts and undertaking a different positioning that would take us into the realm of being the trainer of the trainers, coach to the coaches and evaluators to the evaluator.

Building upon the expertise that had been built with Bvalco, where some of the difficulties of working in the field of board evaluation had been exposed, the authors sensed a need for clarity and commitment to focusing on the dynamics of the boardroom and not the more technical aspects of board evaluation.

The late John Mulryan, former Head of Finance at the Tavistock Institute of Human Relations, had connections with Wedlake Bell LLP whose team had been involved in drafting corporate governance codes. We contacted Edward Craft there and discussed the idea of the Tavistock Institute having some form of collaboration with Wedlake Bell in board evaluation. He liked the idea and we shared the programme with him, the target audience and explored the benefit to both parties. Ed took the proposal to his partners to get agreement. It was an overwhelming 'yes' to the idea and in the first instance they offered to host the first cohort. The structure of the programme was going to be four one-day modules taking place during office hours (09.00–17.00) once a month, to be held at Wedlake Bell premises. As well as providing venue and facilities, Ed was going to take up a visiting faculty role.

Collaboration

Discussions were held about offering joint approaches bridging the legal aspects of governance oversight by Wedlake Bell with attention to behavioural dynamics by the Tavistock Institute and this remains an opportunity. Ed set up a structure of 'round tables' sharing governance stories in which the Tavistock Institute participated in a number, sharing expertise, ideas and challenges.

First cohort

Ed acted as a proper host, appearing towards the end of the day to hear about the deliberations and to offer ideas. The cohort appreciated the location of the venue as easy access for international travellers, the facilities that were very good and the generous catering.

At the review at the end of the first cohort and while looking at the possibility of making the modules two-day residential events, Ed retained his role as external faculty in order to keep the partnership going. His contribution was both technical and facilitative. He was helpful to the cohort in skilfully managing his role as visiting faculty, by paying attention to the dynamics within the cohort at the time of his visits, whilst also preparing and delivering the UK-centred technical input to a global audience.

Ongoing developments

Ed continues to be around as a friend to the enterprise. Our relationship with Wedlake Bell also underwent changes as they have been retained as the lawyers of the Tavistock Institute benefitting from their expertise in other areas of the Institute's work, e.g., with China and Europe.

Introduction to *Dynamics @ Board Level*

Mannie Sher and Leslie Brissett

Background

This book focuses on the cultural, behavioural and emotional dynamics of boards. The book contains a collection of papers written by participants of the Tavistock Institute of Human Relations programme Dynamics @ Board Level. The core method of learning on Tavistock Institute professional development programmes is learning from experience. Consequently, the programme, and hence this book, is less concerned with governance and administration, important as these are. Rather, we attempt to enlarge our understanding of the dynamics in the boardroom through studying its culture, behaviour and emotions and their unconscious determinants and how these affect leadership capability and decision-making. We believe knowledge of 'dynamics' is central to effective board functioning.

The financial crisis of 2008 formed the background to the establishment of the Dynamics @ Board Level programme; we realized that role and behaviour should be the basis of a critical examination of board effectiveness. The Walker Review (2009, p. 9) states explicitly that an understanding of behavioural dynamics is preferable to the introduction of new legislation:

> [I]mprovement in corporate governance will require behavioural change in an array of closely related areas in which prescribed standards and processes play a necessary but insufficient part. Board conformity with laid down procedures such as those for enhanced risk oversight will not alone provide better corporate governance overall if the chairman is weak, if the composition and dynamic of the board is inadequate and if there is unsatisfactory or no engagement with major owners. The behavioural changes that may be needed are unlikely to be fostered by regulatory fiat, which in any event risks provoking unintended consequences. Behavioural improvement is more likely to be achieved through clearer identification of best practice and more effective but, in most areas, non-statutory routes to implementation so that boards and their major owners feel "ownership" of good corporate governance.

In this extract, Walker uses the term 'dynamic' to refer to a generic type of leadership, engagement and behaviour. It was outside the scope of the main part of his review to be more specific than that. Instead, he proposed involving specialists in the study of behavioural dynamics into banking in order to introduce improvements in this area of board functioning. Indeed, he invited Mannie Sher and Ali Gill to write an annexe to his Review outlining in greater detail what 'dynamics' would look like in the context of board behaviour (Gill & Sher, 2009, pp. 139–146). The annexe received wide coverage in the press with some expressing astonishment that a treasury report would include a statement about the need for greater understanding of behavioural dynamics. Subsequent to the publication of the Walker Review, Gill and Sher were invited to meet representatives of regulatory authorities like the Financial Reporting Council, the Financial Services Authority, the Bank of England and senior personnel of a number of commercial banks, to discuss and advise on subjects such as boardroom dynamics and their links to organizational culture and change. Some of Mannie Sher's ideas were written into corporate codes that were emerging at the time. Mannie lectured to groups of non-executive directors (NEDs) at the *Financial Times* and a number of legal firms. As a result of these talks it was clear that many aspiring NEDs were ill-equipped to understand – let alone work – with dynamics. They had a great hunger to learn about the mysteries of behaviour, on integrating board thinking with empathy, and fostering greater openness in boards, facilitating interactions, communicating complex messages succinctly, collaborating across boundaries and other related topics. At the same time, and during the previous decade, Leslie Brissett was taking part in governance processes as a non-executive director in Further and Higher Education and in the National Health Service. He worked as a board adviser to the UK housing associations, facilitating the merger of two housing associations to form one of the largest housing voluntary sector bodies in England. He worked in the USA, with two start-up tech companies and assisted the leadership group to prepare for stock market floatation for one and for the acquisition by another.

When developing the programme Dynamics @ Board Level, we pondered over the definition of 'dynamics' in relation to boards. We asked ourselves how we could increase knowledge of 'dynamics' that went beyond lectures in half-day or one-day training events. From our experience of working in other Tavistock Institute professional development programmes, we knew that embedding an understanding of dynamics leading to changed behaviour would require more time than was available in a one-day training event; it would need a different, somewhat non-traditional approach to teaching and training. We also decided that we needed to be clearer in our definitions of terms such as 'culture', 'dynamics' and 'learning from experience'.

Culture

There is increased public interest in the topic of culture in boardrooms (Financial Reporting Council, 2012, 2016). The FRC report stresses the need to improve trust in the motivations and integrity of business and the role that corporate culture plays in delivering long-term business and economic success. The report states that a healthy culture protects and generates value and that businesses should focus on culture, rather than wait for a crisis, because 'a strong culture will endure in times of stress and mitigate the impact'. The report encourages connecting purpose and strategy to culture, supporting values and driving correct behaviours and it makes clear that boards should be responsible for *overseeing the values and culture* (emphasis added) of the company. The report adds to our understanding of this area because it emphasizes the board's role in overseeing the cultures of others. However, it does not address how boards should understand their own cultures, nor how the cultures of boards influence the cultures of their organizations.

Within the report, 'good cultures' and 'healthy cultures' are defined simply as being aligned with business strategies to generate value. The report goes further by claiming that strong governance, openness and accountability and constructive engagement with stakeholders are areas that lead to a 'strong culture'. The FRC Report does not set out how and by what means 'culture' should be created and managed. Rather, the tone of the report suggests that 'culture' is an objective tangible reality 'out there', potentially pliable and controllable under the company's leadership. An organization's culture may certainly be dependent on statements and the behaviour of the board, but there is little acknowledgment in the report of the extent that culture possibly 'manages' us, that when we enter or join an organization, we step into a built-in culture, made explicit when people say: 'this is how things are done here'. These are powerful attitudes, to which almost everyone subscribes *unconsciously*, and are drawn to as a way of learning and surviving in the new environment. 'Strong culture' (Gabriel, 1999) implies strong commitment to a set of shared values and meanings. While many organizations claim to possess such values, few are genuinely committed to them and indeed most are working to a set of unconscious values that run counter to those espoused by the organization.

Organizations are often pressed to adopt short-term views, opting for 'quick-fix' solutions; they easily compromise their values in the interest of profit or other quantifiable objectives. This tendency to lose sight of high-minded aspirations in organizations is the result of simplistic definitions of 'culture'; of course, it is not an object, rather a 'second skin'. Culture refers to taken-for-granted behaviours that develop from processes of socialization and group behaviour with natural tendencies towards conformity. Culture is absorbed into the minds of the people, becoming part of them inasmuch as they become part of the culture. The term 'culture' usually denotes one overriding set of behavioural and attitudinal norms. However, organizations are made up of diverse cultures, for example, the culture in the engineering workshop of an airline would be different from the culture of its sales force.

Thus, boards in taking responsibility for developing and overseeing their organizations' culture, should first attend to their own. Boards should be asking themselves:

- Is the culture of our board open or stultifying?
- Is it stimulating or numbing?

- Inspiring or de-motivating?
- Supportive or controlling?
- Rigid or flexible?
- Imaginative or reactionary?
- Is the board a custodian or directing? Or a board of guardianship, inspection or policing?

Answers to these questions can be obtained from regular board assessments led either by the board's chair or by external board assessors, which would give boards the opportunities for learning, growth and change. By boards examining their own cultures, they act as models for self-examination by the rest of the organization – a 'physician, heal thyself' philosophy.

Dynamics

In the field of physics, 'dynamics' is the study of the causes of motion and changes in motion; it is the study of the way forces produce motion and why objects are in motion. Dynamics are the forces that produce activity and change in any situation or sphere of existence; simply, the scientific study of movement. The opposite of 'dynamics' is statics or kinematics – the branch of mechanics that is concerned with forces in static equilibrium, i.e., describing objects without considering the causes leading to their motion. In the boardroom, not paying attention to 'dynamics', in our view, may cloud executives' minds and lead to them missing the fundamentals of their operations.

However, in the study of human behaviour, of inter-relationships between people in groups, of power and status between people living or working together, 'dynamics' describes the interplay between conscious and unconscious forces. In systems psychodynamics, a term coined by Eric Miller (Tavistock Institute 1992/93 Review, 1993, p. 42), dynamics is the study of the systemic *and* psychological forces that underlie human behaviour in families, groups, organizations, communities and society. Generic definitions of 'dynamics' can also usefully be incorporated into our understanding of group life – liveliness, enthusiasm and determination, energetic, continuously changing, growing and developing.

What are the 'dynamics' that concern us? How do they manifest themselves in boards? How do we explain them and how are they to be worked with? Structure and dynamics are like two wheels of a bicycle – one is impossible without the other. Structure is the frame that allows for the emergence of dynamics; it makes them visible and available for study and use. Some people have a natural flair and an intuitive understanding of dynamics; for others, dynamics are difficult to comprehend, and are sometimes unbelievable. Leaders who struggle to understand the dynamics of their boards often prefer to rely on hard observable facts that provide a degree of certainty. Undeniably, knowledge of dynamics can be a constructive instrument to explain board behaviour and bring about change in the direction of greater efficiency and effectiveness.

There are dynamics present in the evaluation of the dynamics of a board. How would a board evaluator work with the dynamics inherent in an evaluation process? How does a consultant square the dynamics of consulting with a chair's dynamics of leading? Self-examination and self-scrutiny are different processes to supervision or examination by an outsider. It would be rare for a board to react with equanimity towards being reviewed by external people. The turbulence caused by being reviewed would be linked to feelings of either pride or shame, depending on how well or how badly the board believes it is doing.

It is natural that boards will be recipients of strong emotions from the organizations they lead, and from the stakeholders and communities they serve. Boards may fear: "what will the reviewer find out about us that we don't already know?" "What will be done with the information gleaned about us – will it be used for, or against us?" "Why could we not find it out for ourselves?" The answers to these questions will not be straightforward.

The impact of being observed

Dynamics are mostly transient, are mainly inferred by observing behaviour and having discussions and may be viewed divergently by different people with different board roles. Evidence of dynamics usually emerges from hearing different accounts of episodes or situations by members of the board. Reports about dynamics will usually be accompanied by strong emotions. In turn, dynamics may be exposed by these emotional reactions, by what is said and what is not said, what is avoided, denied or repressed, and other interloping events that say loudly to the trained evaluator – 'this is a dynamic'. Observing emotional and behaviour patterns like hubris or domination or whining, obsessional repetition, meaningless rituals, the presence of special relationships, lack of respect, bullying, scapegoating, repeated lateness, would lead the consultant, or board members for that matter, to conclude that the type of behaviour observed defines the culture of the board. Using knowledge about the causes of dynamics and the reasons for their presence, a 'working hypotheses' might be offered, i.e., a short statement that behaviour 'x' was happening for reason 'y'. The board may be experiencing thoughts and feelings that may be on people's minds, but which cannot be articulated. In Tavistock Institute language, we would call this a collective anxiety against which the board is building a defence. The aim of a 'working hypothesis' is to provide the means for the board to articulate the anxiety *and* the associated defence. The theory behind this is that making unconscious fears and unconscious behaviours conscious helps to remove them, not magically but slowly, piece by piece. Hidden thoughts and feelings and dysfunctional behaviours stand a better chance of being made conscious when they are made unintentionally as an unmistakable part of the communication. The evaluator's skill in these types of communications comes from having had training in investigating and analysing dynamics, respecting the client, keeping the client's interests uppermost, being unafraid of disturbed and disturbing behaviour at any level, always being open to new learning and having a deep commitment to transparent standards of professional practice.

The focus of the study of the Dynamics @ Board Level programme is always on the many different *sets of relationships* between members of the board, between the board-as-a-whole and the organization it leads and the organization and its environment. The focus is not the individual in isolation, not the board in isolation, not the organization in isolation, not the organization's context in isolation, but the dynamic inter-relationships between them all, happening at the same time and in complex ways.

We conceive of the programme in three key phases: (i) recruitment and entry, (ii) delivery during the programme, and (iii) post-programme application. We pay attention to 'dynamics' at each phase of the programme. The cohort is constructed with a view to the seniority and nature, identity and characteristics of participants and the potential dynamics between them. During the programme, their interactions with each other, and with us as directors are data for exploring the dynamics in the programme as a temporary board. Utilizing action learning methodologies, participants extrapolate their learning into their day-to-day work with boards – whether in role as chairs, executive or non-executive members of boards or as catalytic agents of boards like evaluators, consultants or mentors/coaches. We believe that a teaching and training programme based primarily on the study of dynamics in the 'here-and-now' assists the programme participants in their work with boards. The participants' learning, by extension, would contribute towards effective functioning of boards at all levels – culture, behaviour and increased collegial responsibility of boards. The aim of the programme as stated in the brochure is to:

> explore and elaborate individual, group and systemic dynamics, of which no groups are ever fully aware and are never fully free from their influence. The Tavistock Institute offers chairs and members of boards, trainers, evaluators, consultants and coaches working in board development, access to a unique depth of knowledge and practice that comes from advising those in positions of power and authority. For those boards seeking help to diagnose, evaluate and remedy blind spots, engaging someone trained in the methodologies of dynamics of the Tavistock Institute is often the answer. After the programme, graduates will be able to help boards explore resistance-to-change, stifling cultures, dynamics that can affect strategy setting, succession planning and remuneration levels and other anomalies at board level.

Designing the structure of the programme

In order to make visible the properties of dynamics, any programme studying dynamics involves a degree of relaxing – even removing – formal structures, temporarily setting aside business-as-usual goals and objectives that are typical of everyday meetings. It is rather like putting the behavioural processes to be studied under a microscope and as far as possible barring extraneous variables. This setting aside of agendas allows for the study of interpersonal interactions, group and cultural dynamics, thoughts and ideas and overall general board performance. In regular board meetings, these interactions, thoughts and dynamics would ordinarily be goal-focused, cognitive and reaching after reason. All too often, reason is privileged over feelings and emotions. Feelings originate in a different part of the brain that is more associated with creativity, vision and inspiration. In boards, these emotions tend to be suppressed and ignored in favour of fact and reason and comes at a cost to the board. A useful resource that could potentially help reach more mature levels of behaviour and decision-making is thus neglected. Providing safe structures for learning about dynamics is important because when organizations experience periodic crises, emotions like frustration, competition, fear, confusion or panic, can produce primitive states of thinking in even the most experienced board members and lead to impulsive or defensive decision-making. Without appropriate structures to contain the welling up of emotion and to provide a reasonable degree of safety, the work of learning cannot be done. 'Structure' here brings us to the concept of boundaries as 'containers' (Bion, 1959). In the programme, acting as a temporary board, as with permanent boards, there are multiple layers of boundaries that move about in unpredictable and often chaotic ways. In all human systems – individual, group, organizational, societal, as well as in a programme to study dynamics – it is possible to identify two types of boundaries – outer boundaries and inner boundaries. This helps us to understand, for instance, that a chair would 'hold' the boundary between the board's inner world of beliefs, values and fears and the board's outer world of responsibilities of guardianship, direction-giving, overseeing financial probity, representing its multiple stakeholders. The Tavistock views each individual and the board-as-a-whole as having inner and outer boundaries. For example, as individuals and as a board, we present a persona or image that we hope will reflect well on us, but behind an inner boundary, lie feelings of anxiety about acceptance and the fear of being ignored, rejected or criticized, i.e., shamed. These anxieties are kept well out of view, tucked away behind our inner personal or collective boundaries for safe-keeping.

Boundaries, both inner and outer, while permeable and separate, are often breached because of unconscious forces acting on and within boards and the organizations they lead. It is the business of consultants, coaches and evaluators when working with boards to name these unconscious forces and facilitate discussion of them in open and frank ways. Consultants and evaluators of boards will often experience the conflicting push and pull of board dynamics. For example, a board having called in outside assistance, may feel antipathetic towards themselves and their helpers for not being able to be independent. The fear of dependency often lies at the root of a board's determination to soldier on boldly, even if senselessly, rather than face the potential humiliation that comes from calling for assistance to unravel its dynamics.

Learning from experience

The most instructive experiences are those of everyday life.

(Friedrich Wilhelm Nietzsche)

Tavistock Institute post-professional development programmes rely on *learning from experience* philosophy and methodology. This can be roughly translated as using the individual's and the group's observations, thoughts and emotions – head and gut, as it were – as experienced *in the present*, to widen and deepen understanding of the programme's overall theme and in the minute-by-minute issues under discussion. This can be an unsettling experience because we are used to traditional learning, which assumes that the audience has met in order to learn from or be instructed by someone whose knowledge is in advance of the audience. This kind of learning can be called *learning from others' experience*. Research shows that passive learning of this latter kind is unsteady, evokes resistance and is impermanent and has almost no value in transferring knowledge gained from the lecture room to the back-home work situation.

In constructing the Dynamics @ Board Level programme, we aimed to deepen layers of learning by following a *learning from experience* methodology. We therefore constructed the programme-as-a-whole as if it were a temporary board with responsibilities for engaging in the task of learning. The programme directors 'hold' the outer boundary by taking responsibility for securing a good learning venue, recruitment and selection of participants who would be suitably matched according to age, gender, nationality and roles on boards, designing the programme, inviting external faculty, defining the different tasks in the programme and keeping the programme on task and to time; and reviewing and judging written assignments. As far as is possible, internal decisions like how the sub-committees are formed, the order of presentations, emergence of leadership, off-line work and research assignments are taken by the cohort itself, acting as a temporary board. The directors, in directors' role, offer their opinions and interpretations on the emerging dynamics as the directors experience them in the service of the group-learning task. Common examples of group dynamics would be emergence of alliances and anti-alliances and deals made, consciously and unconsciously, between participants around gender and age; the influence of nationality and race; the meaning of seating arrangements – who sits next to whom and why; the meaning of empty chairs; punctuality or lateness around the start and ending of sessions; the manner and order of speaking; the words chosen to express ideas; tone of voice and body language; the emergence of and function served by 'scapegoats'; the rise of hierarchies and the cohort's transference feelings towards the two directors. These dynamics highlight issues of authority, power and status at one level, and denial, splitting, idealization and projection of negative feelings at another – all of which are open for scrutiny and discussion.

The Dynamics @ Board Level programme is an educational event that takes place in a post-professional educational venue and the directors are the 'educators'. Course content covers five modalities of learning, which are integrated into one overall programme: (i) *intellectual knowledge* via reading seminars on psychoanalytic theory, group dynamics; organizational and systems theory; lectures on complexity theory, strategic governance, the legal basis of board roles and tasks and board succession; (ii) experiencing, accessing and owning *feelings, emotions and relationships* via study groups, social dreaming matrices, nature walks and experiencing senses in the open air; (iii) *case-based study* seminars in which examples of participants' on-going work with boards are presented for comment and learning; (iv) two *written assessed assignments* that are completed four months after the end of the programme; and (v) *rigorous in-depth reviews* that follow all events during the programme.

The programme aims to help chairs of boards, board members and board catalytic agents like evaluators and consultants to recognize and strengthen positive dynamics and address negative dynamics.

Further developments

For most of our consulting careers, the editors have been members of or worked with top teams including boards, attending to the nature of boardroom dynamics and the impact of their morale and functioning on the behaviour of executive teams and by extension further into the organization, i.e., the board, in our view, reflecting the organization and the organization reflecting the board in a dynamic reflexive loop. Our exposure to the cultures and functioning of boards has led us to the view that although boards are themselves part of hierarchies, accountable to others above and around them, they often behave as if they are either quite separate from or unhelpfully merged with the organization. Boardroom dynamics and boardroom behaviour need regular assessing because group dynamics tend towards extremes – either towards fusion or towards detachment. Despite our best efforts to systematize knowledge about board dynamics, we are only at the beginning of our understanding of them, usually due to the use of vague and ill-defined terms that impede thinking. Gosling (2004) argues for clarity in the definitions of the objectives of board leadership, sometimes referred to as 'direction setting', involving the arts of persuasion and intuition as much as scientific analyses, synthesis and design. The problem with defining board leadership as 'direction setting', he claims, is similar to the problem of defining strategy as competitive positioning – it becomes too cerebral, theoretical and may be little more than wishful thinking. Boards must consider problems of facilitating emergent strategies and human and group dynamics associated with the processes of change. Boards must go beyond the intellectual activity of setting directions to the pragmatics of getting things done. The study of the distribution and exercise of boardroom power usually divides along psychological or sociological definitions. We challenge the domination by either psychological or sociological approaches that often reduce leadership to so-called 'people skills'.

The theory and practice of group dynamics and understandings that derive from Tavistock socio-technical systems thinking, offers the promise of further developments in the study of board behaviour. Future challenges centre on extending our knowledge into practical means of helping boards manage the uncontained, and sometimes uncontainable dynamics and forces in them. The hope is that a Tavistock group dynamics approach will help clarify blocks and resistances to authority that would make board relationships less toxic. 'Keeping your head down' and 'keeping it in the family', in the case of family businesses, are accepted as behavioural norms in boards.

Work on the role and function of boards is likely to increase in the future. This would necessitate the development of conceptual frameworks to guide people on the size and complexity of boards, especially of interlocking global companies and the greater possibilities for things going wrong. Participatory boards typically involve all stakeholders in organizational strategies to ensure that products or services meet needs and are usable. The term participatory engagement is used in a variety of fields, for instance software design, urban design, product design, sustainability and planning as a way of creating environments that are more responsive and appropriate to the users' cultural, emotional, spiritual and practical needs. Participatory design at board level has a political dimension of empowerment and democratization.

Further research work is suggested to establish why the boards of certain banks did not get into difficulties during the financial crisis. Regulators, politicians, academics and board members themselves are interested in knowing more about what kind of banking milieu existed and what kind of mindset boards relied on that led them to remain prudent, cautious and solvent. Surviving shock will, in future, depend on a number and type of inter-dependent variables that many in the field would like to know and be able to discern what they are. Tuckett and Taffler (2008) and Tuckett (2011), illustrate that emotions really mattered in the financial crisis of 2008. They argue that economists' explanations for what happened in the financial crisis miss the essence because they ignore deep flaws in the organization of financial markets, which are influenced by dynamic components of human psychology. Tuckett suggests that emotion can be systematically incorporated into theories about financial markets and their understanding can be used by boards to create policies to make them safer. His argument is that the crisis resulted from finance leaders' failure to understand and organize markets so that they control the human behaviour they unleash. Financial dynamics have an intrinsically uncertain quality and easily provoke exciting and then frightening stories, thus creating 'divided' mental states and 'groupfeel', not unlike Janis' 'groupthink' (1972).

These aspirations for the future work with boards reference the place of emotion and affect, and caution against the common but unhelpful split between 'individual' and 'society', psychology and sociology. In seeking to overcome such splits, understanding dynamics increasingly illuminates core issues in boards, e.g., role of loss and mourning, nature of identity and culture, experiences of rapid change and negotiation of ethical dilemmas.

Part I

Introduction

Dynamics

The programme Dynamics @ Board Level focuses on 'dynamics' so it is not surprising that a number of authors have focused on the importance of this topic. It is all too easy to seek and find solutions to boardroom functioning in leadership studies, governance regulations or financial oversight; it is more difficult to examine in detail the interactions between roles and people in those roles, and the wellspring for action that comes out of hopes and fears and competition of the board members.

In Chapter 1, Ashley Harshak weighs up the role of the board in ensuring good governance and how a group dynamics perspective can contribute to the debate on good governance. He examines how group dynamics has been integrated into mainstream application of board effectiveness by means of thorough board evaluation. Harshak describes group dynamics as a set of behavioural and psychological processes that occur within a group or between groups – quoting Cartwright and Zander – the "nature of groups, the laws of their development, and their interrelations with individuals, other groups and their institutional environments".

Joe Binnion, in Chapter 2, writes about the need for practical guidance to boards through training, consultancy and the measurement of effectiveness in order to provide insight into the relational dynamics at play. He sets out the case for the relational dynamics of boards and the risk of focusing too much on the 'technical' aspects of board operation. Binnion proposes an early stage balanced framework for board development with some practical implications. Bringing unconscious dynamics to conscious understanding of the board may be the first step in liberating board members and enabling improved board performance.

Vincent Dominé, in Chapter 3, outlines how in the past very little was expected of corporate boards of directors. In theory, board directors had ultimate control of their organizations, but in practice they were chosen by and subservient to management. The board was commonly viewed as a ceremonial add-on to the company and was not considered important to a company's success. Times changed and the general trend towards lean and effective organizations has put pressure on boards to prove their value. Institutional investors now play a greater role in the marketplace and are holding boards accountable. Moreover, robust boards are seen as a way to avoid high-profile and enormously costly corporate scandals. Dominé reasons that boards of directors today have the responsibility and opportunity to be high-performing teams that can be a critical part of company success.

In Chapter 4, Beatriz Boza notes that usually corporate boards are composed of the most qualified, diverse and business-savvy directors, yet they end up underperforming. Enron had a top notch board and so did Lehman Brothers, Northern Rock and Halifax Bank of Scotland. Boza asks why this happens. Applying Wilfred Bion's theory of group dynamics, Boza explains that when boards work to make a company successful, they can get stuck in particular internal dynamics, which are usually dismissed or overlooked. Thus, despite the board being very busy and being convinced that it is performing its task, the possibility of engaging in effective board work is set aside, roles are relinquished and the sight of reality is lost. Understanding such internal dynamics and learning to manage them may provide the necessary vitality boards need in order to deliver their mandate in an ever changing and challenging world.

Maria Claudia Benassi wonders whether a consultant can undertake the herculean task of tackling major socio-political, economic and cultural issues at a national level via a psychodynamics approach, in Chapter 5. How does the consultant engage the nation's leadership in understanding and dealing with these issues? The perspective of systems psychodynamics offers useful supporting arguments. Benassi frames the consultant's role in a coaching-like association in which a light is shone on the quagmire of political intrigue that consultants in this kind of work would find themselves in.

1 Group dynamics and enhancing board effectiveness

Ashley Harshak

"The root causes of most company failures lie in the boardroom".

(Whitehead, 2013)

What is meant by board effectiveness?

In the UK there have been major reports and recommendations for changes in governance with a focus on boards to ensure there would be no repeat of the governance issues that occurred during the crisis (Walker Review, 2009; Board Effectiveness, 2011; UK Corporate Governance Code, 2012).

Group dynamics is regarded as a set of behavioural and psychological processes that occur within a group or between groups. It refers to the "nature of groups, the laws of their development, and their interrelations with individuals, other groups and their institutional environments" (Cartwright & Zander, 1968, p. 19).

Despite the need for greater board effectiveness, it is hard to find an agreed definition of what board effectiveness means. The 1992 Cadbury Report on "The Financial Aspects of Corporate Governance" defined board effectiveness as:

> a board made up of a combination of executive directors, with their intimate knowledge of the business, and of outside, non-executive directors, who can bring a broader view to the company's activities, under a chairman who accepts the duties and responsibilities which the post entails.
>
> (p. 20)

Over time, what is meant by an effective board has moved from a narrow description of who is on the board to one that lays out its important characteristics. In 2011, the Financial Reporting Council (FRC), the body responsible for the UK's corporate governance code, stated that: "An effective board develops and promotes its collective vision of the company's purpose, its culture, its values and the behaviours it wishes to promote in conducting business" (Board Effectiveness, 2011, p. 2; Committee on the Financial Aspects of Corporate Governance, (December 1992). It lists a set of non-exhaustive characteristics, such as providing direction, demonstrating ethical leadership, creating a performance culture, making well-informed decisions and so forth.

Nevertheless, there is no consistency around these characteristics. In 2012, the FRC updated the UK Corporate Governance Code and in its section on effectiveness, it states that to be effective, "[t]he board and its committees should have the appropriate balance of skills, experience, independence and knowledge of the company to enable them to discharge their respective duties and responsibilities effectively" (p. 6). In contrast, other definitions emphasize the importance of clarity of roles (both of the individual and the board), process management, company strategy alignment, and team dynamics, in addition to composition (Dutra, 2012).

This lack of a common definition, or even common attributes does not make the task of enhancing boards' effectiveness easier. In this light, it is interesting to compare the differences between the UK corporate, the central government department and the voluntary sector codes. Of the three, the voluntary sector code states that "an effective board will provide good governance and leadership by working effectively both as individuals and as a team" (The Code Steering Group, 2010, p. 10). The central government code, however, shows no recognition for the role group dynamics plays on boards.

The relevance of group dynamics for board evaluations

In contrast to the divergence of views on effective boards, there is broad consensus around the need for board evaluation. Although there are differences around what should be included in the evaluation and whether this needs to be undertaken by an external evaluator, the UK Corporate Governance Code, 2010, requires all FTSE 350 company boards to undergo an evaluation process at least once every three years, undertaken by an independent external evaluator.

Since 2010, there has been progress as boards have tried to adapt to incorporate governance changes and put in place mechanisms to evaluate board performance. On the whole, the view of board chairs and company secretaries is that evaluations are worthwhile (Muir, 2012). The key areas included in evaluations tend to cover board processes, committee performance, communication, culture and behaviour, risk management, non-executive director (NED) performance, performance of the chair, diversity and succession.

Group dynamics is often seen as one of the numerous aspects for board examination; the National Audit Office's Board Evaluation Questionnaire lists 49 questions that are part of its 'best practice' list and only two of them relate to board (group) dynamics and behaviours (National Audit Office, 2009). In other instances board behaviour is barely mentioned (Heidrick & Struggles, 2014).

Nevertheless, the importance of group dynamics has been one of the key learnings for chairs, "[a]s most companies have improved their governance, the focus for evaluations appears to be moving towards behavioural issues and how behaviour influences overall performance. While chairs recognize the importance of behaviour, few have found an easy way of dealing with the issue" (Muir, 2012, p. 6).

What further contributions can group dynamics play in board effectiveness and evaluation?

From the discussion so far, it is clear that thinking about boards and their effectiveness is continuing to evolve and develop. To date, although aspects of group dynamics have been integrated into practice there is still considerably more that can be applied, specifically in terms of articulating what an effective board might look like and how to evaluate it. Some of the areas where group dynamics thinking and practice can be applied include the meaning of a group, the purpose of the group and its behaviours, roles and skills.

What is a group?

Wilfred Bion, the British psychoanalyst and thinker on group dynamics, in his ground-breaking book *Experiences in Groups* (Bion, 2004) laid out the importance of considering both the individual and the group as a unit of study. This perspective emphasized that individuals cannot be understood, or changed, outside the context of the groups in which they live. "An aggregate cluster of persons becomes a group when interaction between members occurs, when members' awareness of their common relationship develops, and when a common group task emerges . . . when an aggregate becomes a group, the group behaves as a system – an entity or organism that is in some respects greater than the sum of its parts" (Banet & Hayden, 1977, p. 156).

This way of thinking has found its way into many fields, including team effectiveness. Katzenbach and Smith (1999) define high performing teams in ways that are applicable to boards: "A team is a small number of people with complementary skills who are committed to a common purpose, performance goals, and approach for which they hold themselves mutually accountable" (p. 45). Although this definition does refer to key aspects such as skills, purpose, and performance goals, and despite reference to holding themselves mutually accountable for outcomes, it does not do full justice to the relevance of group dynamics.

Katzenbach's and Smith's definition is a useful starting point for a practical definition of board effectiveness. It implies that a board that incorporates a group dynamics perspective would demonstrate behaviours that would enable them to work productively towards their agreed purposes and achieve their performance goals, whilst holding themselves mutually accountable. This approach is a significant advance on more commonly used definitions of board effectiveness that either describe the makeup of a board or focus on results.

Group behaviours

As noted, board chairs acknowledge that behaviour is an important aspect of board performance, which is coming under increased scrutiny, and is an area that they find difficult to deal with probably because of lack of training. It is enlightening to refer to the work of Kurt Lewin, who first used the term *group dynamics* in the 1940s. Lewin, (1947) through his ideas on Field Theory, identified an important dynamic in group behaviour, viz., an individual's level of conduct may differ from the level of the group's accepted conduct by a permitted amount. This idea acknowledges that accepted group standards and behaviours may either enable or constrain individual behaviours. For instance, in the case of the Royal Bank of Scotland board's decision to acquire ABN Amro, the board's directors did not demand detailed due diligence, or question the necessity of this acquisition despite it going against their own strategy, which they had reaffirmed prior to the acquisition (Financial Services Authority, 2011).

Applying Lewin's ideas in order to optimise company performance would imply that boards recognize and tolerate individual variation, which would facilitate open challenges of behaviour, increased diversity and openness. This would demand that boards define, clarify and encourage behaviours that are acceptable and desired in practice.

Lewin demonstrated the effectiveness of his idea that group pressures to conform – as compared to individual commitment to change – can be used powerfully to facilitate and drive behavioural change. In one important study a group of mothers were shown the benefits of giving their children orange juice for nutritional purposes and under group pressure 100% of them conformed. In contrast, where mothers were provided with individual instructions and left to their own devices, only 40% conformed (De Board, 1978). This has important implications for boards, showing the importance of working collectively to change and challenge their behaviours rather than through one-to-one discussions, say between the chair and individual directors.

Group purpose

Group behaviours and ways to understand, influence and shape them are skills that have to be deployed simultaneously as the board is engaged with the business content of its meetings. In this area, Bion offers helpful insights. He understands that there is an explicit purpose of the group – the conscious reason for its existence, and that the group is also subject to unconscious forces acting upon it. Bion argues that in every group, two groups are present at the same time; one he calls the "work group" and the other the "basic assumption group". The work group is that aspect of the group which has to do with the real conscious work of the business of the group that each member has joined and to fulfil its purpose. According to Rioch, "The group constantly tests its conclusions in a scientific spirit. It seeks for knowledge, learns from experience and constantly questions how it may achieve of its goal" (Rioch, 1970, p. 58). For this to be the case, the board needs to be clear what its purpose is and how it is going to operate to fulfil that purpose.

Bion argues that all groups, while engaged in their business, i.e., while being the "work group", also operate under the influence of what he calls a "basic assumption", a dynamic that is outside of individual and group awareness. Although the work group is what has brought the members of the group together, they also often behave as if the "basic assumptions" are more important than the work they have come together to do. Bion developed the concept of basic assumptions to explain why this happens and what its characteristics are. The issue is the degree to which dynamic dominates the group. He believed that there are three distinct emotional states of groups from which it is possible to deduce three basic assumptions: dependency, fight/flight and pairing.

When a group is under the influence of dependency, it behaves as if the purpose of the group is to be sustained by a leader on whom it depends. In this scenario, the group blindly follows the leader who is seen as all-knowing and all-powerful. However, when the leader fails to fulfil the group's expectations, as surely they must, it arouses disappointment and hostility. It is not hard to see how this dynamic may be experienced in a board where a strong CEO or Chair dominates, often ending in failure. An example of this phenomenon can be seen in the 2002 WorldCom bankruptcy, where the CEO and CFO undertook a $3.8 billion accounting fraud. According to the bankruptcy examiner, one board member referred to Ebbers (the CEO) as "God", "Jesus Christ" and "Superman" (Hopkins, 2003).

The second basic assumption is that of fight/flight. In this mode, the group behaves as if it exists to either fight against or flee from a threat. Fight or flight are the only techniques the group is aware of. If a group is preoccupied with this assumption, it will ignore other activities and possibilities and only focus on the perceived threat, or it will attempt to avoid the threat completely and concentrate on peripheral matters. The group in this frame cannot develop or do useful work; all its energies are concentrated on the dominating assumption, to the detriment of its attention to its purpose. It is easy to appreciate how this can apply to boards when, for instance, the board focuses on one topic and believes that 'outsiders are the enemy', or situations where boards ignore or avoid the major issues they are facing and find other less important areas to concentrate on. In the case of the collapse of Enron in 2001, it was a whistle-blower who brought to light the risky accounting practices and concealing of debt that resulted in the company's collapse. When the board was notified of the whistle-blower's letter, no director asked to see the letter or sought to understand what the range of questionable practices were. In essence, the board chose 'flight' and so remained ignorant of the most damaging disclosures (Byrne, 2002; Permanent Subcommittee on Investigations of the Committee on Governmental Affairs US Senate Permanent Subcommittee on Investigations of the Committee on Governmental Affairs US Senate, 2002).

The third basic assumption is that of pairing. Here the assumption is that the board has met for purposes of reproduction, to bring forth a new idea or new product that will save the company. It is engaged in a messianic saviour-type behaviour in which two people usually get together on behalf of the group to 'save' it by providing the ideal solution. The pairing basic assumption group is characterized by great hope, yet within this hope lies future disappointment when it is not fulfilled. The majority of the group steps back and eagerly follows the lead of the two paired members. The dynamics allow the group to deny difficult and painful situations and decisions. In terms of boards, it is possible to imagine a chair and CEO (or potentially a strong NED) 'pairing', painting the picture of a rosy future possibility, ignoring difficulties in the current reality. The rest of the board colludes with the pair in imagining a trouble-free future. Part of the failure of HBOS, a major British bank, can be understood through recognition that the board sat back and allowed the executive team to drive its discussions. Challenge was expected to come from the executives, rather than the non-executives or the full board, yet one of the NEDs went on to state that HBOS' board "was by far and away the best board I ever sat on" (Parliamentary Commission on Banking Standards, 2013, p. 29).

The fact that boards take on a life of their own and can get waylaid into unconscious basic assumption behaviours is enlightening and concerning. This is a challenge for the board to understand and tackle. The presence of these hidden basic assumptions is the reason why self-evaluation is not recommended and the services of an external independent evaluator is thought to be more useful.

Group roles

It is commonly acknowledged that the effectiveness of the board can be determined by the extent to which people are effective in their roles. Board evaluation should devote time and attention to an examination of roles, how clearly the roles are understood and the inter-relationships between roles and role-holders. Usually, attention is focused on the roles of the chair and the CEO. However, more focus is beginning to be given to NEDs and the senior independent director.

Specifically, the chair is seen as setting the agenda and the tone of the discussions. "Good boards are created by good chairmen. The chairman creates the conditions for overall board and individual director effectiveness" (FRC, 2011, p. 2). Although undoubtedly true that the chair plays a critical part in the dynamic, the argument that the chair is the deciding factor misses the point that chair will "both influence and be influenced by . . . the actual and anticipated behaviours and demands of others on the board. Susceptibility to group and social influence is not a trait of those who lack willpower; it is hard-wired into all of us" (Walker, 2009, p. 140). It has been long understood that organizational roles result from how individuals seek to operate within the boundaries set for them by the organization or others (Katz & Kahn, 1966).

As highlighted in the FRC's guidance on effective boards, the CEO is the most senior executive director on the board with responsibility for proposing strategies to the board, and for delivering the strategies as agreed. Thus, the CEO's relationship with the chair is important. The challenge for both parties is to liaise effectively and respectfully within a sphere that encourages transparency, allows for challenge and ensures that the CEO does not dictate to the board. Undoubtedly this is a vital relationship that needs examination in any evaluation.

In evaluating boards the effectiveness of NEDs is also relevant. NEDs often feel that given their limited understanding and day-to-day involvement in the organization they are at a major disadvantage to the CEO and other executive directors. A considerable danger for NEDs is insufficient knowledge about a business to be able to challenge an executive proposal. "Directors frequently do what they do to avoid looking foolish, to avoid angering the CEO, and to be liked. The deference afforded CEOs stems from the perception that, as one director put it, 'when we are in the boardroom, we are on his territory'" (Zweig, 2010, p. 4). Unsurprisingly, therefore, one perspective on evaluating NEDs focuses on the amount of time they devote to their role (Zweig, 2010). Some have argued that there should be a senior independent director (or super director) whose role should be to ensure that there are sufficient levels of understanding and challenge.

Group skills

In addition to evaluating the roles of the board, skills need to be included as well. The importance of skills was highlighted in the case of Paul Flowers, chairman of the Coop Bank, who resigned in the wake of allegedly buying illegal drugs. Mr Flowers was appointed to the role of chair despite a lack of banking experience and limited commercial experience (Goff & Jacobs, 2014).

It is widely recognized that boards need to be made up of people with the required skills if it is to be effective and that this needs to be part of any evaluation. The types of skill generally highlighted are industry knowledge, finance and accounting skills, and the legal/regulatory requirements of corporate governance. Along with this are often added specific functional skills such as marketing, strategy development, etc., which individual NEDs add to the board makeup.

What generally does not get thrown into the mix is an understanding of group dynamics and processes, particularly as it pertains to power, decision-making, appointments to the board and risk. Gill and Sher (2009) argue that "as part of qualifying to be a chair, Executive Director or NED, individuals should be trained in how to take up roles, manage role boundaries, and understand the difference between power, authority and group dynamics" (Walker, 2009, p. 142).

Conclusions

From this discussion of board effectiveness and evaluation, a number of points emerge. The first is the need for greater clarity in the characterization of board effectiveness and the importance for such a definition to include group dynamics as a core element. There has been substantial development in research, which needs to influence boards but is not yet applied. We should therefore be concerned with the continuing need to develop a meaningful definition of board effectiveness, applicable to all sectors.

Secondly, under corporate governance codes, there is a growing requirement for boards to undergo external evaluation. However, there is an element of uneasiness in doing so "because of an underlying fear that a review might destabilize a board that is functioning effectively or perhaps expose one that is not" (Sher, 2011, p. 8). Self-assessment of the unconscious processes that operate in boards is difficult, if not impossible, to achieve. The hesitancy to use external evaluation stems from the wide disparity in quality and outcomes, as well as the lack of an agreed way of undertaking evaluations (Sher, 2011).

Finally, there is a need to develop board capabilities in understanding group dynamics and how they can be influenced. Board chairs have recognized that this is an area in which they are increasingly struggling and for which they lack the skills to handle. Only when boards have the ability to understand and act in a manner that optimises their group dynamics, will boards be able to operate openly and transparently in a challenging and learning environment that supports effective outcomes.

It is clear that despite the focus on boards, board effectiveness and evaluation, this is still an undeveloped area of study. Group dynamics and some of its core principles have a tremendous amount to add. The question is whether boards are up to the challenge.

2 Improving board dynamics

Towards a balanced framework

Joe Binnion

Introduction

Boards 'lead' our public and private institutions. They are populated by the people who we perceive to be leaders – those with the brightest minds or particular talents. The role of the directors, manifest in the activities and decisions of the board, is set out in statute. In undertaking this role, the directors enact their roles with a mind towards their individual responsibility brought to bear through their membership of a group.

Much practical board guidance and board member training is biased towards statutory responsibility, board process, structure, role definition, evaluation and succession. Limited practical guidance and training is provided in the working dynamics of boards (or indeed the executive teams who deliver on the board's behalf). People are left to fend for themselves to understand the dynamics at play, often misinterpreted as 'politics'. It seems the expectation placed upon them is that because they have 'made it' to the board, they somehow understand what is going on. There is significant unconscious processing at play in any group dynamics – it is possible that 'everything' really does matter when considering what is happening within a group.

It is the argument of this chapter that in a very practical sense, too much emphasis is placed on factors such as process or governance and not nearly enough on the dynamics between individuals at the board table – and therefore, a more balanced framework is required to help develop and assess the performance of boards in the future.

Board members: an eclectic mix

It is important to understand the mix of people that might form a board. The people appointed and indeed their number will vary across organizations, but when all things are considered, there will be an eclectic mix.

'Inherent' and 'acquired' diversity

There has been much discourse about the diversity of boards when considering gender. Whilst the 'old school' tie is increasingly fading, it is still present. There has been an increase in female company directors over recent years, particularly as institutional investors have put a spotlight on gender diversity. A decade ago, women directors held 16% of seats in the S&P 500, compared to 22% in 2017 (Spencer Stuart, 2017). There is much work needed to improve the composition of our boards, and initiatives such as the 2020 Campaign seeks to eliminate all-white boards by the end of this decade (Diversity UK Editor, 2014).

The 'inherent diversity' factors such as age, disability, gender, race, and sexual orientation have informed our response to diversity to date and whilst there is a long way to go, there is an increasing awareness in organizations of the conscious and/or unconscious biases that arise as a result of these factors (Diversity, 2016). It is a conceptual step to understand how 'acquired diversity' factors such as education, experience of overseas cultures and work experience more generally, might influence people and their perceptions.

Even only considering the factors that are visible or that can be easily understood from someone's CV, directors today need to become increasingly able to deal with a diverse range of people and the impacts that this diversity may have on group dynamics. A significant proportion of the behaviours or misinterpretation of behaviours is due to lack of knowledge or understanding (Diversity, 2016).

Styles and types

Understanding one's type preference enables one to approach work in a manner that best suits one's style (myersbriggs.org, 2016). Psychometric frameworks, such as Myers-Briggs, appeal to the cognitive processing of leaders and have become accepted methods for development of people and teams within organizations.

The range of tools that helps people to recognize their own and others' 'types', communication styles and behaviours whilst under pressure, is helpful. However, it is not the purpose of this chapter to evaluate these tools, whether successful working together comes down to a 'type', whether people change behaviours as a result of their 'types' and/or whether 'types' change over time. The prevalence of these frameworks is proof enough that people accept and understand some diversity that is hidden, perhaps only revealed through a questionnaire, some coaching and discussion.

Sensual perceptions

Diversity and 'types' are not enough. We also need to consider our hidden and sensual perceptions. From early childhood we create banks of experience that are called upon in subtle ways (Bowlby, 2005). Emotional reactions can be invoked as a result of our attachments to important figures, or our responses to sound or smells, for example. We may need to continually ask ourselves what impact our environment, or the presence of other people, is having on our own responses.

By way of a practical example, in my early consulting training, I was encouraged to never wear strong aftershave because the smell could invoke emotional, sometimes primitive, responses in a client. The risk that the response could be something significantly detrimental was too great.

This type of more primitive response is on the boundary between our conscious and unconscious selves. Most of us are aware of what we hear or smell, and more often than not, the emotion that is evoked. However, we can be taken by surprise and may indeed be impacted at levels we do not fully understand.

The glorious eclectic mix

All of the above, diversity (inherent or acquired), types and our sensual percep-tions provide for a glorious eclectic mix on walking into a board room. Before any business has started, there is already a lot going on in the space between people. Any board member unaware of this will be ill-equipped in their role.

Board dynamics: the prevalence of the unconscious

Moving away from the mix of individuals, types and sensual perceptions in the room covered in the previous section, we now turn our attention to the uncon-scious processing actually going on for each of us as individuals.

Childhood influences

Some of the basic tenets of psychoanalysis are helpful in pointing us toward the significance of our unconscious responses and the pathways toward liberation (Brissett & Sher, 2015):

1 Besides the inherited constitution of personality, a person's development is determined by events in early childhood.
2 Human behaviour, experience, and cognition are largely determined by irra-tional drives.
3 Those drives are largely unconscious.
4 Attempts to bring those drives into awareness meet psychological resistance in the form of defence mechanisms.
5 Conflicts between conscious and unconscious material can result in mental disturbances such as neurosis, neurotic traits, anxiety, depression etc., and conflict in groups.
6 The liberation from the effects of unconscious material is achieved through bringing this material into the conscious mind via skilled guidance.

Even though there is a range of theoretical frameworks that explain board behav-iours, there is overwhelming evidence to support the view that our ways of being are influenced by our early experiences, especially the nature of early attachments (Bowlby, 2005).

The uniqueness of individuals around the boardroom table means peoples' responses and motivations may not always appear as they seem.

Non-verbal communication

The idea that 60–65% of interpersonal communication is conveyed via non-verbal behaviors is now commonly accepted (Burgoon et al., 2009). The bulk of commentary in this area concerns our body language. However, our non-verbal communication is much more than that. Within the non-verbal domain, there are many other considerations such as touch, distance, eye contact, our measure of time, and our paralanguage – the rhythm, pitch, quality, volume of our speech. Non-verbal communication is essentially modes of expression with the exclusion of words, and yet it impacts our communications profoundly.

Not all non-verbal communication is unconscious. For the purpose of this chapter it is assumed that there is a correlation between non-verbal and unconscious processing for it to warrant recognition as a major contributor to group dynamics in the boardroom.

It is important to consider how non-verbal communication impacts others in the boardroom and how other people's non-verbal communication impacts us. If 60% of everything everyone says is non-verbal, and predominantly unconscious, there is a lot being said and heard that we are not cognizant of.

The inner voice shouting loudest

It has not been possible to consider all of the potential inner dialogue that exists for the directors within a board meeting. It is my intention to explore this more and to thereby suggest areas of potential research.

The following vignette has particular resonance – a retired senior civil servant who has chaired a number of public and private sector boards is speaking:

> Firstly, I'm choosing where to sit. I'm wondering if where I sit in relation to others is going to work. Am I sitting too close to a particular person, or does another care I'm not sitting close to them? Where will I best see what is going on? Should I just sit down and relax? Should I sit forward or back? How do I look? Professional, interested, calm and ready for this?
>
> The meeting begins. With a good process and Chair, it begins on time. There is an agenda. There is a procedure people are familiar with – it requires adherence to a set of accepted behaviours, nods, noises of approval.
>
> I'm paying attention to the order of the meeting. I've just heard something I want to contribute to. I'm here for a reason – I have a point of view. Wait though, I might wait to see what others say. I agree with this, I don't necessarily agree with that. Frankly, I don't understand that – but can't really ask what on earth they are talking about (that would disrupt the process).
>
> I've crafted my point. I've rehearsed it several times in my mind. I'm certain about my point now, I'm going for it. Then someone says it for me – better or worse. Or I get the point in and, regardless of whether I bumble my way through my articulation or not, I'm left playing it over, wondering if people understood it. Did I say something as incoherent as some of the others before

me? What will the 'important' people in the room think of my perspective? I'm not sure it landed quite right.

I'll spend the next ten minutes processing what I said internally. I'm not listening fully to the conversation. I don't hear the content. I'm not interested in the dynamic between us. I've got my inner dialogue to attend to. I've missed a significant number of the points – or at least wasn't in full attendance to them.

This cycle might repeat itself, or business may have moved on to something else.

However, before long, the meeting is over and I've spent about half of my time processing what was going on internally for me rather than what was going on in the room.

(Fieldwork notes of a consultation)

The above account highlights the prevalence of the inner voice and all the processing that is going on. Whilst it may not mirror everyone's experience, people have an inner dialogue going on of some kind and the impact of that inner voice on the overall group dynamics is at least interesting if not profoundly important in understanding the overall set of board dynamics. It is where individual thought meets group process.

Bringing the unconscious into consciousness

Processing unconscious dynamics in boards requires consideration of what is happening within and between people. Helping boards to be aware of their behaviour leads to change. The liberating effects of unconscious material are achieved through bringing this material into consciousness – this is critical to the work of consultants or advisers to boards.

Creating a better dynamic – toward a balanced framework

Given everything going on in groups, the following practical guidance is offered:

Technical vs interpersonal factors

There is significant literature focused on the 'technical' factors relating to boards, including board composition, governance, structure and roles, processes, agendas, forward planning, reporting, statutory responsibilities, succession and that the achievement of strategy. There is a lot to refer to, all saying roughly the same (we need order and structure) and is developed to respond to the cognitive/analytical thought processes that dominate our board structures. However, this chapter highlights the influence of dynamics of boards and questions why the subject of dynamics is not given more prominence. This is a gap that must be addressed by consultants in their work with boards. These 'technical' vs 'inter-relational' factors form the first dimension in the balanced framework below.

A risk to note is the positing of 'technical' vs 'inter-relational' factors as 'hard' vs 'soft'. In the cognitive worlds of leaders, there is a bias toward the 'hard' factors and this perhaps explains why 'technical' factors are dominant in the literature. It is this imbalance that must be addressed. Using vision as a metaphor, it can be said that the piercing focus of 'hard' factors is myopic; peripheral vision or 'soft' eyes are also necessary for survival.

Individual vs board

Another key dimension is the individual vs the board-as-a-whole. Performances of both are relevant. As directors, board members are individually responsible, but they also contribute to overall board effectiveness. Improvement in board dynamics and functioning comes as a result of improvement both at group and individual levels.

Towards a balanced framework – an initial model

Considering technical, interpersonal, board and individual factors leads us to the framework shown in Table 2.1. The content of each of the boxes may be debated and developed but for the purposes of this chapter, it is the implications of the framework that are most important to consider.

Implication 1: A re-balance to account for the 'interpersonal' is necessary in our consideration of board effectiveness. If boards are to become more effective when in session, at least 50% of the solution lies in the interpersonal factors – yet little attention is placed in this area at present.

Table 2.1 An initial model for a balanced framework

	Technical	Interpersonal
Overall board effectiveness	• Board composition & diversity • Governance • Structure & roles • Agendas/forward planning • Reporting • Succession • Statutory responsibilities • Organization performance	• Styles & types • Unconscious dynamics • Over-ridden or ignored dynamics • Group interrelations • Group collective awareness
Individual board member capability	• Individual performance plans • Chairman performance • Individual assessment • Bonuses/incentives	• Awareness of self and others • Internal processing – inner voice • Styles/skills • Sensory perception • Nonverbal communication • Diversity awareness

Implication 2: Individual board members are as responsible for their 'inter-personal' development as they are for their 'technical' development. Failure of a board member to pay attention to their own 'interpersonal' development in the context of their board dynamic, could be interpreted as a failure in their duty of care to that dynamic.

Implication 3: The role of the chair in establishing an improved dynamic is key. There is a 'technical' requirement or a process that could be implemented by chairs, to ensure enough attention is paid to the 'interpersonal' by individual board members.

Implication 4: Developing tools that can assist in understanding and improving the relational dynamics is key. Some tools already exist. Others could be developed to highlight to boards the inherent unconscious bias or processing that takes place. These tools should be as prevalent and easy to use as those that support the 'technical'.

Conclusion

This chapter argues for the re-balancing of our understanding and development of boards and integrating the 'technical' aspects with the 'interpersonal or inter-relational'. Without such a rebalance – training, consulting and evaluation of boards will be deficient. Will boards improve as a result of this re-balance? There are a few indicators that this might be the case. In an associated domain – diversity, for example, there is evidence of improved board performance when a board is more diverse (Green Park, 2016; Barta et al., 2012). If we can assume that diverse boards are more aware of their relational dynamics, then there should be a correlation between improved relational dynamics and improved performance.

There is a movement towards assessment of relational dynamics. What if boards needed to be assessed on their dynamics as much as their technical processes? Perhaps there are learnings from other domains (e.g., school evaluation) that could be applied to boards – for the good of our public and private sector organizations.

Finally, it is clear that focus on the 'inter-relational is different from the 'technical'. However, we hope that the adoption of techniques such as the Myers Briggs Personality Type Indicator means that at least the door is open for discussion on dynamics. As always, there is a balance required – a stick and a carrot – the stick: making it the responsibility of directors to focus on their personal development and group dynamics; the carrot: evidence-based improved board performance.

3 Mastering group dynamics

Embedding a learning and coaching culture in board work

Vincent H. Dominé

What is the best way to produce effective boards?

One approach is the approach of good technical corporate governance: to produce a strong board, you need to identify the features of effective boards and get boards to adopt these features.

Following the technical approach, a strong board should consist of directors with diverse, complementary skills and expertise. Directors should have a wealth of experience and be both well-connected and respected. A strong board should also implement the right procedures and practices. For example, directors should attend meetings regularly and arrive prepared for meetings; the board should consist of an optimal number of directors, including a minimum number who are independent; the right sub-committees should be established; the board should hold regular executive sessions and annual self-evaluations.

The trouble with the technical approach is that it does not necessarily produce effective boards. Practices like the ones described above may often contribute to board effectiveness, but on their own they are not enough. A board can meet most or all accepted standards and still not excel. Unfortunately, there are no easy-to-follow formulas that guarantee strong boards (Behan, 2006; Sonnenfeld, 2002; George, 2012).

How is it possible for a board with the right procedures and with competent, experienced, well-intentioned directors to fall short of the mark? Boards are groups of people, and all groups, including the best-constructed boards, are affected by dynamics that can inhibit them from achieving their aims. A board is a social system made up of individuals, and each individual's unique identity and ways of operating contribute to the overall group dynamics.

If a board is to excel, it must have a positive group dynamic that supports and enables its efforts. Findings from the Conference Board Governance Center have shown that "collective board behaviour" has an 800% greater impact on firm performance than the characteristics of individual directors (Charas, 2014). Industry experts and directors themselves now widely recognize that good group dynamics are key to board success (Lorsch, 2012; Sonnenfeld, 2002; Merchant & Pick, 2010; Forbes & Milliken, 1999; Cairns, 2003). As Ram Charan (2005) puts it: "Group dynamics underpins the board's ability to do all the components of its job – whether it's compliance and monitoring or making contributions to strategy and CEO selection".

What are good group dynamics on a board?

Before we can consider ways of improving group dynamics on boards, we need first to understand what group dynamics are and how they affect boards. In my work with boards and executive teams, I have adopted an understanding of group dynamics that is inspired and informed by the theory of the psychoanalyst Wilfred Bion.

Bion (2004) writes that groups come together to fulfil a purpose. The purpose of a board is to fulfil the roles and responsibilities that are expected of its directors. These roles and responsibilities include supporting and challenging management, protecting the organization's assets, managing CEO succession and taking leadership in times of crisis. When a board carries out its roles and responsibilities, it is pursuing its primary task or the task that it was set up to fulfil. The primary task is the board's *raison d'être*.

When a board is pursuing its primary task, the board is in a state that Bion calls 'the work group'. Bion understood that when a group is working together towards achieving a task, it can easily be sidetracked or distracted from achieving its goal because of the dynamic within the group. When a group has been distracted, it is pursuing secondary tasks, i.e., tasks other than the ones it is supposed to be pursuing.

How does a board become sidetracked from pursuing its primary task? The answer is simple: boards are teams of unique individuals, each with their own sets of experiences, beliefs, preferences, desires, needs and fears. When working on a board, directors strive sincerely to advance company interests, but they also have their own emotional life with needs and interests that must be met and protected. In some cases, directors are fully mindful of these interests and needs, but in other cases they are unaware. When the emotional needs of one or more directors are not being adequately met, directors may act out. This in turn may lead other directors to react and this can force the board's attention away from the work it is supposed to be doing.

Sometimes it will be obvious to directors that a board is going off track, e.g., if the board is mediating between two directors who are unable to get along. Instead of focusing on its primary task, the board is forced to spend time and energy on relationship management. What makes Bion's theory profound is that in his theory, individuals within a group are generally unaware of the impact that their emotional lives or "mental phenomena" are having on the group's work. They often fail to recognize when these interests have diverted the group from pursuing its primary task.

Take the extreme example of a board that is subject to groupthink. When groupthink sets in, a group that is highly cohesive and insulated from outside influences achieves consensus on a decision without carefully considering the various options (Brown, 2000). Because decisions made under the influence of groupthink are detached from reality, they often turn out badly. Assume that members of a board are dealing with a crisis and have agreed on a decision because they are anxious and are unconsciously seeking a sense of security in consensus. In this case, the directors may think that they are pursuing their primary task, but in fact the board has been thrown off track. The directors have been diverted to a secondary task by their need to manage their own anxiety. A board under the influence of groupthink lacks the kind of diversity that matters most: not diversity of gender or culture but of thought.

The anxiety that directors must deal with often stems from external causes. However, Bion believed that being part of a group in itself is a fundamental source of anxiety. According to Bion, we all have a deep-seated ambivalence towards participating in groups. On the one hand, participating in groups is an essential part of life. As humans, we have a need to belong to groups and to be recognized and affirmed by them, and we seek out groups to fulfill this need. On the other hand, because we are dependent on groups for this recognition, we are concerned about how the group perceives us and this can lead us to resent the group or be anxious about our involvement in them.

Bion (1961) explains that our relationship to groups is essentially paradoxical: we join groups so that we can belong, but we also want to stand out and be recognized as individuals within those groups. When a group forms there is an expectation on the part of the individuals forming it of achieving some satisfaction from the group. However, one of the first things they are aware of is a sense of frustration produced by the presence of the group of which they are members. This tension in our basic attitude towards groups – this clash between our need for relatedness and our need for autonomy – is a source of anxiety and frustration that can manifest itself in and influence the group dynamic of boards.

It should be clear from this discussion that having good group dynamics on a board is not the same thing as directors merely getting along well with each other. On an effective board, it is undoubtedly helpful, even necessary, for directors to respect each other and work well together. But as we see from the groupthink example, a group can work well together and still be sidetracked from pursuing its primary task.

A good board dynamic is not one in which directors are merely cohesive but one in which directors interact in such a way (a) that their emotional needs and interests do not interfere with – and ideally align and support – the board's performance of its roles and responsibilities, and (b) that allows the board to perform those roles and responsibilities optimally.

Promoting good board dynamics

To summarize, a board exists to serve an organization, but a board also has an emotional life. If the emotional needs of the individuals on the board are not being met adequately, these will interfere with the board's functioning and the board will be unable to do its job properly. In contrast, if a board can attend to the emotional life of the group, this can help the board to prevent problems from arising in the group dynamics.

Perhaps more importantly, a strong board that cultivates a good group dynamic and a positive emotional environment can enhance its performance even more and make itself exceptional. This can put in motion a virtuous cycle: a strong group dynamic on the board allows directors to accomplish more, which in turn strengthens and reinforces the emotional life of the group.

To promote strong board dynamics, directors need to develop a learning and coaching culture that enhances collaboration on the board. Establishing a learning and coaching culture involves three components: acknowledgement, awareness and action.

Acknowledgement

Few boards give their own group dynamics the attention that they deserve. Instead, directors focus most of their time and energy on task-related work. For directors, responsibilities can be great and their time limited, but to optimize their performance boards should be concerned not only with getting the job done, but also with tending to the board's emotional life. The first step for directors in establishing a learning and coaching culture is to recognize and acknowledge that group dynamics impact board performance and that directors should invest time and energy in cultivating good group dynamics.

Boards are distinct from other types of corporate teams in at least two important ways. These distinctions make it even more important for boards to be deliberate about finding ways to better function as a group.

First, directors are usually very senior with extensive professional experience and solid reputations. A lot is expected of directors and they can feel pressure to appear strong and in control. Even today, boards function often in an atmosphere of elaborate civility, decorum and with reserve. This is not an ideal context for directors to discuss how they are feeling and to divulge potentially sensitive issues. Directors must recognize that group dynamics have an impact on board functioning even in the rarefied air of the boardroom and they must be open to ways of making the boardroom environment more conducive to learning and understanding how directors interact as a team.

Second, unlike the members of most corporate teams, directors do not work together full-time. Boards meet only a handful of times each year and there is sometimes little personal contact among directors between meetings. This makes it difficult for directors to get to know each other well and to learn how best to work together. Because directors do not connect regularly with each other outside of meetings, it is especially important for directors to find creative ways of developing social bonds and spaces for dialogue and courageous conversations. The opposite of this can also be true, where some board members know each other really well, may work together on other boards or have converging loyalties or family-ties. This might lead to collusion between some members of the board and create imbalances within the board at large.

Awareness

When directors are working together in a board meeting, they are generally concentrated on and fully aware of the content of their discussion. But in any board meeting, a lot is happening that directors are often either less aware of or not aware of at all: in particular, how participants are behaving and how this behaviour is impacting the board's work. To have good group dynamics, board members need to have a clear sense of what the group dynamic is and this requires that directors pay attention to it.

In their book on Bion, French and Simpson (2015) distinguish between two types of attention. When directors are fully engaged in their work, they are primarily exercising focused attention. With focused attention, they block out extraneous features of their environment and inner experience and zone in on the task at hand. In contrast, evenly suspended attention is not concentrated but wide open. It is a more passive form of attention in which a person takes in what is happening in the moment, both all around and within. Part of evenly suspended attention is the capacity to experience emotion without being overwhelmed by it.

Awareness of group dynamics – of the subtle facets of behaviour around us and our role in this behaviour – requires evenly suspended attention. If a director is too focused on what is being discussed, that person will be unable to pick up on his own behavioural cues and those of other directors. Or to use a different analogy, a director at times needs to 'get off the dance floor and get onto the balcony' for a different, more distanced perspective on what is happening (Heifetz et al., 2009, p. 252). If a director is uncertain about what is happening during a discussion, the director can "press the pause button" to get some perspective by stopping the conversation and asking questions about what is going on in the here and now. For example, a director may say to the board: "I'm struggling right now. What is the question we are trying to answer?"

To increase their awareness of the board dynamic, directors should strive to be aware of four aspects of group interaction.

A. Non-verbal communication

Non-verbal communication, including gestures, body position, facial expressions and vocal tones, is a crucial component of human interaction (Furnham & Petrova, 2010).

To gauge group dynamics effectively, directors need to be aware of non-verbal signals, both their own and those of others. A director's body language can clearly communicate how that director is feeling. For example, psychologists know from studies on both primates and humans that open, expansive body positions and gestures communicate power and confidence, while enclosed body positions and gestures show that the person is feeling powerless or threatened (Carney & Hall, 2005).

Body language can impact the mood on the board. Directors will pick up on and react to the body language of others in group, often unconsciously. Observing the body language of other directors is a good way not only to assess the board's emotional state but also to identify ways in which directors can improve their non-verbal communication and create a more positive board dynamic.

B. Informal roles

Formal roles are roles that are assigned to people and are explicit, such as chairman, lead director or CEO. Informal roles are adopted unofficially by individuals within a group. Informal roles include task roles that help enhance group productivity, such as initiator-contributor, opinion seeker, devil's advocate and maintenance roles that help to keep up group cohesion, such as encourager and compromiser (Franz, 2012). Our personalities influence the informal roles that we play, but so does the context of the group. For example, one may usually play the role of devil's advocate, but within the dynamic of a different group someone else might assume that role.

It is important for directors to be aware of the informal roles they are playing within the board. Sometimes a director can get stuck in one role and not contribute as effectively to board discussion as may be optimally possible. Awareness of the roles directors are assuming is the first step in adopting new roles. Also for a board to function optimally, it needs directors to take up a wide range of informal roles within the team. By paying attention to the roles directors play, they can identify important informal roles that are perhaps missing on the board and ensure that the range of roles is properly balanced.

C. Context

The context of a board meeting is the sum of all the events and circumstances that can have an effect on the board's dynamic. It can include recent incidents within the board, events affecting the company and global economic and political events. It also includes the environment or physical space in which the meeting is being held: the atmosphere of the boardroom, the seating order, etc.

Being aware of context can help directors to understand the group dynamic and even to anticipate how the group dynamic might unfold. In board simulations that I observe, I am always amazed that hardly any participants question the sequence of agenda items, even though this sequence can clearly affect the decision making process. For example, assume the board is slated to first decide on an acquisition and then to hold a discussion on executive compensation. If the board decides against the acquisition – one that management has spent several months evaluating and stands to gain from financially – management will likely be demotivated during the compensation review and this in return may influence the decision of the board.

Unspoken issues

Sometimes the way a board functions is affected most not by what is being said but by what is not being said. Directors may avoid addressing certain important issues because raising them could provoke anxiety or conflict. When the issue is one that all or most of the directors are aware of, it becomes the proverbial 'elephant in the room' issues like these do not fix themselves and tend to get worse with time.

Unspoken issues are a barrier to transparency and can be a source of frustration for directors and can reinforce a culture of passivity on the board. If there are important unspoken issues, directors should identify them so they can be addressed and they should be aware of how these issues might be impacting the way directors are interacting.

Action

Acknowledgement and awareness of group dynamics are important, but on their own they are not enough. A board must agree on and put in place measures and regular practices that promote and maintain good board dynamics. This can be challenging, since boards meet infrequently and have tight schedules. But in my experience, it pays to invest a reasonable amount of time and energy to understanding and improving how the board functions as a group.

Below are some of the ways that boards can embed a learning and coaching culture in their practices.

A. *Practice checking in and checking out*

In most board meetings, directors get straight down to business. By taking time at the beginning of every meeting for directors to check in with each other, boards can make sure that their meetings get off on the right foot.

When checking in, each director should have a chance to talk about 'where they are at': how they are feeling, important events that have occurred in their lives, expectations they have for the meeting, any concerns they may have and so forth. If the checking in process is to be effective, it should not be rushed and it should not be a mere formality. Directors should be candid, transparent and not afraid to share details of their personal lives.

By checking in, directors are able to:

- Connect with each other and get into sync for the remainder of the meeting;
- Get to know each other better and build trust;
- Better understand the perspectives of other directors;
- Identify issues that may be a source of concern and anxiety for certain directors.

This checking-in period is particularly important for boards because directors often do not have a lot of opportunity for personal interaction with each other between formal meetings.

Similarly, directors can bring proper closure to their board meetings by taking time at the end of the meeting to 'check out'. This is an opportunity for directors to reflect as a group on how the meeting went when it is still fresh in everyone's minds. As with checking in, directors who are checking out should discuss not only what they are thinking, but also what they are feeling. Did the board accomplish what it set out to accomplish in the meeting? What was the dynamic of the meeting like overall? Pleasant? Relaxed? Intense? Did everyone get a chance to participate? Are there any unresolved issues from the meeting that still need to be addressed? What did the board learn from the meeting about how it functions? What would the board try to do differently the next time?

B. Experiment with different informal roles

We have already seen that directors can get stuck in particular informal roles and that boards need directors to play a variety of roles if they are to function well. To promote a well-balanced and complete range of informal roles on the board, directors can:

- Address the issue explicitly by taking time to discuss informal roles and the role dynamics on the board;
- Identify if there are holes or role imbalances on the board. Is there enough devil's advocate? Is there a supporter who encourages others and sets a positive tone? A coordinator who connects the ideas of others?
- Experiment during meetings by making informal roles more formal. Appoint directors to play roles like the devil's advocate for a meeting and rotate these roles among directors from meeting to meeting.

These exercises can help the board to develop a more complete and well-rounded dynamic. They will give directors a chance to enhance their repertoire of roles and ensure that the range of roles on the board is evenly balanced.

C. Seek professional development for directors

Some leading business schools offer executive education programmes tailored specifically for directors. Of particular interest are programmes that focus not just on the technical skills directors need but those that also offer modules on people-oriented skills, such as leadership, emotional intelligence and group dynamics. These programmes can help directors develop the awareness and knowledge they need to better understand how boards work and enhance their interaction.

INSEAD's International Directors Programme, with which I have been involved for several years, includes a board process simulation for participants. In the simulation, participants adopt the role of a director and take part in a meeting that replicates the workings of a real board. For example, the simulated board may be meeting to consider a proposal by management to acquire a significant stake in a new company. Participants are given materials to prepare for the meeting. After the meeting, they have a chance to reflect on and assess their individual and collective performance and to discuss their performance with a coach that has observed them. This type of exercise is an excellent opportunity for participants to become more aware of group dynamics and to practice new roles in a board setting.

D. Make the most of board assessments

Annual board evaluations are becoming commonplace and are increasingly encouraged or required by governments and exchanges. Board assessments, however, are only as good as the effort that is put into them. Often board assessments involve only a tick-box type of survey form. These types of assessments may allow boards to meet their reporting requirements, but they generally do not reveal a lot about how the board is functioning.

A board assessment is a great opportunity for directors to give and receive feedback about each other on strengths and developmental areas, and to give input on the board dynamic as a whole. This is best done through confidential, one-to-one interviews with each director, conducted ideally by a third party. After receiving a written summary of the feedback, directors then meet as a group to discuss the assessment results. Through this process, directors can:

- Learn about themselves and how their contributions to the board are perceived;
- Discover new ways in which they can better interact with the board and enhance the group dynamic;
- Surface hidden issues within the board that need to be discussed.

E. Leverage the support of a board coach

The use of coaches is growing worldwide (Bresser Consulting, 2012) and with good reason. Excellent coaches are trusted partners who bring a high-level perspective on a person's situation and who have the know-how and experience to guide executives on their professional journey. Board coaches are familiar with the context of board work and have the necessary credibility to accompany board members individually and collectively. Board coaches can work with individual directors to support them, identify their development goals and enhance their participation on the board.

Board coaches can also work with the board as a whole. In addition to conducting the confidential board assessment interviews described above, coaches can:

- Observe board meetings to assess the board dynamic;
- Work with boards at meetings to establish practices that can enhance group dynamics;
- Facilitate discussions with boards that allow directors to share perspectives, surface hidden issues and have courageous conversations.

4 Board dynamics

A powerful tool to deal with uncertain times

Beatriz Boza

Strategy in uncertain times

Companies relate to society in different ways and at different levels. Be it through their shareholders, workers, clients and suppliers or through their receptionist, the delivery man or garbage disposal worker; relations are built that permeate the company's life and future. By approving and monitoring the company strategy, the board of directors determines the framework of such exchanges and in doing so, builds the foundation for the sustainability of the enterprise.

Defining the parameters of such a framework and setting the company strategy is an increasingly demanding and complex task in our most volatile and uncertain business environment, marked by unprecedented societal and technological changes, which challenge the fundamental tenets of 'doing business as usual'.

Those fundamentals dwell not only on economic, social and technological drivers, which may be assessed and managed – when properly identified and backed by adequate resources – but also involve internal dynamic board processes, which cannot be readily identified and managed. Those internal dynamics involve natural human resistances that board members are not regularly trained to observe, as they emanate from and operate at an unconscious level, as Bion (1961) observed.

Bion is a pioneer in the study of group dynamics. At the Tavistock Institute of Human Relations (hereafter, "Tavistock"), Bion pioneered an understanding of the internal processes that occur within groups that help or hinder the group's capacity to work effectively.

At the heart of this century's biggest corporate scandals were companies with the most highly qualified boards. Enron, for example, had a top notch board in 2001, comprised of a professor emeritus of accounting and former dean of a US university Graduate School of Business, a former US future commodities trading regulator and director of regulatory studies at a US university, the chief executive of a computer services company, the chairman of a cash management and investment company, the chairmen of oil and gas, property development and manufacturing companies, former chairmen of several companies, a president emeritus of a US university, and a member of the British House of Lords and former British cabinet member (The Guardian, 2002).

Lehman Brothers had eight independent board members out of ten, which in 2008 included, for example, the former chairman of Citibank NA and chairman emeritus of US Bancorp, a former vice chairman of Salomon Brothers Inc. and former economist at the Federal Reserve Bank of New York, a former senior partner at McKinsey & Co., former chairman and president of the US Eximbank and former CEO of Celanese Corp., IBM's retired chairman and CEO, Haliburton's retired chair and CEO, the former non-executive chairman of GlaxoSmithKline and member of the board of Vodafone, and the retired chairman and CEO of Telemundo Group (Global Investment Watch, 2008; Bloomberg, 2017).

Northern Rock's board included in 2007, for example, the former Group CEO of National Westminster Bank, vice chairman of the UK Statistics Commission and member of the board for actuarial standards at the Financial Reporting Council, a former director of the Bank of England and chief executive and president of Nissan Europe, a former member of PwC's global board, and a former CEO and deputy chairman of J.O. Hambro Capital Management (Northern Rock, 2007; Bloomberg, 2017).

Similarly, Halifax Bank of Scotland's board included in 2008, the former CEO and chairman of Morgan Stanley, the former senior partner and executive board member of Deloitte LLP, the former CEO of Compass Group plc, the former chief financial officer of Legal & General Group, and a former CEO of The Weir Group plc, chairman of the Bank of Scotland plc and member of the board of Shell (FCA & PRA, 2015; Bloomberg, 2017).

Using as a conceptual framework Tavistock's group relations approach pioneered by Bion, the following vignette illustrates how an adverse external context, especially if prolonged over time, makes a highly qualified board relinquish its primary task and provides a basic tool kit to identify and tackle such phenomena. Names and certain particulars have been modified to safeguard privileged conversations and facts.

Hostile external contexts restrict a board's ability to think

The company at hand is a family business which had grown significantly in the last four decades as a result of continuous innovations, strict controls and hard work. Due to global external factors in the last several years, the value of the company was halved. Some of the older family members (such as the aunts) pressed for dividends as they relied on them for their livelihood; others (cousins) were looking for the right time to sell their stock or, even better, the company or control thereof; whilst those holding management positions, responsible for the company's past success, could not envision their lives outside the company. The chair complained that she had no energy to go to work; and that for the past years all she dealt with were huge hurdles and difficulties. During that period, payroll was frozen as the company attempted to survive, according to her.

The company had a highly qualified and diverse board. The majority of the board were seasoned, non-executive directors, whose backgrounds, experience and seniority covered all aspects of the company's performance. One third of the board were highly regarded independent members. The board met regularly for a couple of hours. Interestingly enough, the board had not revised the company's medium and long-term plans in the last five years despite all individual board members being aware – and the majority of them convinced – of the need to revisit the company's business model. In fact, when asked about their three main concerns about the company, all non-executive board members spontaneously mentioned the absence of a future-driven corporate strategy. One stated that "there is no strategic plan. We need to see where the company will be in 3, 5 and 10 years". Another one commented, "[I]f the company stays where it is [now], in ten years it will be worth only half; if it invests in [new] ventures [which may turn] risky, it will be worth 20 times more". A third one mentioned, "[T]here is no shared view of the future. Which type of company will we be tomorrow?" According to another one, "the company will not grow because of external factors but through the development of its own competitive advantages", highlighting that the company needed to migrate to higher value added services. Company competitors were aggressively revising their corporate strategy to deal with the changing and challenging business environment the industry was facing worldwide. Board members were highly qualified, business savvy and well aware of said factors; however, they did not seem to act upon it. Why? Why were they reluctant to tackle that strategic risk? Similarly, for example, Northern Rock board members admitted that in 2007, prior to the crisis, they were presented with formal reports warning about the liquidity risks of the bank but did not, however, make any decisions (Keeley & Love, 2011).

It is a board's fundamental role to envision and provide for the future of the company. The main international corporate governance standards state the board's primary function to be setting the corporate strategy (ICGN, 2017; OECD, 2015; IFC, 2009; FRC, 2016). Furthermore, with a business unfriendly party skyrocketing in the electoral race, it would be expected that a board that had been experiencing a significant loss in company value would work on a Plan B and eventually, a Plan C for the company. This board, however, was not addressing those major strategic issues. Why? Where did the resistances to reviewing the corporate strategy originate from? What was happening in their system?

The board's primary task

Wilfred Bion's theories on group behaviour provide a compelling answer to this in today's challenging business environment. Groups, according to Bion, have a primary task. That task usually has the form of finding solutions to problems in reality. In the case at hand, the task of the board was running a sustainable business, as set forth in the company bylaws and mandated by local law. Bion calls work done by the board in that vein "work group" dynamics, i.e., the board delivers on the work it is supposed to do. The Tavistock researcher observed that parallel to the work group, there are also powerful dynamic informal processes at play in any group – boards of directors not being any different – which may militate against that work being done. Those internal dynamics deal with, and process, the emotional and psychic unconscious energy of the group. Ideally, that energy is aligned with the performance of the group's primary task and hence the group is engaged in effective group work.

However, more often than not, the emotional and psychic unconscious energy of the group gets stuck in a defensive mode and hinders the carrying out of the primary task. That happens when in the normal course of carrying out its primary task, the group experiences anxieties and/or fear. To deal with the unconscious anxiety being experienced by the group, the group's internal dynamic tries to 'protect' itself – as if any progress or change could imply losses to it – and shuts off, somehow seeking to 'preserve' the emotional life of the group 'as is', and becomes 'stuck' or 'frozen' in its status quo. When that happens, Bion noted, the group unconsciously does not allow itself to move on with its primary task, despite members being busy and convinced that they are doing hard work in pursuit of their common goal. Similarly to what happens with individuals, they may desire, decide and even try to do something but unconsciously end up doing something else.

The observable evidence

Bion observed that working groups trapped in these particular dynamics act out their unconscious resistances as a way of dealing with their anxiety, through three types of behaviour characteristics, which he called *basic assumptions*. Each of Bion's basic-assumption patterns is characterized by a distinct emotional state. Hume provides a detailed description of the emotional state of each of the three basic-assumption patterns (Hume, 2010). The three patterns are:

1   *Fight/flight*, meaning that the group unconsciously assumes that it needs to 'preserve and protect' itself by fighting or fleeing. Thus the group engages in rivalry, competition and fighting, as well as fleeing and taking flight from the task at hand; essentially abandoning it. The only kind of leadership unconsciously accepted is one that mobilizes the group for attack or leads it into flight. Any other kind will be ignored as the group is unconsciously attempting to protect itself. Interestingly enough, when the group is heavy at 'work', group members feel tired and even exhausted, although these efforts are not effective in pursuit of the group's primary task, which in the case of a board means they are not in pursuit of the sustainability of the company. It is as if work is being done 'just to be busy'. In the case of a board, Bion's fight/flight basic assumption could be reflected, for example, through major board attention to minor administrative matters, intense prolonged general discussions without concrete references to company strategy and heavy family rivalries played out at board level.

2   *Dependency*, meaning the group unconsciously expects a 'leader' to take care of it and act on its behalf. Individual members unconsciously disengage and just passively expect somebody else to perform their work, relinquishing their own resources, capabilities and capacity for thought and decision-making to

'its' leader. As part of the group's fantasy, the chosen leader is expected to provide 'security and protection,' is perceived to be omniscient, possessing all knowledge, power, resources and solutions. As a result of this, the chosen leader is frequently drawn into making all decisions and thinking for the group, thus playing into the dependency basic-assumption pattern, which obviously is only a fantasy doomed for disappointment as soon as reality kicks in. In the case of a board, it could be, for example, waiting for the founder, the chair or the CEO to come up with 'the' solution.

3 *Pairing*, meaning the group's unconscious idea of a saviour being born. It implies idealization and the hopefulness and expectation of a chosen couple creating the 'expected solution', i.e., the fantasy of a yet-to-be-born-saviour, who will arrive one day to solve all problems and take care of everything. Bion described the "peculiar air of hopefulness and expectation that one finds in the pairing group in place of any real work that could give the group real grounds for a better outcome" (Hume, 2010, p. 105). Members are busy waiting for 'something' to happen, which will relieve them of their perils. In the case of a board, it could be waiting for a new tender promised by a major client, the idea of an innovation led by a top team, a future up-coming regulation or a new government.

According to Bion, these types of basic-assumption behaviour are not voluntary, rational or conscious. They just 'happen', as they emanate from and operate at an unconscious level. From time to time, one type of basic assumption activity may be dominant and then again another may take precedence, depending on the state of the group's unconscious psychic life. For Bion, groups in general are fluid in nature. So are basic assumptions, which may change from one to another in the same group and even coexist at a particular point in time. At the core of Bion's work is the observation that basic assumption behaviour hinders effective board work.

When engaging in basic assumption behaviour, i.e., not engaging in effective work group mode, Bion also noted that groups enter into *splitting* and *projections*, which also help the group deal with its unconscious anxiety. Splitting occurs, for example, when the group simplifies its complex business environment by dividing it between the 'good' and the 'bad', i.e., reducing reality, which by definition is complex, to only one aspect of it – as if that object, person or idea were perfectly good with no unfavorable aspects, or purely defective with no merit to it. There is no possibility for nuances – let alone envisioning that a different perspective could have some or any merit. For example, when a particular company stakeholder is felt to be the 'bad' one, taking the 'good' company (or its board or management) hostage.

Projections, in turn, involve an unconscious process pursuant to which individuals and groups see in somebody else certain characteristics of their own, to deal with their own anxieties. For example, one's own laziness, dependency and greed is 'projected' on to the 'others' as a way of dealing with one's own anxiety of being lazy, dependent and greedy. Both splitting and projections take the group away from working on its primary task.

According to Bion, observing the behaviour of group members within the group implies paying careful attention not only to what is said, but especially the tone, language, way and order in which it is said, as well as what is done, and above all, felt by members and observers of the group. Through careful observation, the Tavistock researcher asserts, one may identify the state of the group's unconscious emotional and psychic life and thus be able to assist the group in escaping its own defensive basic-assumption mode.

Technically, Bion did not imply that one could *identify* the state of a group's unconscious emotional and psychic life, as per definition, the former operates at an unconscious level. He spoke of being able to come up with a hypothesis of what may be going on in the group's unconscious life through the observation of basic-assumption activity. Building on that idea, Garland observes that "Group interpretations, among other things, hope to address the underlying phantasies or assumptions that inform the way the entire group is behaving at a particular moment" (Garland, 2010, p. 22).

Basic-assumption patterns as a way of unconsciously thinking and conceiving reality can become fixed in an organization's psyche and way of thinking as to how to run the business. When that happens, such patterns may end up being formalized in a structure with roles, hierarchies, processes and responsibilities. Such formal structures usually function as a defence mechanism against the anxiety felt by organization members in carrying out their common task. The Tavistock tradition refers to such defensive structures as social systems, following Elliot Jaques (1957) and Isabel Menzies (1960). Especially in the case of life challenges, be it to human beings (as in nursing or the military) or to organizations challenged to bear their existence (due, for example, to technological disruption, major regulatory overruns or financial crisis), primary task anxieties tend to be overwhelming. In those cases, one of the formal defences is, for example, for a company structure to have all decisions made at the 'top' implying that those above in the hierarchy are holding all authority and final say, and those in the lower ranks need to be pushed and persecuted as they are perceived to be not competent or proactive enough.

Applying Bion's insights to board work

In the case at hand, Bion's fight/flight basic assumption was dominant. There was also pairing, splitting and projections, all of which were taking a highly qualified board hostage as an act of social defence to the high-anxiety felt by the board. Let me explain how, using Tavistock's framework:

- *High anxiety*. A major loss of more than half the company value is, in and of itself, a dramatic event. In this case, it was a prolonged traumatic event as external adverse pressures were not only increasing but lasting for already many years and seemed to not have an end. The chairwoman was exhausted and, in a way, traumatized and so was the board. A sense of helplessness was in the air. When group members experience too much anxiety, the group system seizes up and jams itself into a halt. "Freud (1925) makes explicit the way in which being traumatised is the outcome of a prolonged sense of help-lessness" (Garland, 2010, p. 35). Carlyle points out:

> If there are factors that have threatened the security or the safety of the group, for example, threats to the *boundary* or *containment* of the group, then the group will struggle with its capacity for creativity – its libidinal potential – and be acutely aware of the pull of destructive forces operat-ing against it.
>
> (Carlyle, 2010, p. 68)

- *Splitting*. There were clearly 'the good' and 'the bad' ones. The chair was convinced they were facing radical pressure groups, most demanding and un-loyal consumers and incompetent government officials, coupled with an ageing labour force which was not innovative and proactive enough. There were clear boundaries: the good ones were inside the board and the bad ones were outside of it. There was no space for nuances; let alone the possibility of envisioning that a different view could have merit, including that of chang-ing consumer and citizens' preferences. For Bion, splitting was taking place, which is a natural defence taken by groups in anxiety.
- *Projections*. The idea of everybody else wanting money from the company was also present. How can workers expect to be paid more if they are not pro-active and not inventive enough? How can the public expect more from the company if it is not allowed to make a business? Personal interests, including economic ones, were being placed in 'the others'. By applying Bion's con-cept of projection it was clear that this dynamic was at play, allowing for a distorted view to replace reality, thus creating a 'cozy' fantasy to address the anxieties in the board.
- *Fight*. Competition and rivalry existed amongst the board. Particularly between shareholders pursuing very different interests (for example, dividends today *vs.* long term company performance; sale of the company *vs.* continuous innovations to keep the company going). In turn, the chair of one of the main committees made a strong point for more board stewardship, while at the same time not reporting back to the board what the committee was doing.
- *Flight*. There was no follow up on board resolutions and no one at the board seemed to take care of it. A lawyer, who was not a board member, was doing all board preparation and minutes work. Effective work was being projected outside the board. Work was being done by 'hired help' (consultants, inde-pendent members, etc.), who could not get away with not doing their job. They were the ones doing the work and holding the board's anxiety. It oper-ated as a social defence to the prolonged anxiety the board – and the com-pany – was experiencing. The leadership and hard work the company needed required psychic energy, which the board, as the ultimate holder of the com-pany's inside/outside boundary, was not able to provide and thus became disconnected from the rest of the organization and its real challenges.

- *Pairing.* It seemed the board was waiting for the new government to solve *all* problems, as if a saviour was expected to resolve all uncertainties. Another one of Bion's basic assumptions was a powerful social defence to the prolonged anxiety felt by the board. The new government did not solve all company perils.

Best practices and energy levels as key indicators

When energy stops flowing, systems collapse. We know that well in our daily lives. Be it electricity, water, phone lines or the Internet. Any shut-down impacts and stops our communications and other functioning systems. The same is true for our political institutions. The free flow of ideas is a basic component of our democratic process; when freedom of expression and freedom of the press are limited, democracy is shut down. Groups also need energy to flow freely. When that flow is curtailed, the group's life is at stake and it reacts by collapsing, waiting to be taken care of. Basic-assumption group activity signals that process.

Boards, as any group, need energy to flow freely. A board may exist on paper in the company charter, but it becomes alive through the spontaneous interactions of its members, amongst them and between them and management, the business and also with society. Anxiety curtails those unconscious, spontaneous, informal, mental interactions and exchanges. When the head gets cut off its body, it no longer fulfils its role of guiding the body. When the board gets stuck in a 'business as usual' mode it stops its vital interactions with the rest of its system, the enterprise. The case of the board described previously illustrates this point.

Two corporate governance leading best practices are most fitting to deal with the board dynamics above mentioned: *board diversity* and *board evaluation*. Board diversity is not an end in and of itself or a desired result but a means in a dynamic process. In other words, diversity is not only a matter of structure to be considered when forming a board but a behavioural issue. It is a means to provide a board with the necessary energy, new perspective and internal challenge to its status quo, so that the board can have a refreshed look at company work. Diversity is an antidote to groupthink. According to Cherry, "Groupthink is a term first used in 1972 by social psychologist Irving L. Janis that refers to a psychological phenomenon in which people strive for consensus within a group. In many cases, people will set aside their own personal beliefs or adopt the opinion of the rest of the group" (Cherry, 2017). The main international corporate governance standards call for board diversity as a means for the board to exercise independent judgment over company affairs. Staggered changing of board membership is an effective tool boards should avail themselves of periodically. Interestingly enough, board members in the case at hand had been sitting together in same cohort for almost a decade – something common in family-owned businesses.

It is also a good practice for boards to regularly carry out evaluations to assess their performance and determine whether they possess the right mix of talent. The board at hand had never assessed the performance of its work or its effectiveness.

Interestingly, the company at hand had been making a profit from inception. The board could have leveraged that fact when pushing for new opportunities, for revising the company strategy or for reviewing the firm's business model. This did not happen.

Prolonged, perceived external adverse contexts generate unconscious anxiety in a board, which, if not properly identified and managed, may take, as in the case at hand, even a highly qualified and business savvy board hostage and stuck in a 'business as usual' mode. Companies trapped in doing business as usual, be it in adverse or even in friendly external environments, may well learn from Tavistock's approach. Being alert to energy levels, spontaneity, feelings and free flow of inter- actions and informal dynamics at a board may well enhance a company's future and reduce individual board members' legal perils.

5 The role of consultant challenged by national dynamics

Maria Claudia Benassi

Theoretical considerations

In this chapter, I propose to view the concept of 'nation' from the perspective and the filter of an open system. *Open* because such a system undoubtedly works porously, exchanging resources and energy with its surrounding environment, and *open* also because it both benefits from and is blocked by its very own inter-connected components, which researchers find operating in parallel or together. Given the number of levels and units (structure) as well as the locations in which they operate and the spatial distribution of its design (environment), organiza-tions, as well as nations (Thompson, 1967), are fraught with issues arising from complexity.

For the sake of this argument, we have nations operating as complex open systems. These systems behave in very distinct ways: they are surprising and spontaneous; unaccountable and unpredictable (Daft & Lewin, 1990); carry on in non-linear ways and their elements are said to cross-feed one another through a network of feedback loops (Casti, 1994); and are so interconnected that a small change at one of its levels can well trigger a behavioural change in the whole sys-tem (Anderson, 217–224). Thus, evolution in 'complex adaptive systems' (CAS) often happens when frequent small changes are made in an improvisational, non-orderly way. Change may also occasionally cumulate into rapid radical strate-gic innovations. The latter supports the idea that a consultant inserting itself in the interstices of this commotion created by shifts of order and chaos, structure and freefall should find it possible to bring about change. Typically, by being able to stand outside the system-cum-nation to avoid being blinded by its rapid dynamics – hereafter to be referred to as national dynamics – a consultant steps in towards engagement with the goal of harmonizing and integrating that which operates "at the edge of chaos" (Aram, 2016).

The response of a CAS towards that small change can be negative; it can be per-ceived as intrusive, confusing, and deserving of being isolated and defeated. On the other hand, consultants can hope to reach their change goals if they align their approach with the context, generating a force that reverberates through the sys-tem, shaking and re-shaping it as it interacts with other components. As this com-motion fails to reach cyclical equilibrium and instead moves constantly – though in a random state – towards self-orchestrated order, a sort of adaptability comes into evidence. This adaptability and the presence of innate progress finally defines organizations and (in this case) nations that experience evolution.

How then to frame the contribution of a consultant when it comes to these evolutionary dynamics? Prigogine and Stengers (1984) argue that 'autogenesis' or self-organization only happens in systems that import energy from the outside and are directly linked to the non-linear behavior that CAS shows. Following Barnard (1938), Anderson explains that "organisations are seen as dissipative structures that can only be maintained when members are induced to contribute energy to them". Furthermore, Kauffman (1993) argues that order emerges when agents respond to inputs from just one other agent. Thus a two-input system is 'homeostatic' and this indicates a certain tension or balance. Inputs from three or more agents will destroy such a balance and bring the system to collapse. While the pattern of connections among agents is not yet clear, reversing the argument brings us to the case of only one agent and what they can achieve. Due to lack of ties or poor reach of its influence, the agent may not be able to draw in singlehandedly enough energy to maintain dissipative structures responding to various inputs – a conversant state that ultimately leads to "order emergence".

Reflecting on the difference between a participative vs a systemic practice when hailing a complexity approach to organizational change, Shaw, 2003 posits that "life arises from and is sustained by a dialectic between the tidiness and harmony of cooperation and the destructiveness and dissonance of messy competition". This suggests that conversations are not the vehicle, but the engine that powers the movement itself. Shaw leads us back into a concatenation of paradoxes by acknowledging that a consultant's participation in the formation of organizational (or a nation's) experience is as intrinsic and complex as the patterns that give life to the CAS itself. In other words, we the producers of human conversation are responsible for a process of communicative action that has the intrinsic capacity to pattern itself, thus generating a cosmology of interactions (responsive relating, as Shaw calls the process), which one will be unable to control but which may control one in part.

With these elements at our disposal, we can argue that a consultant focused on bringing about transformation within a CAS would do well in positioning itself adroitly *vis-à-vis this* 'complexity quagmire', as it were. As with most quagmires, we often say that those caught in the mess helped to create it to an extent. Both consultant and national leaders will face one another inside the system and awareness of one's motivation and biases are one way to step into the role. Further and loosely following Jung (1969), our agent may easily be driven by a sort of Jungian archetypal energy. Displaying the naivety and the charm of a certain Spanish caballero (Don Quijote de la Mancha) who is not afraid of his own courage, they could overestimate their power and at times struggle with the distinction between fact and fiction. Hence, such agents could be seen by others as somewhat delusional. At other times, they could seem to follow the guidance of a superior force, strongly believing in their position as the elect to save their country. Individualists with a calling, as it were, who can easily arouse envy and competition.

The magnetism emanating from the overlap of strengths and roles speaks of a certain portion of constructive narcissism. They will display the charisma and the strength of personality to lead. Tapping into the collective unconscious while nonetheless empowering self-awareness could be one way to align for successful change.

Case study 1

When our subcommittee experienced Anja's emotions, we were impressed by her courage. Yet not everyone was caring, carefree, considerate and/or collegial when it came to responding to her conundrum. Anja wants to help her northern European country understand and act its way out of a deeply-rooted (historical events), ominous (challenging neighbours) and unsettling quagmire that bodes nothing good for the future (as long as the leadership remains in denial and relies on defense mechanisms). Her excellent skills as a psychoanalyst, in combination with the methodology that she developed from Tavistock, prepared her as a consultant to shed light on the national dynamics that are holding her country back. In the subcommittee, I asked about allies. Anja had lost her allies, she told us. Suggestions were made for her to act independently, but she did not challenge our suggestions. What she explained made sense, but her modus operandi and the acceptance of the idea of a single-handed move, on the other hand, seemed unrealistic to many.

Beyond the emotional bond to her nation, Anja harbours a strong sense of pride. She is proud of who she is, what she has achieved, and what she stands for. Having a would-be *cause célèbre* like the one she has brought to Tavistock (one of our directors having pointed out that there is not much literature on national dynamics), would position her not only as having something monumental to achieve, but would also help her become a pioneer in the field. This success, in turn, would draw attention to her and get her the closeness to Tavistock that she in part already enjoys and unabashedly seeks to further. Undoubtedly, the size of the undertaking is directly proportionate to the amount of envy and competition that such a consultant would be subjected to.

Some helpful insights have surfaced in private conversation with Anja. Her decisions are informed by what she sees as the inability of others to see things as clearly as she does and to act upon these. If allies slow you down, why have allies? Anja grew up in a household where her sisters, unable to deal with her talent and probably confronted with their own deficiencies or insecurities, chose to project inadequacies on to her. With envy and competition prevailing and having been let down by a mother who failed to understand family and group dynamics and to act as an impartial and skilled coach, Anja learned early on in life to fend for herself. It was survival as she put it. She became the expert in psychodynamics that she wished she could have been assisted by. Hence it is no surprise that Anja often undertakes projects on her own and is somewhat blocked to see, understand, accept, and act upon the advantages of letting go and trusting, of seeing people for who they are, and of strategically taking what they offer, to reach a common goal.

Cheered on by some of us, and energized by the courage that only conviction can give, Anja is poised to take on the behemoth of her nation state's political apparatus. She believes that offering the president an initial dialogue infused with the fluidity taught by complexity researchers and then perhaps moving on to working with his closest advisers with a group of Tavistock-trained experts (thereby creating a small think tank approach) could render the understanding of some of the country's dilemmas less daunting and perhaps even solvable. They would explore options that can be worked upon and prepare a report to shine some light on the situation. Such is at this point the high-level understanding of the primary task.

Yet the way to that conversation with the president, which is deemed the most efficient way to gain access, buy-in, and an opportunity to effect change appears fraught with difficulties (and blockers). How does one do the work within oneself to move from 'lashing out' to 'helping'? Pictorially, in our group, Anja depicted herself as an angel-like creature ready to shoot her arrow at the nation. Anja needed to try different routes (and fail) to understand that the energy of her passion and the single-handed effort of her anxiety is not enough to generate the 'stirrings' that will mobilize the right sense of "urgency" (Kotter, 2012). Our learning then is that engaging with national dynamics cannot and should not be attempted alone. Anja is today in the process of creating a network and has joined forces with two academics she respects and whose input can also generate the support of others. The approach will be softer, savvier and more inclusive, but the road may be a long one. Deep down Anja is not totally convinced; for her, as she says, dealing with the primary task is more important than finding allies who may or may not respond as she would like. Change can be hard.

Case study 2

Urban is a Catholic priest whose services to the church and intellectual prowess helped him qualify for training at some of the world's finest institutions. He loves to learn and holds several degrees and specialized certifications. In particular, he has utilized group relations theory in his professional activities. Urban comes from a country in the Caribbean with which he identifies and whose plight and future chances he considers his responsibility to support. His family and contacts are there and while he travels the world collecting accolades, knowledge, and experience, he often returns to his nation to apply his acquired skills. He believes the reality of his island nation, in terms of national dynamics, could be rendered more effective at two levels. Firstly, the Ministry of Public Administration has staff that need to undergo development training (implying a wider initiative that includes open workshops and a conference) to familiarize and equip themselves with a change mindset that can tackle the culture of violence and corruption (Sher, 2013) prevalent within the system. Secondly, most – if not all – board functions in the country are unmonitored, with board members in urgent need of increased awareness, evaluation and development.

Urban felt inspired by Case Study 1. He felt that he could make an impact and contribute by making a significant difference by tackling both levels above from the perspective of a dynamic that needs exploring, experiencing and exposing. It has become difficult to see through the layers of basic assumptions that weave their influence across the nation's leadership (both public and private). Fraught relationships make leaders feel disempowered. Urban felt seriously encouraged when his brother said that he held the key to change.

And the movement got underway by exploring how to approach the decision makers. In part due to his affiliation with the powerful institution that is the Catholic church, Urban's access to government was easier to achieve than the accessibility described in Case Study 1. Furthermore, Urban's understanding of how to navigate the politics of such access is clearer (perhaps in equal measure because of his affiliation with an institution like the church). Urban obtained the access (and soon the ear) of decision makers by focusing on "mutual concern and exploration" and was aware that he had to be consistent when dealing with the Minister of Public Administration, not pushing frontally but "requesting their views and enlisting their support and influence" (as he put it). An advantage working in his favour was that in his nation, the thirst for working with group relations and psychodynamics is strong.

Urban's energy and drive were consumed somewhere else for the better part of eight months and the process slowed down his progress, even though he had more favourable starting conditions than Case Study 1. Urban had become aware early on that a CAS required more than his analytic prowess. After some unfortunate disappointments in terms of trusting others, Urban was introduced to and settled on an ideal partner who shared his training and approach. A woman expert based in his country with whom the primary task became more manageable.

Yet he and his newly found partner could not see eye-to-eye. While it was not easy for him to present his feelings to our group, privately he confessed to me what a toll the clashes had taken. There was competition, envy, dependency, jealousy, blame/shame, insecurities and anger (not to mention lack of trust on both sides) that came to the surface in forms that were shockingly surprising to Urban. This unexpectedness spoke volumes of his lack of preparedness: Urban had not fully assumed he would need an ally as well as an equal to run this show.

The saviour role (especially for a priest) may be hard to resist. Again, when working within a CAS, it is not the individual need or drive but a variety of conflicting inputs that will energize a structure into a 'changed' emergence. For Urban and his partner, Patricia Shaw's argument that "life arises from and is sustained by a dialectic between the tidiness and harmony of cooperation and the destructiveness and dissonance of messy competition", in a way renders clearer what they are steering towards. Progress is slow but steady now, not only between the two of them but between them and the administration they wish to serve. Urban tells me of his colleague's unconscious blockers that still need to be worked upon for her to deliver efficiently. However, two psychodynamics experts should surely be able to tackle that. Change requires persistence and consistency.

Comparison and contrast

Interestingly, both cases are stamped by the strong undercurrent of their post-colonial situation and its concomitant mindset. While a clearly recognizable identity has been sought and in part found (even in the multiplicity and melting-pot diversity of the Caribbean island-state in question), these further developed systems resonate with introjective identification, part and parcel of a survival scheme. At many levels, both societal groups experience the dynamics of fear, shame, guilt, gratitude and even admiration, which creates an interdependence with their former oppressors: either with the oppressor itself or with the idealization of their former ruling ways. This mechanism holds the system in its grip and suffocates long-term transformation through stagnation and paralysis; psychosocial mechanisms, at play at both conscious and unconscious levels, hold sway.

Our consultants have taken different approaches to work with their differing national dynamics and systems, building on the learnings from complexity research and group relations, on the nature of the psychoanalytical services they tender daily, with an overlay of their own biases. Anja chose to work her way to the top, determined to become the adviser to the national leaders. The understanding, as well as the hope, lies in the belief that when advising and influencing behaviour at the top, the CAS will receive the transformative impact through trickle-down or cascading innovative energy.

The work is ongoing – we called it herculean at the beginning of this chapter. After her reiterated offer of services was declined, Anja decided to catch the prime minister's attention by creating a virtual magazine with blog entries and elucidating national dynamics concepts, the link to which was eventually sent to all members of parliament with holiday greetings, four months after its launch. Interestingly – and on a positive note – the prime minister himself and the press from his administration appears to have started to exhibit behaviours, use terminology (albeit in a superficial manner), and issue communications that seem to indicate that either the original letters or the e-magazine have been read and its advice heeded. To Anja's credit, a nation-wide dialogue has ensued along those lines. In our terms, the CAS is seeking self-orchestrated order and adaptability is in evidence. Unsure who is now working with the prime minister (some suggest it could be one of Anja's fiercest competitors, male, and working in the capital closer to the government), Anja is disappointed and wishes she could get the recognition she deserves for the change set in motion. The system seems to be taking control as Anja has not been able to do so all by herself. In spite of her chosen allies, Anja continues to work alone, a habit she cannot shirk.

Urban, on the other hand, undertakes community work at the senior leadership level, attempting to nudge the system one group and one conference at a time. He is taking much longer to see results although the initial reception was very gratifying and the need seems to be enormous. The conviction here is that transformation of the leadership at the national level is made possible through the invitations extended by organizations to the consultant and his partner to initiate change interventions. This grassroots-type of approach will take longer to reach its goal, but may be less fraught with political intrigue, jealousy and competition and may also be more difficult to ignore. Recognition is also coming his way. He is at this point already influencing the work of a few clinicians, consultants, and has recently been called by the office of the prime minister in response to a proposal he presented through supporters some time ago. He still has to win decision makers from the corporate world and effectively execute all of the above. However, the expertise Urban brings from abroad and his impeccable credentials outweigh any potentially damning racial discrimination, professional jealousy, or limitations imposed by his frock. Presently, he will shift his base from Europe back to his country to spend most of his time there, thus accelerating the speed of the badly needed change.

Conclusion

In sum, I would argue that interpretation is admirable (psychodynamics), but action is better: social and organizational change of the kind that upsets power structures are required today if we want to effect a systemic turnaround (Petriglieri, 2017). What does this sort of social activism require of the consultant as an individual? Placing oneself at the interstices of a CAS demands an inclusive attitude towards both clients and allies. Exercising influence without authority proves paramount. Finally, turning fragmentation into integration also requires in-depth awareness of one's motivation coupled with a collaborative ability to listen (and understand), more than to tell.

In terms of approach, what would help to have a chance at systemic change? Based on the cases described here, we can postulate that attempting transformational work at a national level may require honest scrutiny of some of these initial considerations:

1   Understanding the origins of the tension that keep the nation from evolving;
2   Measuring the intensity with which dominance and control have the collective energy and imagination in its grip;
3   Deciding whether a top-down or a bottom-up approach will lead to improved results;
4   Realistically ascertaining the chances to reach change goals by oneself or with the help of strategic alliances;
5   Concretely and honestly weighing the possibility that issues of gender, race, class, etc., can get in the way and preparing for it;
6   Concretely and honestly weighing the possibility that one's unconscious biases, fears, and denials will get in the way and being prepared for it;
7   Understanding the risks involved and tackling them with equanimity, housing anxiety and disappointment in a less personal corner of one's professionalism; and last but not least,
8   Scrutinizing the competition both as a challenge or a realistic force which, if you cannot beat, you should consider joining. Painful as that may seem.

Part II

Process, growth and performance

This section is concerned with process, growth and performance, which are aspects of board behaviour that may receive inconsistent and unequal emphasis. The chapters in this section challenge us to be alert to the distractions that may sway a board from its main role and task.

In Chapter 6, Wayne Mullen investigates the appeal of high-growth and hyper-growth companies to investors and employees. He says that for adventurous investors the early years may provide the best return on investment and the opportunity to invest, making a significant return and exiting quickly. For employees, there is an appeal about working for a hot new brand, the 'new kid on the block' that is overtaking its established rivals. The reality for leaders and the executive committees or boards is that they may find themselves running an organization they no longer recognize or are ill equipped to lead. Innovators and entrepreneurs may not always be the best people to lead sustainable organizations. The demands of taking a company public, the quarter-to-quarter expectations, may increase people and governance responsibilities that cannot match the heady, adrenaline rush of early success.

Toy Odiakosa, in Chapter 7, writes about teams as complex adaptive systems that operate on very few rules. The topic of rules within the same space as a non-linear entity, such as a conversation, is multifaceted and remains fervently researched. Based on studies involving a senior management team and a board, Toy identifies a frame for two forms of dynamic so far not mentioned in the literature, but which are critical to successful working in teams. Toy describes key dynamics that show up in forces, such as an attitude or a feeling held by the group as a whole. The key dynamics coalesce from generic dynamics into new forms and in the right conditions, key dynamics catalyze and coalesce to form a driving dynamic. Recognizing the two forms of key and driving dynamics are pivotal to recognizing motivations and how both team and board perform on real tasks.

Paul Schanzer in Chapter 8 explores how unconscious behaviour influences the dynamics of high performance and how individuals can develop their existing skills through a greater self-awareness of the unconscious. He describes enhancing the existing skill set individually and collectively with an initial focus on communication and decision-making skills.

In Chapter 9, Martin Palethorpe draws our attention to decision-making as the number 1 dysfunction impacting the effectiveness of boards. He looks at real-life examples of poor decisions and their catastrophic impact and then explores the deeper aspects of what prevents quality decision-making in the boards of Britain and beyond. He uses three organizations as examples to bring practice and real life to the theory.

Rachael Etebar, in Chapter 10, describes how a seat on the board is seen as a symbol by the HR profession of the value and respect in which the profession is held. She notes how the business press increasingly questions whether HR deserves such a seat, due to a perception of a lack of strategic influence and understanding of how businesses run. Rachel explores board dynamics as an explanation for why the HR profession's aspiration to be on the board is facing hostility and rejection.

In Chapter 11, Grant Taylor asks what board performance is and how it can be measured. Do boards have common characteristics? Grant argues that the pace of change is increasing and organizations need to be able to look over the horizon and adapt. The board sets the context for enabling change, bringing the outside in, stretching ideas and managing risks. Grant asks that given that governance has improved over the last 20 years, and most boards have people who understand their duties and appreciate their fiduciary responsibilities, why are some boards still driven by process and risk management rather than performance and achievement? Unquestionably, robust governance is important; we need the bolts on the wheels to be secure, but have we ever seen how fast the car can go? If we spend too much time checking to see if the car is well maintained, we may find that it is travelling in the wrong direction!

6 Caught between vision and memory – the impact of high growth on board dynamics

Wayne Mullen

Trouble at the top

One tech company was founded in one European country but as it grew, headquartered in another. The success of the company's products was unprecedented and prior to its public offering, leaders with experience in running public companies were brought on board to help it become investment ready. There were, understandably, concerns about maintaining the culture and sense of belonging as the company grew but some of the founders struggled with the idea that people from outside their country could understand their company culture – seen very much as a product of their national culture.

As the organization grew, so did the need for larger support functions in other countries with different responsibilities and priorities from the creative areas. Newer and geographically distant employees did not participate in the founder hero worship seen in longer serving employees. There were differing models of success between functions accompanied by inevitable politics and competing interests.

Whilst communication from the CEO focused on keeping everyone aligned to the company's purpose – to make great products – at executive committee level the rapid growth had introduced dynamics with which they were struggling. The executive committee was divided; those from the founding country and those who were not; and those who were part of the original team and those who were not. The latter happened also to be managing support functions. The lack of a global mind-set and the locating of the culture and identity of the company in one country served only to alienate the executives and indeed employees that were from elsewhere.

Original executive committee members from the founding country bemoaned the need for support functions:

> When we were small, if a bulb needed replacing we replaced it. We didn't have facilities people.
> Why do we need people booking travel for us?
> Why do we need all these HR processes? Before, everyone just got on with what they needed to do.

Why do we have to have our logo on name cards? Everything is so corporate.

(Personal communication)

There was a sense that the founders feared the company they had created was slipping away and perhaps that they unconsciously doubted their own ability to lead a global business. These technical leaders struggled to grasp issues that were not of a technical nature. With the executives unable to find a leadership language for their experience of organizational growing pains, the phrase "that's so corporate" was thrown around until it became a dominant organizational narrative that served only to denigrate support functions. The general manager of the founder office (a founder himself) berated employees from outside that country and became obstructive, for example refusing to allow employees global access cards to permit them to enter his building if they were not based there.

The new executives were critical of the way in which the company was run, viewing the founders as inexperienced and immature. The new executives' lack of acknowledgment of past efforts and struggles that contributed to the company's extraordinary success made them appear as if they were simply 'throwing stones from the outside'.

The technology sector values loose, flexible, organizational structures along with creativity and agility and so its leaders also need to maintain an agile and creative stance. Here however, the executives' defensive faculties were more evident than their need to be creative or flexible. Unable to respond to the pace of change, some executives clung to their romanticized past; their unconscious holding them prisoner to a time when, perhaps, they felt a greater sense of control. As for the new executives, they too continually referenced their own pasts idealizing their previous companies and CEOs without recognizing their own entrenched positions.

The tech company actively and successfully cultivated a culture of fun, but to the extent that no one felt able to say that, at times, working there was anything but fun. Real conversations tended to happen 'offline' and it was difficult to determine which relationships were authentic.

Friends without benefits

The investment banking sector values much more stable structures but has to respond to changing and often volatile markets. One emerging markets investment bank became the number one global investment bank in its country. The majority of its managers, once regional heads, were now global leaders of a business with growth in excess of 50% per year. It was a compelling story; a group of young managers working together at one bank set up a competitor bank that became a global success and its country's national champion. They were close – the founders became friends and they and their families socialized and even holidayed together.

However, executives that joined from other global banks found the bank bureaucratic and domestically entrenched. Its culture was collegiate and informal but there was little evidence of direction setting or strategy and there were fundamental disagreements about where the bank should be focusing its efforts, the type of deals it should be doing and even the countries in which it should be operating.

Two bodies – a global operations committee and a business executive committee, managed the organization. One was cautious and concerned with governance and regulation, the other entrepreneurial and ambitious. Needless to say, decision-making was challenging since agreement was needed from both bodies before any company-wide activities or initiatives could commence. Each body, however, had different primary tasks and concerns. After some years of feedback and frustration it was agreed that a single management board above both the committees would be established with a focus on strategic decision-making. Several hours were spent with the CEO talking through the composition of the new board. Despite encouraging him to think in terms of roles rather than people, he found it hard to conceive of a management board without all of the original founders. Finally, exasperated, he said "but we're a family".

Impediments to the leadership needed for sustainable organizations

What explains the struggle entrepreneurial leaders have in the transition to leading a sustainable organization and what prevents founder boards from understanding organizational growing pains and managing growth effectively? Certainly, research has found no evidence that professional managers perform better in high-growth firms than founder managers (Swiercz & Lydon, 2002).

Narcissism is a level of functioning prevalent in start-up environments and perhaps understandably so. It can take a degree of single-mindedness and self-confidence to take the kind of risks needed in a start-up environment. The charismatic, maverick CEO and the founder DNA that runs through many start-ups are often compelling drivers of engagement and motivation in those early days. As the organization matures, they may be less helpful especially if the CEO and executives are unable to get in touch with the constructive narcissist that can get them to do their work effectively in a changed environment.

If we understand that narcissism demands surface stimulation (Grotstein & Symington, 1993) then it is easy to see how chasing temporary highs can take precedence over engaging in the dialogue necessary for sense-making or initiating the change processes needed to create a sustainable business. One of the great tragedies of narcissism is that it consumes the energy that could otherwise be used for creative problem-solving. The downstream impact of leader narcissism on organizational culture can be seen in the extravagant parties for every product launch, continual pursuit of awards and proactive PR that ensures executives are regularly profiled in the industry press.

Other aspects of leader narcissism may be seen in some of the cult-like and somewhat unhealthy cultures sometimes present in start-ups and particularly present in the tech sector. Diversity is espoused and employees are encouraged to be themselves, but only as long as being themselves aligns with the unspoken but very specific organizational norms, established by the founders. The lack of a dress code for example, may suggest coherence with the rhetoric of 'we don't care what you wear, it's what you do that matters', but the protectionism sets in as soon as anyone from outside the industry walks in; woe betide anyone who turns up for an interview in a suit. What happens if you are a finance or human resources professional? Can you contribute and be part of the tribe if you are not a self-proclaimed 'geek'?

Narcissism also hinders the capacity to speak and hear the truth. A focus on the successes of the past, the continual re-telling of early success stories in place of a clear vision and coherent strategy for the future may be telltale signs of narcissistic denial at board level. Ignoring the warning signs of organizational growing pains may unconsciously protect boards from the painful realities of running large organizations, but it also prevents them from metabolizing present anxieties into forward thinking and constructive ideas and actions. Acknowledging that failure could be a part of the organization's future may be considerably more helpful than dwelling on its past.

At the tech company, there was something else getting in the way of the executive committee working together effectively. The division across the committee was replicated down through the organization; the same division between founder committee members and newer executives could be seen between employees located in the founder country and those in the new corporate centre. This geographical fault line was recognized but never addressed; the constant emphasis on having fun became an organizational defence against conflict even though it was suppressing the diversity of thinking needed to create a culture and identity that was globally inclusive.

The rupture in this executive committee may have served a purpose; perhaps there was collusion to perpetuate interpersonal rivalry in order to avoid managing the tension that becoming a public company had thrown up. There was no longer a single primary task – to make great products – there was a double task: to satisfy the analysts and shareholders as well. Both tasks needed to be accomplished in an industry that was new, and in a company whose technology and subsequent success had no precedent. Executive committee members could not ask the question 'How do we work without knowing?' or even 'What kind of company are we now?' Instead the fight became the repository for their anxiety.

In the investment bank, as growth tailed off, so too did confidence among some of the original executive team members. Senior leaders complained about the 'inner circle', the excessive bureaucracy, and questioned the competence of some of the executives to lead the bank going forward. Despite tacit recognition of the problems associated with members of the executive team, there was reluctance from the CEO or indeed the chairman, to confront those problems. As the bank stabilized, the executives brought in to build the business found that the on-going maintenance of a smaller emerging markets business to be less challenging than the global banks they had come from. The board seemed to be in denial about the fact that the bank would never compete with the bulge-bracket firms it had tried to position itself alongside and it was unable to manage the vision for the organization when the realities did not stack up.

The response from the CEO of the bank – 'But we're a family' – reveals another unconscious primary task of boards: to stay together. In a start-up environment people get very close and very intense very quickly; those bonds are sealed so early and to such extent that it can be difficult for the board to acknowledge when one or more members are no longer contributing in the right way. The excessive bureaucracy too may have been an example of "social defence" identified by Menzies (1961) where the continual development of policies and endless approval procedures, etc., may have been serving the psychological defensive needs of the executive to experience control in an otherwise chaotic and volatile setting. Like the tech company, the bank became caught between vision and memory. Without a clear purpose and direction, its employees engaged in what some called a 'Christmas Tree Strategy'; picking up any deals they could find like bright, shiny baubles.

The challenge for executive committee and board members

The board is the ultimate authority whose first task is to find its role. Only then can it hope to have the clarity needed to develop the strategic capability of the organization. If the primary injunction for leadership is to 'know thyself', then it is true also of executive committees and boards. The executive whose mind is focused on logos, on name cards or who books their travel, is unlikely to be operating optimally at board level. The leadership body needs to be sufficiently self-auditing to be able to identify its members who are not philosophically, behaviourally or strategically aligned and if necessary to exclude them. A healthy board must be able to have brave conversations with those executives who may be at the point of derailing, about their futures with the company.

The non-executive director can help in this area. They bring independence and impartiality, along with responsibilities for guardianship, advice giving, support and policing. The board is a factor of its context and the non-executive director, as an outsider, has a broader environmental awareness than the executive directors, with a clearer perspective of external factors that may impact the company. They occupy a unique position, being able to take advantage of speaking as part of the board and at other times to speak from outside the board. They should work with the board to define the primary task of the organization to ensure that the system beneath supports that.

Along with their connection to the external environment, non-executive directors bring value if they are also able to connect with what is going on around the rest of the organization. It is axiomatic that dynamics at board level will play out across the organization and non-executive directors (indeed all board members) may wish to consider opportunities to listen to what people around the organization say about their experience of working there and occasionally check in on their clarity about the organization's strategy and purpose. What are people saying about the organization's strategy? Do they understand it? What are the narratives running through the organization? What do people say about the leadership? Are there geographical or functional fault-lines?

There is a collusive trap of course; non-executive directors are bound in their commitment for a fixed number of days per year over a fixed period preventing them from thinking about longevity. However, if they wish to leave the organizations they serve in a better place than they found them, it is incumbent on them to deliver the messages to the executive: what the executives themselves have been avoiding.

Receiving feedback at the top of the organization can be difficult; as you move up in organizations, truth may be more difficult to find. Non-executive directors can support boards by encouraging regular, honest, and rigorous assessment of its leaders and through feedback. They need to stay vigilant, observant and pay attention to the dynamics across the board – including their own contribution to those dynamics. Board members may be on better behaviour in front of non-executive directors and so the non-executive directors need to listen – not just to what is being said, but also to what is not being said at meetings. They need to pay particular attention to the CEO and how other executives react to her. Non-executive directors too must model self-awareness, a reflective and flexible stance and strong interpersonal relationships.

The role of organizational development practitioners and coaches

Those involved in organizational development or executive coaching can play a significant role in helping executive committees and boards to be effective. They can:

- Help board members to understand that in healthy systems the past needs be acknowledged in order to make sense of the present. By acknowledging the past but working with the present, practitioners and coaches can help to free executives from their stories.
- Counsel founders and newer executives to 'take back their projections' and to work as a team with the present; as a team it is easier to process complexity and to see the space more clearly.
- Help the board to identify the dynamics that are causing unhelpful patterns in their functioning. Those patterns will continue to exist unless the underlying dynamics are addressed.
- Support leaders in accepting that it is okay not to know – and instead create a safe space for dialogue. Working with not knowing may actually help keep the board in touch with what it is supposed to be doing – its primary task – but they can only do that with each other.

- Encourage new members of boards to acknowledge what has come before them in order that their colleagues have confidence that they will be able to connect their contributions with the organization's past.
- Discourage new members of the board from seeing themselves as separate from the dynamics of the board – however dysfunctional these may appear when they arrive.

Leaders may not want to hear what they unconsciously know and what others can see and that presents a risk if the practitioner is the one to call attention to it. This creates a dilemma for practitioners and coaches who inevitably want their services used again. In a catalytic role one has to say the unsayable and needs to convey those messages without criticizing and blaming or leaving executives paralyzed.

We must avoid labelling what is happening at board level or in the organizational level as 'good' or 'bad' – when we label we are applying the past. Working with 'what is' means that we create an opening in which we can facilitate and maintain dialogue. We can work with executives as people. We can help them to surface their unconscious concerns, make changes in their interactions with each other and with their primary task, and then see how the organization responds. We must try not to see our roles as fixing broken organizations or systems or people but accept chaos and complexity and seek to understand.

No organization can hope to succeed if the executive committee or board is unhealthy. In times of ever-increasing ambiguity and complexity, organizations would do well to give as much priority to board development as they do to other forms of leadership development. The time and energy the board spends on dysfunctional relationships is a significant cost especially when one considers the fact that those dysfunctions are likely to be reflected throughout the organization. Investment in the development of the board is likely to have considerable returns.

For all executives then, an awareness of and attention to board dynamics, particularly during periods of growth, will be invaluable in contributing to the effective functioning not just of the board, but of the organization as a whole.

7 The driving dynamic, board performance and role

Toy Odiakosa

The effects of dynamics

Key dynamics are formed when attitudes shared by members of a board coalesce. They form the right conditions for catalyzing and maintaining a driving dynamic, which is the dominant attitude or feeling in a board that ultimately informs what the board wants, and how it enacts its role through its judgments and performance. The effects of these dynamics are most evident in the creative responses of individual board members, particularly when they faced unspoken elements of conversation that drove judgments and decisions. This chapter concludes by observing that by updating their recognition for their key dynamics, boards can build opportunities to become more agile and competitive.

Through conversations and reflections that were sometimes challenging and often unpredictable, participants in both studies that this article is based on made meaning of their exchanges and their individual contributions to the dynamics in play. Insights were then utilized in future interactions. Dynamics were perceived more strongly during phases of interaction that were unexpected and ambiguous. In both teams, members were invited to reflect on how an individuals' contributions may be affecting the dynamics within the team or the board as a whole, and conversely, how the team and board dynamics may be impacting an individuals' judgments.

Participants described dynamics such as competing, seeking power, and protecting their role and the organization. Not all dynamics observed in play coalesced into key dynamics. By ramping up their tolerance for high-performance dynamics, both the board and the senior management team showed accelerated, sustained results in that they had spent more time on business goals. For example, they were more curious, more able to notice informal assumptions and expectations towards colleagues, visitors and their executives.

Ramping-up team sensory acuity

The first study was of a senior management team (Figure 7.1), conducted over a period of 12 months. Technology had changed the way the team managed and drove the business. The team had been struggling to improve its business results,

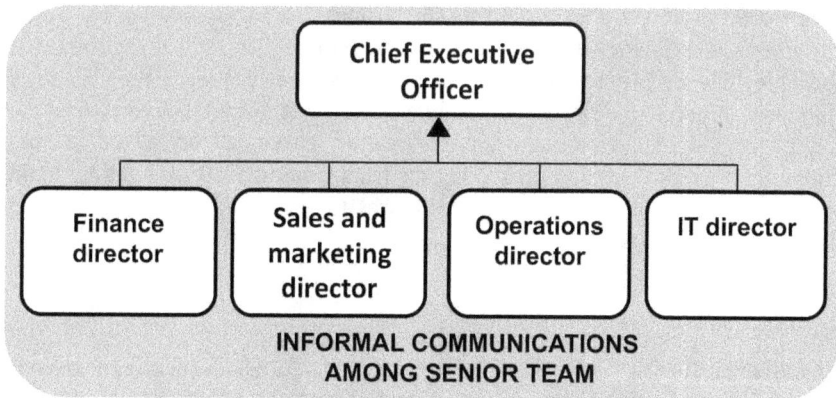

Figure 7.1 Informal communications among senior team

and as part of a turn-around plan, it sought to review its dynamics. My role was to provide consultation to the team.

Initial meetings took the form of individual semi-structured conversations. Here team members could provide their view of the same set of questions and speak freely about their experience of other topics important to them. These conversations revealed each member's perception of what a high-performing team looks like, and how they rated their team in this context of agreeing to its business plan. While each member appreciated the contribution of colleagues, it was equally clear that they struggled to work together. Collectively, the senior management team agreed that its difficulties with agreeing on a business plan signalled an ongoing underlying problem in the dynamics of the team.

We held an open negotiation about confidentiality, so the team could agree on the forms of information that would not be shared between the chief executive officer and the rest of the team. The aim was to cross-fertilize permitted themes and apply learnings iteratively. Four team meetings and four individual meetings were agreed upon, to work with the team as they addressed important business decisions. Reflective spaces were made available, to elicit collective and individual-agent reflections, and identify the contributions these made to coalescing or individuating key dynamics. Learnings could then be applied to future situations. To create the iterative, double-loop learning environment, a Chinese Wall was placed between the CEO's coaching and parallel individual coaching conversations with the rest of the team.

In a meeting to discuss the budget, the operations director, supported by the IT director, disagreed with the sales director on figures she presented. The CEO did not intervene but continued listening. The sales director fired a volley of protests at the operations director including that her function would "not carry more than a fair share", he did "not see the bigger picture", and he should "stop trying to be the CEO". She argued that the team seemed to "have agreed between yourselves to allocate a fixed cost" to her function whether or not they were incurred, and then spread what was not used across the business. She would not agree to such conditions. The finance director, who had said nothing so far, sat hunched over the table with hands in his lap. The pace of exchanges had speeded up, voices had tightened, suggesting a rise in feeling. Eye contact was averted and directed at the CEO, which signalled a retreat from this conflict. This appeared to be the team's formula for gridlock. It was distracting the team from its work and getting in the way of its decisions and performance. It was time to pause and name the key dynamics in these exchanges.

Dynamics

The three elements of a 'dynamic' are that it is an attitude or feeling (Brissett & Sher, 2010, p. 70) that occurs in the context of a person's membership to a specific group, and is consequent to an event perceived to be relevant to the group, and the group as a whole perceives that attitude as appropriate (Goldenberg et al., 2014, p. 581). For example, as a member of the senior management team (specific group), the finance director contributed advice relevant for strategy, forecasting, and execution (perceived as important for the team by the team). However, his experience of team meetings was that they were combative, and his inability to assert his view gained him a reputation (collective feeling) as a yes-man to be ignored.

Key dynamics

Dynamics attract or repel other dynamics either strongly or weakly through coalescing and individuating forces between them. During various pauses the group decided that disagreements among members had something to do with the operations director's meddling in functions outside his remit. His intention had been to protect his part of the business by spying on his colleagues when they were not on location. The new sales director was driven by her desire to bring in high revenues, and a belief that as the first and only female in the life of this senior management team, she needed to be tough until they recognized she was "not to be messed with" (Puwar, 2004, pp. 129–132). After a few uncertain months of the business being positioned for sale, the IT director wanted stability in the team and he found an ally in the operations director. The fourth key dynamic was the finance director's reputation as a yes-man.

In the right conditions, dynamics that attract other dynamics coalesce through the "butterfly effect" (Prigogine, 1997, pp. 30–31). That is, small changes to repeated actions, quickly or slowly over time create small acceptances that coalesce and catalyze into new forms. These 'key dynamics' must be adopted explicitly or tacitly by each individual member, until they form a critical mass that support a driving dynamic. For example, during phases of extreme stress the sales and operations directors egged each other on, colluded by the team, and thereby involving the entire team. With these distractions on foot, the team as a whole also failed to map its behaviours back to its joint purpose. When aggregated, these dynamics contributed to gridlocks in the team's decision-making and performance.

Driving dynamic

A 'driving dynamic' is the consequence of three or four coalescing key dynamics that must be present to form a robust support for the dominant feeling (driving dynamic) in the awareness of a team as a whole. The driving dynamic in the senior management team had to do with 'first protect my part of the business'. Skilful facilitation was needed to get the team to openly acknowledge that its internal competition was real and could be acceptable (Waldrop, 1992, pp. 64–66, 262). In practical terms, most senior executive teams have an undercurrent of individual and team objectives pulling in directions that may compete at the team level. In this study, team members had strong bilateral relationships with the chief executive, and facilitating conversations with them was sometimes challenging.

One year later, the team was still engaging with potentially thorny dynamics but now with increased awareness, and it was exceeding top-line expectations. By ramping up its tolerance for high performance dynamics, members of the senior management team continually returned to its joint purpose as a method of holding individual competitive goals within an adequate check.

Role, decision-making and performance

In the second study, an eight-person board of which I was one, was joined by two consultants. Between the total of eight males and two females there were three to seven cultures. Boards can be unnatural environments for collective ownership, so the board's objectives were to articulate its joint purpose, and secondly, to refine its awareness of its key dynamics by identifying the informal role of members.

The board described 'role' as characteristics that defines the person. So, a recognized role holder would represent the most prototypical member for that role. Role was linked to the common purpose for which the board had convened. Conversations began by considering each person's view but by the end, a lack of focus meant the discussions had spiralled in several directions. This ambiguity set the tone for what was to come (Cavanagh & Lane, 2012, p. 84). One participant expressed his thoughts in the following way:

> I meet this politeness and there is too much politeness. It seems to be very difficult to get into it. It is like dealing with something I can't get my energy around. I want to rip off my shirt! It's there then it is not there, then it is there then it is not there. . . . Very abstract and I don't know what to do about it but that is what I feel.

The comment was met with bemusement, sighs, laughter and head-nods. Energy in the room surged and we discussed what this meant. The member's contribution had been utilized as a pressure valve to relieve an undercurrent of dissatisfaction presumably of this ambiguous, unpredictable phase that had been driving activities with an element of seeking something. We did not know it yet; however, role allocation was already underway (Waldrop, 1992).

Key dynamics

By updating its recognition for key dynamics, boards can build opportunities to become more agile and competitive. In this study, reflective conversation showed that the journey from the board's lack of agreement about task and role allocation was partly navigated through individuating and coalescing dynamics (Waldrop, 1992, pp. 292–294). Three key dynamics showing up were the dynamics of holding something on behalf of the board; competing for role; and seeking something.

Holding something on behalf of the board

The board progressed its role identification task by focusing on the human dynamics attached to process vehicles such as conversation and discussion. Every person engages with the world through their own unique perceptual filters. For example, the person who suffered from too much politeness fit the role of a container, holding something on behalf of the board. This container dynamic was a huge release for the board's less useful undercurrents. It permitted constructive argumentation, debate and conflict, and freed the rest of the board to think clearly and independently. One could argue that the sighs and laughter meeting the container holding these undercurrents partly represented a huge relief by the board in seeking a candidate and finally allocating the role (Waldrop, 1992, p. 262). The container role provided the board with safety valves for open discussions, and various types showed up according to context. That is, role allocation was never accidental. Rather the dynamics creating them coalesced through small acknowledgements, tacit agreements about informal roles that the board needed in order to function well. Without a key dynamic for container roles decisive action by the board would have been compromised.

Seeking something

The board's behaviour of seeking something was a key dynamic during its ambiguous feelings phases. One member described the experience as recursive, in that a lot of time was spent starting on, but not fully engaging with topics. For example, individual board members would contribute, which would be accepted for discussion. However, before the topic was adequately examined, it was dropped because there was "insufficient time" to look at it properly. A fresh contribution would then be offered, and the process would be repeated, only to again end prematurely. Several experts invited to the board received the same treatment. Their contributions were received then criticized after some cursory examination. The seeking behaviour raised the question of – why is new information again being rejected? This is succinctly summed by a member in the following manner:

> Do you know what I am struck with? A sentence was used in relation to the SS that said 'they always want more.' There is something about us as a board . . . maybe nothing is good enough. This sentiment is part of the dynamic found in board rooms where the non-executives and executives can't quite get together on what do we want, and how do we enact our role as a board?

Competing for territory and role

During a memorable visit to the board, experts introduced themselves and so did individual board members. Each introduction got longer and more elaborate as we went around the room. In the conversation that followed, some members sensed a particular struggle between one of the visitors and a board member, such that some exchanges between them seemed not to relate to the topic at hand, rather they appeared to be having a one-to-one conversation.

Since no challenge was brought to the unfolding facts, the exchange had the effect of allocating the role of chair to the individual board member. Subsequent reflexive conversations were not in disagreement, the evidence was simply noticed, which behaviourally systematically allocated the role of chairman to that individual.

Decision-making

Figure 7.2 is an overview of the main decision-making pathways interwoven by the board in recognizing the various board roles. Behaviours, activities and compromises were offered for recognition, and acknowledgment as adequately characterizing a role.

The whole board tested and considered various behaviours and activities over several exchanges and events. Silence was often taken to mean acceptance.

The driving dynamic

The indication from the three key dynamics should have signalled that they might coalesce into the driving dynamic in this board, which was that 'nothing was good enough'. That would have been a problematic dynamic because it ran the risk of accumulating until it posed a genuine risk for the development of behaviours that would produce homeostasis, where no decisions would be agreed. So, compared with the goal-focused key orientation, the driving dynamic had a strong avoidant focus of 'one cannot leave empty handed'. Or put another way, we must cooperate enough to gain something from this experience. The driving dynamic need not always have a negative focus. Whether or not the negative focus is desirable depends on the context. In this case, the feeling of not wanting to leave

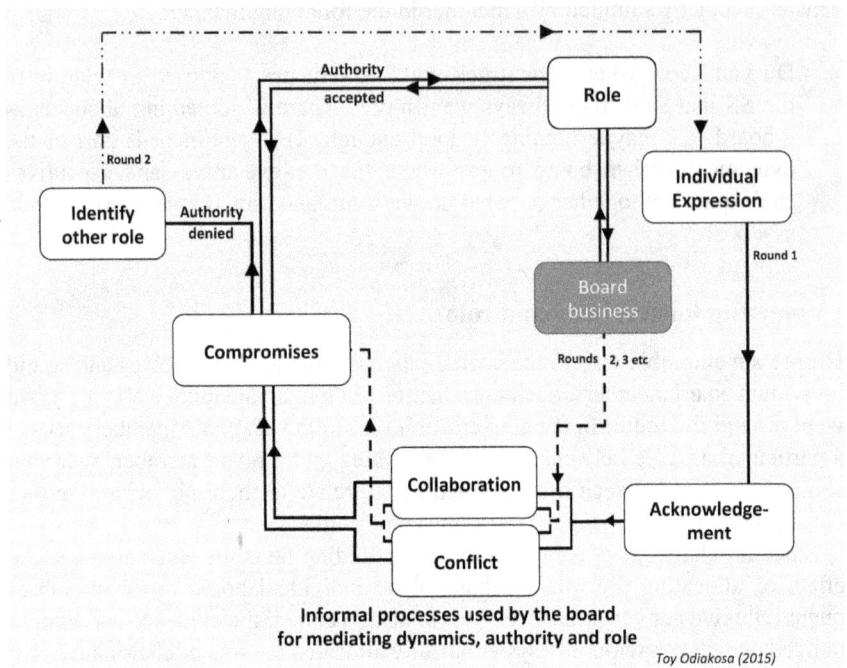

Figure 7.2 diagram labels:

Authority accepted — Role

Round 2

Identify other role — Authority denied

Individual Expression

Board business — Round 1

Compromises

Rounds 2, 3 etc

Collaboration

Acknowledge-ment

Conflict

**Informal processes used by the board
for mediating dynamics, authority and role**

Toy Odiakosa (2015)

Figure 7.2 Informal processes used by the board for mediating dynamics, authority and role

empty handed served to keep the board's key dynamics in check, so the end result worked adequately. At the same time, it would have been preferable to move towards operating from a positive driving dynamic.

General discussion

Neither the senior management team nor the board were in crisis. Most of the time, both had adequate buffering and resilience to meet demands on the quality of dynamics among team members. The approach to both differed because dynamics among the senior management team was so volatile; it was better to focus on working through its business plan and budget. On the other hand, the more developed board was able to work directly on the informal roles of members. Both methods showed improvements in the tolerance for those dynamics needed among members to facilitate them in resonating more as an entity.

The preferred state of most systems is homoeostatic. Unsurprisingly, in the presence of disruption and change this dynamic appeared in both cases. For example, the IT director in the senior management team perceived that stability was too low in the team, so he aligned his views with those of the operations director. Though not a key dynamic, the search for homeostasis was felt across the team. In the board, one side effect of seeking something, and conversations that were not flowing was that the board became distracted from its purpose. For example, the key and driving dynamics got distracted from remaining focused on the tasks, and conversation sometimes spiralled in unfocused, ambiguous directions.

In both the senior management team and the board, comments and questions aired included: What is the point of bringing up difficult and historic dynamics? Noticing these dynamics seems an extravagant way to surface problems. Some things cannot be repaired – why go there? I want to say don't be so sensitive. Who is responsible for difficult feelings in a dynamic – the sender or the receiver? Are decisions always made with the rational task in mind?

Answers to these evolved over time, through seemingly unrelated conversations. Yet everyone agreed that the topics raised possibilities. Senders and receivers felt they contributed to the dynamics in play. In practice, dynamics such as these are already felt within boards and teams although not often surfaced. Where speed was worshiped, suboptimal function increased, compounded by globalizing, scaling up or down, and other forms of restructuring. Joiners and stayers carried legacy dynamics that needed to be surfaced and acknowledged sensitively, in order to avoid less useful dynamics accidentally being included into how decisions are now made.

Not all dynamics coalesced into key dynamics. For example, the solo female on the senior management team had a reputation for being aggressive. She verbalized the gender issue in bilateral conversations, but never in the whole team whose somatic norm was male. Her behavioural response was clear in her masking her femininity and adopting behaviours often associated with the male gender.

Conclusion

This chapter has described how key dynamics are based on coalescing dynamics, which form the right conditions to catalyze and maintain a driving dynamic. It has identified a pivotal role for the notion of key dynamics and a driving dynamic, which were critical to identifying a motivation and how both board and senior management team enacted their roles.

While neither team in these studies was in crisis or distress; splits and dissatisfaction triggered their decisions to review and refresh the informal aspects of their work. Exchanges went through ambiguous phases where dynamics or feelings spiralled in unpredictable directions with no indication of resolution. Facilitated reflexive conversations led to robust accelerated results for both team and board. Through these practical conversations, both entities identified ways of improving how they related to each other internally as well as with their external roles. They improved their tolerance for high performance dynamics. In addition, elements for these results are unlikely to be imitable even in the face of realistic threats.

Ultimately the power to act is in the gift of boards and senior management teams. When a board's competences with tough dynamics are left untested, abilities to listen and be curious become less available as methods of acquiring fresh solutions to volatile, uncertain, ambiguous and challenging environments.

It is akin to never switching a computer off and on, in order to refresh it, until it crashes. In the world of 21st century businesses, high-performance dynamics continue to be critical and scrutinized. Therefore, embracing conflict by refreshing their awareness of dynamics has large pay-offs in added value, relevance, and performance for boards and their senior management teams.

8 High-performing boards – exploring the influence of unconscious behaviours

Paul Schanzer

Introduction to governance and high performing organizations

This chapter offers a rationale to inform the definition of high-performing organizations and perspectives on ways in which unconscious behaviours may influence the dynamics of high performance for public sector boards in the 21st century – the age of 'One Public Service'.

The term, 'high performing organization' (HPO) entered management literature some 25 years ago. It drew upon existing management theories that emerged in the 1970s and 1980s, particularly in respect of models of transformational leadership and whole systems approaches to organizational change. The approach received added impetus as a result of the global economic downturn in the mid-2000s.

There is no generally accepted definition of HPO. One reviewer commented that "researchers approach the topic of high-performance from different backgrounds and angles and with different goals; it makes sense that there is not yet a consistent definition of an HPO". Another noted that of the 63 published papers on HPO, only seven included a definition.

The following two sample definitions illustrate this lack of common definition, though they are representative of those published in the literature:

> an organization that achieves financial results that are better than those of its peer group over a longer period of time, by being able to adapt well to changes and react to these quickly, by setting up an integrated and aligned management structure, by continuously improving its core capabilities, and by truly treating the employees as its main asset.
>
> (de Waal, 2011)

> [Organizations that] generate maximum public value. They are relentlessly citizen centred and outcome focused. Their capabilities and operational activities all support the delivery of outcomes defined by their mission, and they measure their performance based on those outcomes, not just inputs and outputs. At the same time, they are committed to cost-effectiveness. They hold themselves accountable; they actively accept their role as stewards of

the public trust; and they make their operations and results transparent to all. They are innovative and flexible, continually striving to improve value delivery, and are able to respond creatively to new challenges and opportunities. They work in open and collaborative ways, understanding that their organization is part of a larger system, and cultivate working relationships with other agencies, organizations and stakeholders. Finally, they reflect their enthusiasm for delivering public value. This evident passion engages both internal staff and external stakeholders in active support of their organizations mission.

(Accenture, 2005)

Governance in the public sector

Governance is a wide-ranging term that means different things to different people. It encompasses concepts such as leadership, stewardship, accountability, ethical behaviour and control. As a result, it is difficult to provide a single definition that satisfies the expectations of those with a view on this subject. A useful definition from a whole system organization, namely NHS Wales (Welsh Government, 2014). defines governance as: A system of accountability to citizens, service users, stakeholders and the wider community, within which healthcare organizations work, take decisions and lead their people to achieve their objectives.

It refers to the way in which public service bodies ensure that they are doing the right things, in the right way, for the right people, in a manner that upholds the values set for the Welsh public sector. The effectiveness of governance arrangements has a significant impact on how well organizations meet their aims and objectives.

It is expected that effective governance provides the foundation for high-performing organizations, underpinned by the principles of accountability, transparency, probity, and long-term sustainability. Effective governance leads to efficient management and high performance, true engagement with citizens and appropriate stewardship of public money. It is against this backdrop of expectations that public sector boards assess their performance to demonstrate compliance to those for whom they are accountable, within government.

None of this is new, yet there have been worrying and regular examples where the principles of accountability have not been put into practice. Underlying these hopes are assumptions that good boards will facilitate the building of trust and equitable distribution of costs, risks and benefits; can help empower weaker board members and provide opportunities for mutual learning. Research from the Tavistock Institute of Human Relations identifies that boards can generate tensions and risks for members, especially where there is little commitment to common goals or investment in trust or where too many risks are imposed on the least powerful board members. A high-performing effective board may require internal changes to the structures, roles and tasks of its members, something that can pose a real challenge, but without which, effectiveness of the board may be seriously undermined.

The role of boards in governance and high-performance

It is recognized that where the pursuit of profit is not the primary purpose of the organization, culture – and more specifically values – become the key organizing principle. The scope of corporate governance has broadened in recent years, with the overall objective being to enhance organizational performance. The independent Commission on Good Governance in Public Service identifies the following principles of good governance:

- Focusing on the organization's purpose and on outcomes for citizens and service users.
- Performing effectively in clearly defined functions and roles.
- Promoting values for the whole organization and demonstrating the values of governance through behaviour.
- Taking informed, transparent decisions and managing risk.
- Developing the capacity and capability of the governing body to be effective.
- Engaging stakeholders and making accountability real.

Exploration of the unconscious and its organizational impact

To clarify what is meant by 'the unconscious', Sigmund Freud, the Austrian neurologist and father of psychoanalysis recognized that there are hidden aspects of human life which, while remaining hidden, nevertheless influence conscious processes. In treating individuals, Freud (1921) found that there was often resistance to accepting the existence of the unconscious. However, he believed he could demonstrate its existence by drawing attention to dreams, slips of the tongue and mistakes as evidence of a meaningful mental life of which we are not aware. What was then required was interpretation of these symbolic expressions from the unconscious. Ideas which have a valid meaning at the conscious level may at the same time have an unconscious hidden meaning.

Looking at an organization through a psychoanalytical lens is a potentially creative activity that may help in understanding and dealing with certain issues. A key contributor to the understanding of unconscious processes in groups was the 20th century influential British psychoanalyst Bion (1980). He developed a framework for analyzing some of the more irrational features of unconscious group life. Like individuals, organizations develop defences against difficult emotions, which are too threatening or too painful to acknowledge. These emotions may be a response to an external threat such as government policy or social change. They may arise from internal conflicts between teams and departments in competition for resources or from the nature of the work and the particular individuals involved.

Some organizational defences are healthy in that they enable staff to cope with stress and develop their work in the organization. Although some organizational defences, just like some individual defences can obstruct contact with reality and in this way damage the staff and hinder the organization in fulfilling its task in adapting to changing circumstances. At the heart of these defences is denial, which involves pushing certain thoughts, feelings and experiences out of conscious awareness because they have become too anxiety provoking.

Taking this approach a step further, Klein (1959), devised novel therapeutic techniques for children that had an impact on child psychology and contemporary psychoanalysis. She observed that when children are playing, they often represent their different feelings and emotions through characters and animals either invented or originating from children's stories such as the handsome prince, the sly fox, Cinderella and the ugly sister. The action of separating feeling or emotions into differentiated emotions is known as splitting. By splitting emotions, children gain relief from internal conflicts. Klein (1959) provides the example of the painful conflict between the love and hate for a mother, which can be relieved by splitting the mother-image into Cinderella and the jealous sister. Projection often accompanies splitting, and involves locating feelings and emotions in others instead of in oneself. Thus, the child attributes slyness to the fox or jealousy to the ugly sister. Through play, these contradictory feelings and figures can be explored and resolved.

Through this work with children, Klein developed a conceptualization of an unconscious inner world which is present in everyone and inhabited by different characters, each portraying differentiated parts of self or aspects of the external world. In early childhood, splitting and projection are key defences for avoiding pain. Klein referred to this as the paranoid-schizoid position where 'paranoid' relates to badness being experienced as coming from outside oneself and 'schizoid' to the splitting. This is a normal stage of development that occurs during childhood and as a state of mind can recur throughout life.

Sometimes the splitting process occurs between groups within organizations. Structural divisions into boards, directorates, professions or teams are necessary for organizations to operate effectively. However, these divisions become fertile ground for the splitting and projection of negative images. The gaps between directorates or professions can be filled with many different emotions such as denigration, rivalry, hatred, prejudice, paranoia. Each group feels it represents something good and that other groups represent something inferior. In the NHS for example, medics are seen as authoritarian whilst non-executives talk too much; psychotherapists are precious and managers only think about money. You can see how the individual members of these groups are stereotyped just like the characters playing roles in children's games and stories. This results in an organization being stuck in a paranoid-schizoid projective system, whereby emotional disorder interferes with the functioning of the organization, particularly in relation to tasks that require joint working or collective input.

Bion's observations about the role of group processes in group dynamics refers to recurrent emotional states of groups as basic assumptions. He argues that in every group, two groups actually exist: the tendency towards work on the primary task (or work group) and a second, often unconscious, tendency to avoid work on the primary task, which he termed the basic assumption group. These opposing groups can be thought of as a wish to face and work with reality, and the wish to evade it when it is painful or causes psychological conflict within or between group members.

The work group is an aspect of group functioning with the primary task of the group; what the group has formed to accomplish will keep the group anchored to a sophisticated and rational level of behaviour. The basic assumption group describes the tacit underlying assumptions upon which the behaviour of the group is based. Bion identified three basic assumptions: dependency, fight-flight and pairing. When a group adopts any one of the basic assumptions, it interferes with the task the group is attempting to accomplish. Bion believed that interpretation by the therapist of this aspect of group dynamics would result in insights regarding effective group work.

Psychoanalytical ideas offer a particular way of thinking about organizational processes together with influences from other conceptual frameworks to fully understand the function of the organization. A psychoanalytical approach provides opportunities for creating spaces within organizations for standing back and thinking about the emotional processes within which they are involved. This may be considered in ways that reduces stress and conflict and informs change and development. These ideas help individuals to develop a capacity for self-exploration by observing and reflecting on the impact that the unconscious group and organizational processes have on us all and our own contribution to these processes as we carry out our roles.

Mindfulness, a route to the unconscious

For clinical purposes, mindfulness can be considered a distinct state of consciousness distinguished from the ordinary consciousness of everyday living. In general, a mindful state of consciousness is characterized by awareness turned inward, towards present, felt experience. It is passive, though alert, open, curious, and exploratory. It seeks to simply be aware of what is, as opposed to attempting to do or confirm anything. Mindfulness has the potential to offer a positive practical approach by providing a safe and stress-free environment within which individuals are able to explore themselves more deeply.

Thus, it is an expression of non-doing, or non-effort where the self consciously suspends agendas, judgments, and normal-common understandings. In so doing, one can easily lose track of space and time, like a child at play who becomes totally engaged in their activities. In addition to the passive capacity to simply witness experience as it unfolds, a mindful state of consciousness may also manifest essential qualities such as compassion, acceptance and qualities that can be positively brought to bear on what comes into awareness, as highlighted by Almaas (1986) and Schwartz (1995).

Mindfulness is used as the highway to the unconscious, or implicit, pre-reflective consciousness where core organizing beliefs control experience and expression before they come into consciousness. Johnson (2009) generally listens for signs or indicators of a client's unconscious core narrative, the storyteller as opposed to the endless variations on one's story, and often uses these indicators as access routes for characteristic change, as well as the details of the presenting issue.

Mindfulness can thus be used to reorganize deep structures, as well as provide distance and perspective on the inner ecology of our egos. It can be used as the main therapeutic tool within a session, as well as a life-long practice and skill during and beyond psychotherapy. Wilber (2000) likewise endorses the value of mindfulness or the use of the witness in promoting both personal and transpersonal change. Many in Buddhist and transpersonal psychology employ a witnessing or mindful state of consciousness to consider normal mental-emotional life, and move toward the Eastern tradition possibility of the No-Self, or unity consciousness, in addition to using it in the service of the Western tradition of healing the fractured self.

Schanzer's (1990) experimental design highlighted that meditation based relaxation can effectively support psychotherapy by enhancing those factors valued by therapists such as greater awareness of feelings and unconscious behaviours.

Connecting body and mind

John Kabat-Zinn (1996) describes mindfulness as "Paying attention in a particular way, on purpose, in the present moment, without judgement". He further describes mindfulness practice as a way of training the mind to increase levels of sustained awareness; of oneself and others and of the environment. In cultivating this self-awareness we can be more adept in using our energy – mental, emotional and physical, in a way that increases our inner resources rather than depleting them.

Sensory ambling 'connectedness to nature'

Five studies utilizing survey, experimental, and diary methods assessed the effects of being outdoors on subjective vitality. As a species, movement is an important part of our natural state; being mobile enables us to see, hear and feel the world from a different perspective, which can be more fruitful when connecting with others. Neuroscience points to the importance of movement to stimulate our brains to help us think and feel better. Movement offers that 'feel good' factor, whether a hard physical activity or gentle ambling. Evidence from experimental psychological studies undertaken recently links exposure to nature with increased energy and heightened sense of wellbeing (Ryan et al., 2010)

Ryan et al. (2010) noted that participants consistently felt more energetic when they spent time in natural environments or imagined themselves in such situations. The findings identified that individuals were more generous and caring when exposed to nature. These studies highlighted the importance of having access to natural surroundings and of incorporating natural elements into our work environments through the use of natural light and indoor plants.

Mindfulness, a self-help approach in effectively managing unconscious behaviours

There is a growing body of evidence that suggests that the practice of mindfulness can have significant positive impact in the workplace with examples of greater concentration and focus, increased mental flexibility, improved confidence, optimism and resilience cited as just some of the benefits. The research highlights that with increased emotional intelligence developed through mindfulness practice, interpersonal relationships improved Chaskalson (2011).

Mindfulness helps us to be more aware of our feelings and emotions and notice the physical sensations that accompanies them, creating a breathing space for us to respond in a considered rather than reactive way, helping to differentiate between our own feelings and those of others; sometimes referred to as the 'dark side of empathy' (Chaskalson, 2011).

Many global organizations use mindfulness practice at the start of meetings, with others taking the opportunity to practice more informally by taking a few moments during the day to breathe and focus on the body to create moments of stillness.

In 2010, the UK Mental Health Foundation published *The Mindfulness Report*, which highlighted a number of significant benefits. This report suggested that people who are more mindful have the following characteristics

- They are less likely to act defensively or aggressively when they feel threatened.
- They have a greater awareness, understanding and acceptance of their feelings and emotions and recover from bad moods more quickly.
- They have a higher and more stable self-esteem, that is less reliant on external factors.
- They feel more in control of their behaviour and are better able to override or change internal thoughts and feelings and resist acting on impulse.
- They enjoy more satisfying relationships, are better at communicating, and are less troubled by relationship conflict, as well as less likely to think negatively about their partner or colleague as a result of conflict.

Conclusions

Both mindfulness and psychoanalysis have a place in easing the burdens of anxiety, depression and obsessional thinking. It is not unusual to find analytic therapists using a mix of both techniques, sometimes beginning with mindfulness to achieve clarity, and then discussing what surfaced in greater depth. As with most of psychotherapy, the art lies not in dogmatically clinging to one approach over another, but in carefully determining which tool is most likely to unlock the mysteries of the moment for the individual.

There is a significant body of evidence that demonstrates that where individuals have developed the ability to recognize aspects of their unconscious behaviour and actions, this can positively influence their capacity to perform more effectively. Therefore, it would be pertinent to explore the opportunity of engaging with existing board members with whom we already have an established relationship and have already used fairly traditional development methods to date. These individuals may be mature enough to explore further the impact of their unconscious patterns and behaviours and how these influence in a positive or negative way their own contribution, and the subsequent collective dynamics of the group.

I am keen to find a way in which mindfulness can be used as an intervention for holding the space within which individuals are able, in an atmosphere of trust, to more freely engage in a development process that has the potential to bring greater mind/body awareness to their everyday interactions and therefore enhance their contribution and performance individually and collectively.

I recognize the disruptive and invasive nature that tapping into an individual's unconscious mind can have in this context and the need for a degree of safety to support them as they may surface often upsetting, distressing or conflicting emotions.

That said, having an intervention that enables individuals to explore independently and collectively aspects of their unconscious mind can offer the potential to enhance their ability to think and perform more effectively at work and within their broader personal life. When this is combined with how an individual functions and performs through their conscious actions and behaviours, there is greater potential and opportunity for truly optimum performance to be achieved.

> When they think that they know the answers, people are difficult to guide.
> When they know that they don't know, people find their own way.
>
> Lao Tzu, *Tao* (65)

9   Decision-making – the no.1 dysfunction impacting the effectiveness of boards

Martin Palethorpe

Boards and decision-making

Board decision-making is a critically important part of running an effective organization. There are numerous examples that substantiate this claim by reflecting on the calamitous impact of some board's decisions. Over the last few decades, corporate disasters have included Enron, RBS, BP Oil, Columbia space shuttle, Tesco 'Fresh & Easy', the Co-op Bank and Lehman Brothers. After each disaster, a lengthy independent review follows with a few hundred-page report citing what had happened. Often a key component is poor decision-making by the board.

Tesco

Tesco spent 20 years considering a move into the US market, and undertook two years of intensive on-the-ground research. They even sent senior executives to live with Californian families to observe the way they shopped and ate (Butler, 2012).

However, Tesco's US board ignored much of the research findings and deciding to set-up the stores it wanted and ignored the data that was provided by its potential customers. For example, although US shoppers prefer to buy in bulk to save money, Fresh & Easy offered small pack sizes. The stores also stocked British-style ready meals and relied heavily on self-service tills. This was a big turn-off to American customers, who value good service.

From its launch in November 2007, Tesco never achieved the sales it needed. By April 2013, Tesco pulled out of the US market, at a reported cost of £1.2 billion.

So, what happened in the Tesco Board that led to these seemingly poor decisions?

Decision-making practice

Decision-making methods have been around for a long time. On the face of it, the process of make decisions is a simple one. A classic approach may be identifying the problem, developing an alternative, evaluating an alternative, choosing and implementing the best alternative, evaluating the decision. This decision methodology looks simple. However, if decisions are easy, how can so many calamitous organizational decisions occur? The reason is that decisions made by a board have a dynamic aspect, which contributes to complex results. Boards and their group dynamics warrant far more understanding and mastery than is currently the case on many boards.

This chapter looks at three real-life examples that I have direct insight into: Organization T, Organization W and Board K.

Organization T

The core leadership team of this retail organization has been together for 18 months. The team has concerned itself with merging two organizations with challenging financial objectives to meet their bank's demands. The culture in the team can be described as – too much going on, a lot of internal focus and frustration as identities, systems and processes from the two previously separate businesses were merged.

There are multiple dynamics that impact the leadership team's ability to make decisions:

- Busy-ness – With so much going on, the team does not take time to step-back and reflect on strategic decisions.
- Meeting culture – the members of the leadership team work in different offices. They meet once per month for three hours. Thus, they have limited time together and meetings regularly feature a lengthy agenda. Together, these characteristics restricts their dialogue.
- The CEO, who is effectively the team leader, has an authoritative style. Her approach contributes to people feeling that she does not want to encourage challenging and exploratory conversations. Consequently, team members often do not challenge in group settings.

Organization W

This organization is a charity. It is a wonderful organization doing magnificent work for service to men and women. At the time of writing, the organization is completing a turnaround phase as a result of past poor management and results. They have had two CEOs in a short span of time. The situation has stabilized with a new first-time CEO who has turned the business around.

But there are some deeper aspects worthy of exploration. Challenge is generally not wanted; good news is over-celebrated, and bad news avoided. This stems partly from its history, but also the natural inclination of the first-time CEO to prove that everything is 'just great'.

In this example, the dynamics at board level are as follows:

- The new CEO is trying to prove himself and is over-positive about the situation.

- The Chair who is anxious about any form of challenge, keeps to a tight formal agenda with little room for effective debate.
- Some members of the board undertake excessive challenging behaviours as a counter-balance to working through the positive picture that is always given to them.
- An organization without a clear vision or strategy to which the board can align.

Board K

Board K is the board created as part of the Tavistock Institute diploma course, Dynamics @ Board Level. It consists of two course directors, eight board members who are individual participants in the course. The board's purpose is to work together in order to learn about board functioning.

1   Individual and group anxiety is always present;
2   The group builds defences against anxiety;
3   The influence of the leader;
4   People are the products of their past.

Each factor is discussed in relation to the theories substantiating the factor. Practical real-life examples are taken from Organizations T and W and Board K.

1. Individual and group anxiety is always present

Underlying all behaviour within a board is anxiety.

Gudykunst – anxiety/ uncertainty management

Gudykunst's (2005) Anxiety/uncertainty management (AUM) theory defines how humans communicate based on a balance of anxiety and uncertainty in social situations. Gudykunst believed that in order for successful group communication to occur, anxiety/uncertainty must be reduced.

Anxiety can be described as apprehension based on a fear of negative consequences. Gudykunst postulates that effective communication involves managing anxiety between minimum and maximum thresholds. Once the upper limit of anxiety is reached, effective communication ceases.

Group (or social) anxiety specifically is the fear of being judged or evaluated by others. It is typically characterized by an intense fear of what others are thinking about them (specifically fear of embarrassment or humiliation, criticism, or rejection), which results in the individual feeling insecure and not good enough, and/or the assumption that they will be rejected by peers.

In board situations, this anxiety exists beneath the surface in many ways and continually impacts behaviour. Two deep-rooted fears in Richard Barrett's model "the Seven Levels of Consciousness" (Barrett, 1998) are: Firstly, the fear that 'I am not loved enough', and secondly, the fear that 'I am not worthy enough'. And with these underpinning deep-rooted fears, the following show up:

- Fear of looking silly

  I worry about saying something that others do not agree with, or that they think is nonsensical, so if I have a point that could in anyway appear silly, I do not share it.

- Fear of offending others

  I do not want to offend anyone, so if I have a point that is potentially offensive or threatening for a board colleague, I simply do not say it, or if I do say it, I compensate and only say a milder version of my main point.

- Fear of not being accepted

  If I am new to a group, I have a desire to be accepted by the group and to 'fit in', so the strategy I take is to keep quiet, to 'ease into the group', and hence I speak only on topics I deem to be 'safe'.

- Fear of being alone in my opinion

  If I have made previous points that the group has not supported, it can affect how I intervene subsequently. I am more likely to only speak on topics I deem to be 'safe', and I actively seek support from others.

- Fear of not being liked or respected, or feeling part of the group

  If I do not feel part of the group, I may withdraw or hold back. I either keep a distance (for example by keeping myself busy with emails), so that I cannot get close to others so that I can't be disliked; or I make a particular effort to make connections with people personally. I often do the latter by pairing with people that I consider to be 'like me'.

- Fear of talking too much or of not talking enough

  This fear exists as a voice in my head, which will regulate how much I talk. This could be considered good self-awareness and regulation, but it could also lead to over-control and over-thinking my involvement in the group. The impact could be that I don't share my opinions that could be of value to the group.

- Fear of conflict

  Especially in a new group, or a group where there is high anxiety, I am likely to be worried about having conflict with others. Conflict increases anxiety. As a result, my strategy may be one of three:

  a. Do not have the conflict and simply keep quiet
  b. Do not have the conflict, but discuss the issue with people in smaller groups afterwards
  c. Have the conflict, then compensate by smoothing over the relationships afterwards

In Organization W, Anthony has developed a reputation for being the challenging one on the board. He brought up contentious issues in the past, raising the level of group anxiety. People made remarks to him in private about his challenges. The chairman found Anthony's challenge difficult to handle. Consequently, Anthony constantly 'manages' the extent of his challenges. In one case, the chairman wanted to change the frequency of the two-hour board meetings, from monthly to bi-monthly. Anthony disagreed with this based on his experience of working in an organization that recently almost went bankrupt. But Anthony is anxious about constantly voicing his contrary opinions. But he has been more than usually vocal in today's meeting, so he keeps quiet. The decision is made. He has a fear of talking too much, of not being accepted, or being alone in his opinion. It is a small, but good example of poor group decision-making.

In Board K, I notice that two members of the group, James and Mary, are speaking excessively and negatively impacting the board discussion. As a result, I voice my opinion, and then experience significant anxiety. I fear that I have offended James and Mary and I fear what the group may now think of me. I find myself compensating in several ways:

- By withdrawing from some of the rest of the board conversation;
- By checking with the two group members in the break if I've offended them and 'smooth things over';
- By looking for assurance from others about my viewpoint. If others agree with me, my own anxiety about what I have said reduces.

Because Board K is a learning group about boards, through the above actions, I find that my views are encouraged. But on an organizational board, I know that I would probably have caused a real issue in the group dynamic. So, the tendency is to keep quiet even on issues that are fundamentally impacting how the Board operates.

In Organization T, through an anonymous feedback session, people said they wanted the MD to be more decisive on significant strategic issues. When she actively encouraged people to tell her what they meant by this, the group was unable to comment. The decisions they want her to take are: what the structure of the senior team should be, and who should and should not be on it. The group has a natural level of anxiety about raising these aspects in the group because the decisions will impact the group members personally. They fear offending others; they fear bringing up contentious topics; thus, their strategy is – keep quiet and hope that the MD will make the decision.

2. The group builds defences against anxiety

This section will describe the socially-constructed defences of boards.

Bion's basic assumption groups

Wilfred Bion's (1961) key question was – what is the task of the group? Bion argued that in every group, there are actually two groups present: the 'work group', and the 'basic assumption group'. The work group is that aspect of group functioning which has to do with the primary task of the group. At the same time, all groups contain the 'basic assumption group', which refers to the tacit underlying assumptions on which the behaviour of the group is based. Bion identified three basic assumptions: dependency, fight-flight, and pairing. When a group adopts any one of these basic assumptions, the task of the work group is undermined.

In the basic assumption of 'fight-flight', the group behaves as though it has met to preserve itself at all costs; it achieves this by running away from or fighting someone or something. In 'fight' mode, the group may be characterized by aggressiveness; in 'flight' mode, the group may engage in chit-chat, people arrive late or any other activity that serves to avoid addressing the primary task.

Basic Assumption 'fight-flight' happens frequently; in Organization T, the UK executive team has short meetings; they work from different locations; when they do get together, meetings have packed agendas; they concentrate on detail, and devote no time to strategic issues.

In Organization W too, board meetings are held only once every two months. This could be a fight-flight response. The agenda is packed and wider strategic issues are avoided. The chair tends to shut down conversations because 'we don't have time'. Because organization W is a charity and depends on volunteers, board members are often absent. Lateness and absence are tolerated; they are also handy flight mechanisms.

Bain's socially-constructed defences

Alastair Bain's work focuses on the socially-constructed defences (Bain, 1998) that serve to protect from the anxieties which are aroused when a group is engaged in carrying out its primary task. Bain says that these social defences may be evident in the organization's structures, in procedures, systems, roles, culture, and in the gap between what the organization says it is doing and what it is actually doing. Social defences are 'created' unconsciously by the organization's members, through their interactions in carrying out the primary task. These defences are increased when decisions are being made. Decisions result in change, which arouses stress since it implies giving something that is familiar for an unknown future.

Argyris' organizational defence routines

Arygyris called these defences Organizational Defence Routines, ODRs (Argyris, 1990). ODRs are any action designed to protect people, so that they do not feel embarrassed or threatened. But ODRs also prevent organizational learning.

'The emperor's new clothes' is a classic ODR. No-one dared to point out that the emperor was naked for fear of embarrassing him and themselves. A 'can do' attitude can also be an ODR by blinding people from seeing organizational realities and inhibiting them from reporting and dealing with serious problems. The

Challenger space tragedy was a prime example, where a faulty design was repeatedly missed by engineers' intent on meeting deadlines.

The board of Organization W engages in ODR by being overly positive and avoiding challenging conversations. The danger is that the organization will miss discussing important topics concerning the organization's future. The potential ramifications of this for the charity are: not being efficient with service delivery, lacking focus on sustainable recurring income, not having a clear focus on their client-base and building a new building before utilizing current space.

Groupthink

Groupthink (Janis, 1982) is a phenomenon that describes group members' actions to achieve harmony or conformity; it results in irrational or dysfunctional decision-making outcomes. Group members try to minimize conflict and reach consensus without critically evaluating alternative viewpoints, by actively suppressing dissenting viewpoints, and by isolating themselves from outside influences. Groupthink is a socially-constructed defence against anxiety.

In organization T, Melanie strongly believed that the board was making the wrong decision in reducing headcount in the operations department. She voiced her opinion. In spite of this, the board went ahead and decided to reduce the headcount and six months later there was a catastrophic impact on customer service. This affected internal morale, customer satisfaction and resulted in lost clients. Consequently, the board decided to re-hire staff within the operations department. After the event, Melanie reminded people of her opinions, but no-one else on the board remembered the strength of her views. Why didn't people hear Melanie? I suggest that Melanie felt anxiety at the time, which prevented her from expressing her views more strongly. But I believe the board suffered from groupthink. The board did not want to hear the alternative viewpoints expressed. They wanted to make a quick decision to take cost out of the business and hit certain timescales.

Eliat Aram on complexity theory

Eliat Aram (Aram, 2012) notes that in complexity theory, organizations are regarded as complex adaptive systems, meaning they tend to be non-linear and self-organizing, with emergent futures. This means their evolution cannot be traced back to simple explanations of cause and effect. Self-organization means that agents act locally; and that in their local interaction, global patterns emerge without any blueprint or design. Large complex systems evolve in an unpredictable manner. The weather is a natural example of a complex system.

The problem is that people, and in particular organizations, do not like the unknown. Knowledge and predictability are preferred because anxiety is reduced that way. Boards therefore may work according to plans and the known, in order to make their complex adaptive systems predictable.

But if boards create excessive order, their organization will tend to be rigid and not adaptable; on the other hand, if they create no order at all, chaos may result and lead to their disintegration. The key, says Aram, is to exist on the 'edge of chaos' – where complex systems develop enough stability to survive, but are comfortable with lack of full predictability in order to continually innovate.

Organization T is part-owned by Venture Capitalists (VC). The CEO operates under significant pressure to deliver financial results. The VC demands predictability, which generates pressure and hence anxiety in the CEO. The CEO passes the pressure to the executive board, which increases its anxiety. Their defence routines to manage anxiety are 'to deliver good results at all costs'. Therefore, they had reduced the headcount, even when it was not the right thing to do. They de-prioritized initiatives that were not revenue-related. They acted confidently and created plans to demonstrate how they were going to achieve them. In this situation, the leaders were ignoring the fact that their organization was a complex adaptive system. Their planning and structure was in danger of thwarting innovation.

3. The influence of the leader on decision-making

Bion's basic assumption group – 'dependency'

The essential aim of a group in basic assumption dependency (ba/d) mode (Bion, 1961) is to attain security through, and have its members protected by, one individual. Group members behave passively, and act as though the leader is omnipotent and omniscient. The group wants the leader to relieve them of anxiety – releasing them from the responsibility of leadership and the accountability for decisions. For example, the leader may make a decision that other members of the board may not fully agree with, but they remain silent.

Basic assumption dependency leaders are idealized as god-like figures who are believed to be able to take care of their 'children'. Strong-character leaders are particularly susceptible to this role. If the 'magical' leader does not perform as expected, then they will be attacked and a replacement sought. Thus, a cycle of leader-seeking, idealization and denigration is a common process in ba/d groups.

Max Weber on power and authority

Power and authority held by the leader (Weber, 1922) are distinct and different concepts, but they often combine together in the role of CEO and/or chairman. Weber defines power as the ability to achieve one's own will in a social situation. Often people at the top of organizations have reached the top because they have powerful personalities. They are often bright and have strong opinions and determination. During their career, they have used power to have others follow them.

Weber outlines three types of legitimate authority: traditional, charismatic and legal-rational authority. All of these can be at play in the decision-making dynamics of boards. Traditional authority stems from authority that arises from 'the traditions' of an entity. Subordinates then comply, based on their loyalty to the 'tradition'. Charismatic authority is a form of power involving people complying with individuals with charismatic personalities. Legal-rational authority is rules-based authority and in organizations, boards will rely on the rules to support their authority.

Combining ideas of Weber's power and authority concept and Bion's b/ad concept, we note that boards' default positions may turn to deference; the group defers responsibility and leadership to the CEO or chair; and the more powerful the individual, the more the board would defer.

Organization T

In Organization T, the executive team was characterized by deferential behaviour. They could not say what they thought even when disagreeing with the CEO, but they complied. Sometimes they reluctantly went along with decisions, and then gossiped with each other outside board meetings about what they did not like. Additionally, they covertly tried influencing the CEO's view in one-to-one meetings.

Organization W

In the board of Organization W, the chairman has the natural authority by virtue of the role but appears to have limited charismatic authority or power. In this board, the chair manages to lead and influence small decisions. The board goes along with a decision on frequency of meetings or content of the agenda. But on important topics, such as CEO remuneration, or organizational KPIs, the board becomes more vocal. In those situations, the chair lacks the same level of power as in Organization T. The chairman becomes a facilitator rather than a leader in decision-making.

4. People are products of their past (and their impact on board decision-making)

Klein on infancy

Klein (1975) claims that people relate to others and situations in their adult lives in ways that have been shaped by family experiences during infancy. A person who experienced neglect or abuse in infancy would grow up expecting similar behaviour from others, especially from those who remind them of the neglectful or abusive person from their past (often a parent). These images of people and events have become internalized and turn into 'internal' objects (in the unconscious) that the person carries into adulthood and are used unconsciously to predict people's behavior in their social relationships and interactions. Later experiences can reshape these early patterns, but internal objects often continue to exert a strong influence throughout life.

This topic is important because individuals on boards have values, beliefs and behaviours that are shaped by their past. And the ability of the individuals and hence the board to contribute to and make decisions may be shaped by unconscious processes. This might influence the level of anxiety a board member feels, which will in turn shape what the board member says and/or does.

Organization E

The CEO, Geoff, is emotionally cold, directive and impersonal in his approach; he shares little about himself with others, is black-and-white in his thinking and is controlling. He was brought up in a tough working-class family with a father who was strict with him, sometimes brutal, who showed few feelings of love or affection. This upbringing has impacted on who Geoff is today, in his leadership and his approach in board meetings.

Board K example

The intervention that I made with James and Mary in Board K is another example. There are factors in my past that influenced how I felt and behaved towards James and Mary. My father was a strong and controlling influence on me. My mother was often dominated by my father, and during my teenage years, I found myself increasingly standing up for my mother. I rebel against controlling or dominating people and I often make a stand against unfair treatment of others. I spoke against James and Mary because I felt they were dominating the conversation unfairly and I took it upon myself, I thought, to play the role that I played with my father thirty years earlier.

To one degree or another, we are all products of our past which shape our interactions in the present. In boards, the interactions, conversations and decisions are a complex web of past histories of each of the board members. Their individual levels of self-awareness and self-mastery have a significant impact on the quality and effectiveness of the board conversations and hence in decision-making.

Summary

At this time in the world – post-credit crisis – there is an increased focus on governance issues generally and on board effectiveness particularly. Organizations are required to manage themselves more predictably, and with more stability. In order to achieve this, boards need to become better at making decisions through a deeper level of understanding and self-awareness about inter-personal relationships and group dynamics.

10 Board dynamics as an explanation for the rejection of the role of HR director from the boardroom

Rachael Etebar

Background

HR as a function is a relatively recent phenomenon, with the term human resources coming into usage during the 1980s to replace the previous title of personnel. This renaming was driven by the implementation of the Ulrich model. Ulrich (1996) suggested that instigating business partnering, handing-over transactional people functions to third party shared service providers and increasingly to managers, would leave HR directors free to focus on strategy. The ultimate prize Ulrich suggested was a seat at the board table.

Twenty years on from the Ulrich model, there is increasing noise in the business press that HR has not earned its seat in the boardroom. The language used about HR has increasingly turned derogatory and hateful: 'Blow up HR' (Effron & Ort, 2015; Harvard Business Review Cover, 2015) and 'Why we love to hate HR' (Cappelli, 2015). Cappelli states that in his view HR does not deserve a seat in the boardroom because of a lack of vision and strategic insight. For Zenger and Folkman (2015) it is because HR is the "corporate punching bag, vying with IT for the dubious title of most-irritating function" or because HR is a "backwater that focused on tissues, teabags, time and attendance" (Woods, 2011). The authors of such articles argue that HR directors should not have a seat at the table unless they are more focused on business strategy, more data driven and talk the language of the business.

There are few such articles accusing the finance director of caring about numbers more than people or telling the chief information officer that there are other things in life than computers or digital data. "Financial analysts mostly display complete disinterest in HR, despite their need to discern the sources of lasting value" (Creelman & Lambert, 2011). This paper aims to use board dynamics to explain why the aspiration for HR Directors to have a seat in the boardroom is the recipient of such denigrating language and violent, sadistic rejection.

A different type of language

Many of the derogatory articles about HR in the boardroom comment on 'HR speak', with an implicit assumption that soft or ambiguous language is of lesser value. HR directors must use rational, business terminology and metrics in an expectation that only this will bring credibility at board level and improve the perception of HR (Harvey Nash, 2016).

The desire to turn human beings into numbers on a spreadsheet, to assert control through formal process is associated with traditional ways of working in boards and is a defence against anxiety, aimed at controlling the stress and fear in the complex adaptive system. The use of analytical and rational terminology is a type of sense making and a defensive position aimed at controlling the stress and paranoid anxiety in the system introduced by the different way HR converses. Despite huge amounts of focus in recent years on leaders requiring emotional intelligence (Goleman, 2005), such intimate interactions may be perceived as a threat to the board, as it challenges them to consider the emotion as well as the rationale in their decision making. If a board does not welcome a range of views and seek a balance of opinions, then it is in danger of the pressure of groupthink. If the board members do not seek to work comfortably between the different modes of communication, a fight-flight response may be invoked, with the minority member seen as a threat to the board and the approval social norms, resulting in rejection.

Van der Veer (1996, p. 250) described how language is used to create a structured world "whose boundaries we cannot transcend once we have stepped into it" and that despite constant dialogue between speaker and listener, they may never fully understand each other because of the different perceptions of what is said. Shaw (2002, p. 15) calls conversations the "patterning of human interaction" and that the focus on structured process-based language in the boardroom such as 'tangible outputs', 'concrete results' and 'solid outcomes' creates pressure and fear as 'a consequence of a way of thinking that has become habitual in corporate and institutional life'. Shaw argues that rigorously controlled conversations create delusions of omniscience and omnipotence. She argues that conversations are the real organizational process and gives examples of how often the true business happens in spontaneous free-flowing coffee break discussions, rather than in formal meetings themselves. It could be argued that HR can add real value to board business through its grounding in the type of conversation that Shaw suggests.

Similarly, Nevis et al. (2003) describes the difference between what they term as strategic and intimate interactions. Strategic interactions concern individuals 'exchanging influence to accomplish a specific task' and is the language in which boards are accustomed to conducting their work, where people are balance sheet assets to be controlled within a structured, formulaic system. HR works more normally within the intimate interaction space, focusing on connections and what people are thinking and feeling as a way of influencing through soft emotional power. Shaw supports this approach, arguing that random, opportunistic connections, made without clearly defined objectives is "instructive of continuity and change as emergence in the complex social processes of communicative action" (Shaw, 2002, p. 65).

The fact that HR directors may accept this criticism and consider conforming, demonstrates a lack of confidence and defensive, subordinate position-taking. It could be argued that HR should resist the pressure to be a follower and should value their ability to challenge groupthink, the different perspective that they bring to the organization and the creativity that comes from their challenge to the system.

A gender issue?

HR is the one profession where women dominate. According to Xpert HR (2014) 74.1% of HR directors in the UK are women. The rise in accusations that HR is not deserving of a place on the board has coincided with the increased political focus on the proportion of women on boards created by the Davies Review (2011).

Given the high proportion of women who are HR directors, it would not have been unreasonable for boards to have addressed the pressure for female representation through promoting their female HR directors to the board. It is evident that this has not happened. The number of women on FTSE100 Boards reached 26% for the first time in 2016; however, this increase has been driven through an increase of non-executive director roles held by women to 31.4%, compared to only 9.7% of executive directorships (Sealy et al. 2016). Below board level, this research showed that on executive committees of FTSE 100 companies, only 19.4% of roles are held by women. This equated to 26 roles, of which only 2 posts were HR.

The attitude displayed towards HR is evidence of high anxiety and perhaps an unconscious psychological rejection of the political pressure to increase the number of women on boards (Sher, 2012). It can be argued that this is a projection of hatred on to the far too often, 'token woman' in the senior team. The apparent lack of progress of HR in to the boardroom may be evidence of a subconscious desire to rebel by boards, against being told to change and suggests an attempt to control external interference.

In order to gain influence, the HR director may try to seek power through taking on a feminine-type role in the board, analogous to that of a mother. They may try to create a dependent, nourishing and nurturing relationship at board level in which the HR director may act variously as coach, counsel and adviser and be privy to their fellow board members' deepest desires and feelings. However, if they allow themselves to be stereotyped in this capacity alone, with no involvement in other board matters, they may become cast solely in the role of mentor, which Klein (1959, p. 300) describes as "achieving vicariously the fulfilment of aims unfulfilled in his own life". Similarly, Woods (2011) says: 'The reason HR directors have carved themselves a position of trust from the CEO is because the CEO will see them as the only director who won't take their seat'. Caldwell (2011) further states: 'When HR Directors have a place in the boardroom there is often an assumption that they invariably listen, council or implement, rather than provide high level strategic input into business decision making'. Acting too much within the stereotype of gender or role could therefore potentially disempower the HR Director and make it easy for them to be dismissed and rejected.

The HR Director may have occasion to castigate individuals for inappropriate behaviour or sooth their worry over a difficult matter, dealing with their infantile anxiety when confronted with frustration. Klein (1957, p. 180) talks about child-like features such as over-dependence and the concept of splitting, with the good breast used to sooth and the bad breast seen as a receptacle for destructive drives. If the HR director tries to move outside of the good object role projected upon them by the board, the other board members may well feel unconscious rivalry, persecution, hatred and anger (Klein, 1959). If interdisciplinary rivalry takes place and the board splits and is in fight-flight mode, then HR will be standing alone and isolated. It is therefore very important that decisions about significant people matters are treated as primary tasks owned by the whole board as the work group.

Anxiety caused by the devolution of people management to managers

An organization is a system domain, for which responsibility for the structure, culture, training and processes often resides with HR. Such processes, argues Bion (1961), are used to make organizations focus on their primary task and to opti-mize performance and organizational sense making. Menzies (1982) argues that long over-elaborate processes are used to reduce the weight of decision-making and to dissipate the ownership of decisions from individuals to the collective as an unconscious social defence. Therefore, a culture might drive such a system to protect itself and, if the HR function is seen as the owner of the processes, it may become the receptacle of blame, if it is cast in the role of inhibitor to the delivery of the primary task.

The devolution of responsibility for most people practices to the line, now means that the HR function is dependent on the opinions and actions of the line manager (John & Björkman, 2015). Separation anxiety and the stress of being forced to be independent can result in attacks on the HR function, as managers resent that they are diverted from what they see as their primary task of running the business by people issues, which they do not accept as their responsibility. Managers may display anger and antipathy that they are required to do people things that they perceive as difficult, and retain the expectation that HR should step in and make the bad thing go away (Ainsworth, 1969, p. 15). Managers may exhibit help seeking behaviour, exaggerating their helplessness in a desire for attention and approval. If their dependency needs are not met, there may be sub-conscious feelings and destructive phantasies of abandonment, alienation and neglect projected on to HR.

The reputation of HR can also be damaged if the board does not signal the value and importance they place on people matters. If the board empowers managers to ignore their responsibilities or find excuses to divert attention from why they have not done their work, the board will be complicit in questioning the legitimacy of HR to operate. This is the equivalent of a splitting process, argues Obholzer (2004, p. 39), with perceived soft elements disowned by the organization and assigned to the individuals with the perceived valency for this sort of work, often as part of an unconscious institutional process. Obholzer argues that this is neglect by the board as 'the health of the entire workforce must fall within the remit of management, who also have a particular responsibility for minimising the effect of 'toxic' processes arising from the nature of the work in which the organization is engaged' (p. 40).

HR as a container for anxiety

Menzies (1982) argued that the system unconsciously needs someone to contain the anxiety on its behalf. In many organizations, rules of secrecy and conspiracy surround people matters; for example, concerning board remuneration, discipline or talent markings. The HR director may become the container of the anxiety about secrets that could potentially damage the reputation of the organization if they become public (Bain, 1998). If things go wrong therefore, HR may be the receiver of projections of feelings of shame or blame. For example, the *Daily Mail* reports (Glennie, August 29, 2013). that in 2013 the BBC exited a number of senior staff with large compensation payments. There were no maximum caps in place, only a rule that payments over £75,000 had to be signed off by the HR director. When the Public Accounts Committee started investigating, the HR director became the target of destructive and persecutory blame for the perceived lack of control over public money, because she signed the authorization for the payments. The director general of the BBC called the HR director a 'toxic asset', dehumanizing her and demonstrating his use of denial and detachment as a defence against the stress and paranoid anxiety of the situation.

The HR director's role as a container for secrets can also inspire jealousy and greed from other board members, which Klein (1957, p. 181) calls 'an impetuous and insatiable craving'. 'How much does he earn?' 'What was his bonus?' 'Is he going to be promoted before me?' The HR director as the owner of the secrets of the remuneration committee, may be seen as omnipotent, holding power and personal knowledge over other board members. Rivalry and sadistic impulses may create a drive to spoil and destroy the HR director. Deprivation, says Klein (p. 183), increases greed and persecutory anxiety. An understanding of these feelings and reactions will help the HR director in relating to board colleagues. The HR director must not rush to pander to feelings, attempting to sooth too early, if they are going to face the reality of the situation. Temporary states of envy, hatred and grievance will help develop feelings of gratitude later (Klein, 1957, p. 187).

The relationship with the CEO

Bain (1998, p. 2) described Jacques' research into splitting and pairing, using the analogy of the first officer having to take all the shit and be a shit, in order that the captain is idealized, which is a comparison that could equally be applied to the relationship of the HR director and the CEO. Often the CEO will make a decision that he or she will distance themself from, in order to retain their mystique. The HR director will become the 'holding environment' (Winnicott, 1965) for the resultant organizational distress, feelings of stress and persecution engendered.

Many HR directors seek to gain their power and thus their seat at the table via the relationship they have with the CEO. Often their aim is to help create a phantasy of a powerful, charismatic leader, whatever the reality might be. HR directors may collude with the CEO about the image they want to present, and how they use their power to promote, reward or punish. This can create a fantasy of the HR director as the power behind the throne or the go-between. There is a danger for an HR director in being too closely associated as a follower of the CEO, as they can become the focus for the stress, anxiety and transfer of feelings of unconscious greed, rivalry, hatred and powerlessness experienced by the other executives. Being a CEO can be lonely and it is important that the HR director is a confidant for the CEO, allowing them to express their feelings and provide advice. However, HR directors should be cautioned against becoming too inextricably associated in the power politics at play, in order to keep a measure of independence.

Conclusion

Board dynamics are proven to be a useful lens through which to look at the possible drivers behind the claims that HR does not deserve a seat in the boardroom. It is evident that there may be a paranoid anxiety aimed at protecting the system from the challenge HR may bring to the board. A different type of soft conversation, and lack of conformity with normal business terminology creates anger and violent, sadistic rejection. The stress in the system may be enhanced by managers projecting destructive phantasies of abandonment and neglect on to HR in order to avoid taking responsibility for managing their people. Unconscious greed and envy caused by HR being the holder of organizational secrets, may also be a driver; as could be jealously if HR has a close relationship with the CEO. That this is a profession where women are successful could be a cause of violent rejection, due to the increasing political pressure to increase the number of women on boards. As Caldwell (2011, p. 58) says: 'The boardroom is a social space that operates through symbolic power; it tends to reinforce and reproduce legitimisations of boardroom access. It defines why HR or any associated function does or does not deserve a seat on the board'.

11 Modern boards

Grant Taylor

Discharging fiduciary duties and generating new thinking

The risk management groundhog-day board agenda that reassures us that we are discharging our fiduciary duties is only one part of the board's role. The car needs its wheels to be secure and its tyres to have tread, indeed, but what about its potential? Can it go towards another direction? Could a tune up, or would a new engine be a great investment? Which would be better in the long term? What if we used the car for a different purpose or shared it with other people? If we put wings on it, would it fly? Sometimes the focus of the board is inward and pedestrian, but increasingly, boards today recognize that their role is to be strategic, to generate new thinking, and for board members to contribute more broadly to the fulfilment of the organization's vision and mission. On occasion, everything is set up for the board to be proactive and strategic, but it just doesn't happen. Human dynamics may instead be stifling the ability of a board member to contribute to their fullest potential.

It can be a complex picture; thus, investing in governance needs to be well thought through. Particularly in the charity sector, where any investment in infrastructure is heavily scrutinized when funds raised are often felt (by the public) to be best spent on directly supporting beneficiaries. Failure to gain a return on investment can be particularly damaging for charities, or worse, a governance failure can lead to a loss of confidence from donors, falling income, loss of contracts, and ultimately the demise of a charity.

So, back to the opening questions. What is board performance? How can we measure it? Are high-performing boards recognizable in a modern digital age, and if so do they have common characteristics?

Having read around the subject, and having tried to get behind the buzzwords, I have not found meaningful definitions or definitive answers. Perhaps I was over-optimistic in my expectations. Although I would have settled for a good overview of what a high-performing board's characteristics are, what I found instead is what constitutes advice for good governance rather than anything inspirational.

Why is it that despite process and structural improvements – in recent years – to the way that boards operate, they are generally no more dynamic than they ever were? Why have the innovative and disruptive business practices that we see in new organizations, that we often aspire to adopt, do not filtrate the boardroom?

Some say that because boards have fiduciary responsibilities and compliance-heavy environments, they are not places where innovation can easily thrive. However, surely boards have responsibility for strategy development and must generate new thinking that will keep an organization relevant? After all, what's the point of managing risk in an organization that has stagnated and become irrelevant?

If a board delivers its fiduciary role well, it can go to the next stage and actively support a successful future for the organization. This is where the excitement is. Excitement comes from creative thinking, doing new things and taking risks, not the maintenance of the mediocre. When board members are recruited, we think about their skills in the context of what the board wants to achieve for the organization. We want their skills, expertise, networks and potential contribution, and therefore we must enable them to have impact, rather than having the enthusiasm and excitement squeezed out of them by bureaucracy, process, and box ticking. Boards, if well-run, can be a hot-bed for innovative thinking and a place for exciting debates. It is where creative discussions not only *should* happen, but *must* happen.

High performance in the workplace is about hiring the right people and creating a culture that enables them to perform. When looking at team performance, we add in behaviours. This applies as much to the boardroom as anywhere else.

I feel fortunate to have had broad exposure to many different types of boards as a consultant working with boards to recruit executives and non-executives, as well as undertaking board reviews and as a trustee myself. This has given me an insight into the boards of charities, membership bodies, social enterprises, governing bodies of schools, colleges and universities – and albeit to a lesser extent – the boards of commercial organizations. My knowledge, observations and ideas have been brought together in a concept that I describe as the '21st Century or Modern Board.' It is not rooted in academic theory, so if you are looking for that you will not find it here. I use the 'modern board' as a benchmark when undertaking my board reviews and find it serves me well as a practical, sensible and logical framework that can be implemented to raise performance.

Every board is different

Before discussing the benchmark content with you, we must appreciate that every board is different. Significantly different in fact. Just as every organization is different, the board will often reflect the unique nature of the organization; its hierarchy, history, social standing, external environment, strategy, management and the behaviours and attitudes of its members. Sometimes the board reflects the style and approach of an over-dominant chair or CEO or the limited ambition often seen in a geographically isolated location where there are fewer cultural influences. Sometimes a board operates effectively and sometimes not.

We must keep this in mind when looking at the features of a modern board, where the relevance of each element of the benchmark will vary depending on the organization. Some of this will resonate, some will not. That said, I am confident that you will get a good sense of what a high-performing modern board looks like and how to recognize strong performance, whatever board you are a part of.

The best way to consider what follows is to imagine a continuum or line with marks from 1–100, with 1 being the worst type of out-of-date board and 100 being the modern board that we are all aiming for. Most boards are likely to be between middle ranges between 25 and 75. Where would you be with each part?

Key features of the modern 21st century board and how it differs from the 20th century board:

The board

In the 20th century board, most decision-making happened at full board meetings with little work, and minimal engagement of board members occurring outside of the main board meeting. There were few committees, and those that existed tended to be toothless or were marginalized. Whilst the older boards did have a strategic view and deal with crises, the modern board has both a strategic and tactical view (bottom-up as well as top-down), prevents and plans for crises through well-defined roles, responsibilities and committee structures. Committees are empowered (they have teeth), with power distributed amongst committees. The modern board becomes the nexus that unites the committees. This structure prevents tasks from becoming everyone's responsibility, but nobody's job. The key difference between the two boards is that the work of the modern board is continuous and ongoing, with work distributed to effective committees.

The focus of the 20th century board was fiduciary. In other words, the board's work was concerned primarily with compliance and managing risk. You would often hear people say "nothing will go wrong on my watch". The problem with this approach is that it stifles the board's ability to support the organization in achieving objectives. It restricts innovation, creativity and blunts entrepreneurialism. The 21st century board, however, appreciates the fiduciary role, as well as its legal, ethical and social responsibilities. It is also focused on what will be happening in the future, looking to understand trends in the sector and economy at large, in order to stimulate ideas and innovation, maintain relevance and even perhaps to enjoy first mover advantages. 21st century boards are set up to spark ideas, support calculated risks and deploy the expertise of their members in a more expansive way to expedite the reaching of organizational objectives. As such, the board will have people with relevant skills and experience in modern marketing, communications, income generation and digital matters, so that the board can ensure that the organization is relevant in the way it engages with the modern world. The board will contain people that understand modern technology to take advantage of new developments, as well as to avoid the pitfalls of investing in the wrong area.

I am often asked about the optimal board size for an organization. In the past, boards have tended to be too large and unwieldy, or too small and lacking vital skills. As a rule, having 12 board members* is a good benchmark size for three simple reasons:

1   Modern boards should have the executive team present and engaged in a meaningful way with the work of the board. This will usually consist of two or three people (CEO/finance director/plus one or two specialist executives in operations, marketing & communications and business development & income generation). These executives can rotate depending upon the agenda and may not attend all meetings. This leaves space for around nine external board members (more could make decision-making slow and a challenge to manage), of which up to two or three people may not be able to attend meetings on any occasion. Having more than 25% executive board members to non-executive is not appropriate for both robust board dynamics and associated governance. Thus, purely from a numbers perspective, having less than 12 people, if three are members of the executive, could be problematic when there are vacancies and absences.

2   To have the range of skills and experience needed to oversee, scrutinize and add value to a modern organization, you need people who understand and have experience of entrepreneurship and growing modern organizations, technology and its possibilities for an organization, marketing and communications (including digital), income generation and human resources, which would include talent management and people and performance. Additionally, change and transformation, high-level and strategic financial and commercial skills, governance and risk, as well as specialist sector skills, knowledge and relevant networks.

3   To be diverse enough to have a range of genders, ages, cultural backgrounds (we live in a globally connected world and you cannot be an internationally focused organization with a board made up of older white males, as most still are, regardless of where they have previously lived and worked). Constructive debate and discussion also requires a range of thinking styles, attitudes to risk and approaches to business.

Board size needs to be appropriate to serve the organization effectively. Membership associations and professional bodies, for example, have more complex structures with a cohort of members, some elected, often present, but I've left that aside, instead generalizing to make a point.

Board members

A 20th century board will have board members who act through their status and are unlikely to take ownership of their performance, the performance of the board, or of the organization. As a team, they are a homogeneous group of individuals likely to share similar perspectives and often tend to agree with the CEO rather than adequately scrutinize the executive team's performance. They usually have business or relevant sector skills, but rarely have people who are active entrepreneurs with real currency in modern markets. They are hands-off and keep their distance from the executives and staff. They are also likely to be committed to several other boards and may lack focus or time. Boards still stuck in the past focus on having the right names and titles over and above competence, relevance, skills or potential, attention or overall contribution of members.

In the 21st century, modern board members are a diverse and challenging group of people, tough minded, shrewd and bring business insight. The board has a good number of fast-thinking, nimble and creative entrepreneurs present who can see opportunities that staff may not, liven up the boardroom and encourage different attitudes to risk. They stretch and challenge the CEO's thinking and executive team performance. They not only scrutinize the organization's performance but are comfortable reviewing board performance and reflecting on their own performance as a part of that team. A modern board member acts with professionalism and takes ownership of issues. They are happy to have objectives and be measured against them, show resilience and are open to challenge. They are happy to have a fixed tenure and aware enough to move on, when they feel that they have made their contribution, even if this is after just one term. They always put the needs of the organization first and demonstrate awareness that somebody with a different background or thinking style, may be able to add more value. Modern board members are engaged with executives, and are valued by them as their 'critical friends', so they should be encouraged to challenge and thereby seek to be of service to the organization. They want to spend time amid the organization, building their knowledge, understanding and considering how they can best add value. 'It's what we do rather than who we are'.

Behaviours drive performance, and high performing boards and their members behave in ways that build their organization's strength. This means that motivation, expectations, personality styles and behaviours require careful assessment in the recruitment process. Accepted behaviours and establishing a culture for high-performance must be set by the chair and communicated in the recruitment process, reinforced by induction and monitored on a regular basis by the chair.

Unwin (2015) suggests the following personal styles exist to enable high-performance within boards:

The Peacemaker asks – can't we find a common way? Surely there is a different approach?

The Challenger says – can't we do better? Has it always been done this way and if so why?

The History holder says, do remember where we come from. We need to go back to our roots, and remember what worked in the past.

The Compliance person will always say, what will the auditors think? Is this legal?

The Passionate advocate will respond, for goodness sake, surely, we must take a risk?

The Data champion says – all the evidence shows that however often we do that, it makes no difference to the outcomes.

The Wise counsellor says, we are not the only people trying to tackle this issue, we need to think carefully, plan properly, and take this step by step.

The Inspiring leader will describe their vision, will point to the hills, will enthuse and excite.

While the Fixer says, I think we can get together outside the meeting and sort this out.

And the Risk taker says, the case is there, let's just spend the money, and it is such a good idea that it will work.

While the Strategist says, we need to think about what will happen in 2025, and recognize that if the Government makes the changes that they are planning, then our position will be much stronger and the whole environment will be different.

And the User champion says, I am worried that we are ignoring the interests of our beneficiaries and customers. We haven't mentioned their needs all though this meeting.

All those voices and questions make great boards. High-performing boards have the diversity to hold in balance the strategist, passionate advocate and entrepreneur with the risk-taker, the compliance person and the data champion. In Julia's words: "I have seen boards that are entirely entrepreneurial and they are pretty scary. I have also seen boards that are entirely compliance driven, and they are terrifying".

Recruitment, induction and development

In the past, personal nominations were the way to find new board members. This could be described as the 'Country Club approach' as it served to propagate familiar views and the feel of a social club environment. The emphasis was on recruiting people with status and experience who can offer advice from their preceding career, rather than bring dedicated skills that may help the organization in the future. There was rarely a committee dedicated to open recruitment of new board members. This is still prevalent, with too many people thinking that getting high-profile people on their board means they are succeeding, irrespective of the input of that person.

The 21st century board places the emphasis on recruiting people who are current leaders or emerging future leaders in their careers with specific talents in modern business such as digital marketing and communications or technology. Skills and current experience are the focus. This helps to promote a diversity of ideas, backgrounds and approaches so that the ideal board culture feels like a pit-crew where each member brings something specific to the board team and delivers with precision. They have a committee dedicated to ensuring a robust external recruitment process, with succession planning and board member development programmes in place. Recruitment is strategic; actively seeking a high-level of diversity to ensure a board is made up of people with different skills and perspectives.

Induction and development has for many boards in the past been haphazard, ineffective or in some cases non-existent. Modern boards ensure induction and development is organized, consistent and well-structured, with ongoing learning opportunities for board members. Board members, however, will take it upon themselves to self-orientate by requesting information, site visits and asking peers for information on the background of the board and relationships between board members. Peer mentoring relationships exist to support new board members to get up to speed quickly.

Board meetings

Board meetings in outdated boards can run for hours with little meaningful debate or outcomes agreed. The structure of the meetings and the tradition of how they have been run in the past is important. The board can feel like a shadow of the chief executive or chair, where energy is not distributed evenly, thus holding the organization back.

The modern board feels like an independent entity with collective energy and everybody motivated, with personal objectives or areas of responsibility that they own. Form follows function – and the level of structure and formality is only what is required, no more and no less.

Board meetings and committees use technology, efficiently utilizing the time and expertise of board members. This results in actions and decisions that make a difference being taken quickly and efficiently. For example, the use of chat rooms and remote communications shifting the main fiduciary business towards a virtual board or committees (outside of core meetings) resulting in plenty of space for strategic and generative discussion.

In fact, the way the organization is run from its core is driving this change in the board. Roles become blurred, with the focus on achieving the vision. Porous boundaries occur but that is acceptable if you have the right people with the right attitudes on your board. Dialogue takes up space, and rather than the default position in the boardroom of yesterday being a squeezed agenda, space is created for more meaningful debate by having just a few agenda items. Review, reporting and decision making must be balanced with discourse and exchange.

Wouldn't it be great if the board set three important strategic issues every year and really attacked them? Wouldn't it be great if these took precedent over the governance themes at the board meetings? The lower-priority tasks would be delegated to the CEO or committees so it can invest its attention on other issues that could be more critical at that time. This takes a strong chair, committed to actively managing the work of the board and recognizing the value of the board members. A good scheme of delegation will need to exist. The chair understands that risk management is not seen as the primary role of the board in the 21st century, and whilst risks need active managing, the board should also be measured by the organization's growth, social impact or progression towards its vision.

The modern chair

For the avoidance of any doubt, the CEO runs the organization and the chair runs the board. How the chair runs the board is probably the single most important factor in whether a board (and organization) can perform at a high level. The chair of a modern board will set high standards, see performance management as an opportunity to facilitate the ongoing development of the board and each individual member of it. They will help the board member to have a clearly defined role and responsibilities, a clear understanding of positive behaviour and will motivate and stimulate ideas and innovation in others. Equally, they will challenge low levels of commitment and recognize that change is rapid and constant and seek to update the skills and experience of the board regularly. To do this well they will need to understand the organization's position in their market sector and how the mix of expertise relates to that as well as the future direction of the organization. Modern boards leave space to recruit people with skills that they need to acquire quickly, and pay significant attention to succession planning.

A modern chair's focus should be on five key areas of responsibility:

1) Leadership of board of trustees by developing objectives for both the board and individual board members, ensuring induction, development and appraisal processes are in place, and by being accessible to, and supportive of, all board members.
2) Ambassadorial representation by acting as a figurehead to represent the organization and seeking to raise the profile of the organization at every opportunity in professional and social circles.
3) Preparing the agenda (with CEO input) and chairing the meeting effectively by finding a balance between people, time and issues. If any one of these dominates, a meeting can run overtime, create resentment. By also guiding the direction of the meeting so that all members of the board can share their ideas, concerns and expertise to ensure that dialogue moves towards actions and positive outcomes.
4) Ensuring actions, the strategy and business plan is delivered by setting the strategic direction, and ensuring that targets for board, board members and CEO are agreed, monitored and met.
5) Challenge and support for the CEO by being a critical mentor and adviser and allowing the CEO to deliver their role without interference. Being available and communicating openly and transparently with the CEO and directors as well as having the courage to ask tough questions on a 1:1 basis behind closed doors is critical. The chair will act quickly on risks or when standards and performance is slipping.

The chair can delegate or share some of these responsibilities with other board members, committees or the CEO and directors, but is ultimately responsible for all the above. Neglecting or badly managing any of the above will severely restrict organizational progress and performance.

Final words

It is clear that there are many complex and inter-connected factors that will contribute to a high-performing board. The quality of the chair, each board member and their understanding of the role, the diversity of people, the structure of meetings, committee structures and how they interplay with the board, the way the work of the board is distributed all year around, induction and training, attitudes and behaviours, and importantly, relations between board members and staff all have an impact.

Setting standards, recruiting well and having objectives to work to are all critical and offer a decent starting point. Maintaining standards, keeping the board fresh and the meetings exciting, is hard work. It needs investment in time and resources. It needs board members that are willing to support and challenge each other, and it needs the commitment of everybody involved in the organization's leadership to make it work. However, if you value your time, and that of others, it is a worthwhile journey to embark on.

Part III

Introduction

States of mind

The following section contains descriptions of the 'states of mind' of boards that can be discerned by the trained observer. The section contains chapters that describe various emotional states of boards, which can impact their effectiveness to carry out the work they are there to do. The authors of the chapters in this section offer insights into the states of mind of boards and the possible reasons why certain states of mind may interfere with board functioning. Obstructions may range from a board composed of people who are not aligned with the values of the organization for which they bear responsibility or who are not conscientious in their approach to the work, to a board that cannot find or take up its role appropriately in relation to overall strategy. A board that is overly competitive, rivalrous, passive or opaque in its functioning fails to serve the organization and potentially could lead it into crisis.

Steven Phillips in Chapter 12 draws on the ideas of the poet Keats on "being in uncertainties, mysteries and doubts", and the application of the concept of negative capability in boards, "when a man is capable of being in uncertainties, [m]ysteries, doubts, without any irritable reaching after fact and reason ". Phillips takes us to Bion's slightly expanded definition as the ability to tolerate the pain and confusion of not knowing, rather than imposing ready-made answers, inappropriate certainties or other panacea upon an ambiguous situation or emotional challenge. Phillips describes how by avoiding anticipated painful experiences, a board can unconsciously collude, employ strategies and tactics that prevent or evade their anxieties, which in turn inhibits learning and decision-making.

In Chapter 13, Paula Wilson describes the role of humour in the boardroom, suggesting a critical look at the states of boards that are sometimes a little too serious. She suggests that humour and laughter are natural elements of real dialogue and that humour should have a clearer role in boardroom interactions and conversations. Humour may even assist the most 'stuck' boards to make beneficial changes.

In Chapter 14, George Th. Fischer-Varvitsiotis describes narcissistic states of mind in boards, pointing out the difference between healthy narcissism – a fundamental function of the 'self', ensuring a healthy self-confidence, performance capability, charisma, etc., and narcissistic disorders that are expressed as hubris, the underestimation of risk, arrogance and inaccessibility to criticism. Also useful is the idea that narcissistic disorders often cause the emergence of 'criticism-free zones', leading to unbounded risk-taking. For this reason, knowledge of personality traits can be helpful in establishing a 'good' board mandate.

Boards may be in disarray, paralyzed and in chaotic states of mind with a number of members taking literal flight from the board. Tammy Noel in Chapter 15 writes about the effect of such a board on her personal health, feeling unable to be an effective contributor, feeling drained, crippled and wrung out. She concludes that the board's state of mind resembled a pattern of corruption, competition and collusion, driven by a desire to stay close to the group's key source of power – a holy trinity of unhelpful unconscious behaviour – that was impossible to change.

Increasing board effectiveness is everyone's business – authorities, board members, and employees all look to boards to carry out their work effectively. Toya Lorch in Chapter 16 distinguishes between learning *to* experience and learning *from* experience. She points out how boards fail to learn from experience by turning a blind eye to their underperformance. Lorch claims that board members may have limited capacity to learn *to* experience the challenges of working in groups. Reasons may include their level of seniority, diverse leadership styles, incompatible interests and time constraints. She describes the states of mind of arrogance ('*I know*'), insecurity ('*I should know*'), narcissism ('*I need to run the show*'), and fear of leaving their comfort zone ('*Why should I take risks?*').

12 'Being in uncertainties, mysteries, doubts'

The application of negative capability in the board

Steven Phillips

Negative capability

The concept of negative capability was described by the poet John Keats, (Simpson et al., 2002) in a letter to his brothers, as 'when man is capable of being in uncertainties, mysteries, doubts, without any irritable reaching after fact and reason.'

Harris Williams (2010) expands Bion's definition of negative capability as the ability to tolerate the pain and confusion of not knowing, rather than imposing ready-made answers, inappropriate certainties or other panacea, upon an ambiguous situation or emotional challenge.

Keats is suggesting – from an artist's perspective – that artists need to be able to suspend their seeking out of beauty and truth, so that the beauty and truth of nature can make itself known to them – and through them. The author's belief is that Bion, from his psychoanalytic perspective, is recognizing the pain that we feel from 'not knowing' and our desire to introduce already available knowledge. This already available knowledge enables us to avoid the painful experience of experiential learning, or coming to 'know' something through our live experiences in the here and now.

To avoid this anticipated painful experience a group or system can unconsciously collude to employ strategies and tactics to prevent or evade this experiential learning, through what has been termed social defences against anxiety (Menzies, 1960; Bain, 1998). 'Negative capability' is perhaps describing the ability to overcome the unconscious pull of these social defences and to be able to sit with, or contain, that anxiety.

I have been involved in designing and directing leadership development programmes with members of the middle and upper-management populations of very large, international and commercially successful corporations for over 20 years.

I only mention this length of experience to highlight that *in spite of it*, I am still awed by the confusion, lack of clarity, lack of clarification, unclear intentions, unclear purposes, duplication of effort, micro-management, boss-pleasing (concern for actions that deliver approval from one's line manager, above any strategic relevance) and otherwise unproductive activity that seems to be the undiscussable lived experience and norm of corporate life. No longer surprised – but nevertheless overwhelmingly impressed by the normalization of what seems a 'mass emperor's new clothes' collusion.

In the fog of day-to-day uncertainty and volatility, people in organizations look to the certainty of any clear task that is on offer to them as an opportunity to perform, to demonstrate their capability, to achieve something discrete and have success that is specifically attributable to them. When this appetite for a clear primary task, i.e., the work with which a person is explicitly tasked, is combined with leaderships' "irritable grasping after fact and reason", a powerful cycle of supply and demand is fuelled and maintained.

The 'fact and reason' sought from the boardroom as the demand-side of the equation is often in the specific form of data, business cases, PowerPoint slides, or presentations in person. I am not suggesting that these factual and reasoned inputs to decision-making do not have a place. I am observing that there comes a point at which individual and, especially in a board, collective *judgment* is required.

It is at these moments, in which judgment rather the reductive analysis is required, that negative capability may be of great value to the functioning of the board. An increase in negative capability would also reduce the demands made on already busy people for more data, more slide packs, more business cases and so forth.

At these times I would argue that in order to be sufficiently present to the *patterns* of information already available amongst data, experience, individual sensing and intuition, a degree of suspension of reductive analysis, suspension of knowledge, suspension of needing to be the ones who know, is required.

In considering this I am bearing in mind that the "irritable grasping after fact and reason" is also a social defence against the anxiety of the circumstances. Some of those circumstances being the challenge of suspending habitual patterns (i.e., of imposing pre-conceived answers) *and* the impossibility of actually meeting the expectation of others and themselves that the board can be 'the ones who know'.

A case of irritable reaching

I am facilitating the board of a company in the media sector, which is meeting for the first of a series of two two-day strategy workshops. Their business was founded in 1767, but now this historically print-based media business faces the challenge of fundamentally re-inventing itself for a digital media world. The challenge of the workshop, to identify the details of a strategy for not only reinventing the organization but to also create new market demand too, is enormous. Their tough starting point is to be part of the most rapidly declining segment of the most rapidly declining commercial sector.

The directors express that no-one has done this before and it feels to them both enormously exciting and, given the business's long history, a massive responsibility. They are also very aware that there is poor morale amongst the bulk of the 3,000 strong workforce. The changes required to modernize the traditional working practices have led to ill feeling and a distinct 'us and them' relationship between a unionized workforce and the senior management.

The majority of the directors are recent appointments (within the last 12 months), typically chosen for their digital media experience, and not necessarily experienced in the role of director, in membership of a board or of working together.

At a point in the flow of work over the two days, the directors need to clarify their strategy amongst themselves and reach agreement. Specifically, they need to identify their level of commitment and investment to their very wide range of existing print media titles compared to their approach to new digital media development. This is not as easy as deciding at what speed to shift from an 'old world' to a 'new world' media. The brand value of the titles of existing print media are a critical part of the *new* media proposition and so cannot all simply be allowed to wither at varying speeds.

The group work together to consider different approaches to strategy and investment. The CEO and the finance director (FD) in particular want to focus on the available data, which is in the form of directories of financial and sales performance. These documents concern the performance of several hundred individual publications, each reported in several different dimensions. It is therefore, a very large volume of data.

Having recently been an attendee at a Tavistock programme entitled Dynamics @ Board Level, I am more aware than I would have previously been, to my own experience of the here-and-now of this group. During this particular strategy workshop, I took the opportunity to practice applying that potentially raised awareness of the dynamics of the group. In particular, I am attending to my own felt experience; how might what I am feeling represent something that is unconsciously in play for the group-as-a-whole? The group-as-a-whole refers here to a web-like *collective* unconscious of the group.

In the workshop, I noticed that the team is very intellectual in its approach and this is most strongly demonstrated by the chief executive officer (CEO). The CEO, Tony, is an intellectually powerful, highly rational and engaging figure.

I also notice that I am feeling confused about the conversations about strategic direction and feeling lost as to what the group is trying to do, and how their exploration of detailed figures is going to help resolve larger scale issues. For example, what is their stance about *what* they are trying to do and *why* they are doing it? What are the principles that they will apply in making investment decisions? How clear are they on what question they are trying to answer and how they will answer it?

The FD and CEO discuss possible scenarios with what I feel is a significant level of detachment. Whilst one part of me feels this is an admirable necessity – i.e., not being personally invested in a specific direction – I am more struck by the lack of foundation from which we are working. The conversation, whilst on the one hand being about using hard data, feels paradoxically ungrounded and abstract. The data is discussed as being very important in enabling us to decide 'how to place our bets'.

In discussing their future approaches to technology, a member of the group describes their approach as 'platform agnostic', meaning they are not wedded to any one technology and will work with whatever media is appropriate.

This comment consolidates a thought I have about the group's discussion – it is agnostic. *They are agnostic.* I feel frustrated and even disappointed that I am not getting any idea as to what the people here fundamentally believe. Is the group seeking a *calculation* that will define their direction, perhaps in the absence of having some personal clarity? Being such an intellectual group, I feel I could be witnessing an MBA class discussing what to conclude as part of a case study exercise. They seem exercised and engaged by this discussion as if it is an abstract puzzle to be solved, a cerebral exercise and not connected to a human enterprise with human consequences and opportunities.

I am considering the possibilities that:

1   This discussion is enabling the participants to avoid the dreadful responsibility, that their decisions will have big and sometimes negative impact upon the lives of the workforce.
2   I am feeling something about the lack of clarity, on behalf of this group, about the why, how and what we are trying to do.
3   I am feeling something on behalf of the workforce who are unclear on where the business is going and for whom the board feels detached, unfeeling and ungrounded in their reality.
4   I am being influenced in my reaction by an upbringing in which social justice, left-wing politics and the disempowerment of labour were dinner table conversation and currency.

The desire to get into and stay in the facts, the data and the desire to avoid a personal point of view by using a calculation could be a social defence against anxiety – and perhaps some negative capability is being called for. The *suspension* of the desire to get to 'decisive action' might lead to sufficient space, in which to have some reflection on what is happening here and now for these individuals and this group. And that reflection might lift the attention from the detail to some time spent 'living in' the larger questions and feeling the emotions of the situation in ways that might also inform decisions and actions.

I decide to intervene by describing what I am experiencing, as I have above, and inviting others in the group to respond and say what is going on for them at the moment. This is a deliberate and careful choice of words because I do not want this group, who are together for the first time, to feel that this is a critique of their process.

The FD, Angela, does respond very quickly, in a manner that feels defensive to me, to say that dispassionate and rational decision-making is exactly what is required and that a full examination of the numbers will tell them what a profitable business is and what is not. She says that she is very clear in what she believes and that she feels that there is good alignment in the team.

The human resources director (HRD), David, asks whether that *is* the basis of their investment decisions, i.e., that we are going to back profitable titles and withdraw from non-profitable ones? He goes on to question that logic by stating his understanding: that the strategy we are discussing requires the support of titles that have high brand equity, *not* necessarily only those with current profitability.

Three other members of the group say that they are not clear what we are doing at the moment. They do not feel that there is a fundamental agreement amongst the group and that more time is needed to get clearer about what kind of business we want and, more importantly, clarify its purpose.

The HRD speaks up very passionately at this point to say that he joined the business because whilst he recognized the challenge that it faced commercially, he felt that it fulfilled an important role in society and that he is concerned that they have a responsibility to exercise some stewardship, to ensure that it continues to serve that purpose.

The group's conversation is now about the desire to *not* be driven by a purely commercial goal but to be clear about the degree to which the chosen strategy both depends on and upholds a legacy that dates back to 1767.

The CEO now leads the group in a discussion to identify *what* it is that they really need to get clear about in this session. There is a shift in the subject of the conversation to now being about what they believe about the organization's purpose, the function it serves in society and how the strategy delivers that. This then leads to some decision-making criteria to apply to investment decisions. The tone of the conversation is also different, with more voices participating, as the subject matter seems to be more personal and less abstract.

By the end of the two days the group report that they have a quality of conversation that those with longer experience say they have not had before, and issues were discussed that do not otherwise get talked about. The CEO is pleased that a greater depth of alignment has been achieved whilst the FD is not really sure whether it has been helpful or not, but is pleased to see that "some people here have had a chance to catch up with the thinking that frankly I feel has already been done and agreed, and to get on to the same bloody page!"

I feel satisfied overall, not least that the client, as represented by the HRD and CEO, believe this to have been a valuable investment.

My intervention in the case described above was based on the belief that my experience and expression of confusion, disappointment and frustration were feelings that I had on behalf of the group as a whole. In other words, the group's *collective* unconscious held an unexpressed set of reactions to what was happening. When I spoke of my experience I was raising something that may have been true for the group as a whole but which lay below the surface of their conscious awareness.

Looking back at this now, I note that I felt especially energized and rewarded by seeing a small intervention, which perhaps reflected my feeling of the need to express *the team's* discomfort at the 'irritable reaching after fact and reason', having an impact upon the group's perspective and orientation to their work.

A useful frame?

Is negative capability a useful way of framing the ability to resist the otherwise unconscious gravitational pull of our social defences against anxiety?

I am experimenting in current practice to see whether introducing the concept of negative capability is a useful way of encouraging a group to resist taking refuge in 'decisive action' and spending longer in 'reflective inaction'. The premise is that it will be more accessible for a board to be actively engaged in practicing this capability consciously, than it is to reflect or report their methods of avoidance back to the group *after* the fact. These two approaches are not mutually exclusive and a combination is most likely to occur in practice.

The notion of developing a useful and perhaps even sophisticated 'capability' may be more attractive or ego-syntonic, especially to people who may identify themselves as business leaders, than the discomfort of feeling apprehended in the practice of a collective deficit.

There is also a degree of opportunity to be found in the zeitgeist of leading in a more VUCA world (Volatile, Uncertain, Complex and Ambiguous). I would argue that a board can be more readily engaged in (a) reflecting on the degree to which they are developing their negative capability, in order to be more 'fit' for the emerging demands of the VUCA world, than it is to engage them in (b) reflecting on how they have been avoiding the existential discomfort and dread of being in the present moment.

Negative capability has the useful benefit of being able to suggest 'an appealing ambition' rather than pathologize a norm of group dynamics, both in the philosophical stance of the practitioner and in the way that they might describe it to their clients.

Reflective inaction – in action

By raising negative capability, or reflective inaction, as a practice to explore with a group, I am proposing that this can be a means to encourage and enable the group to practice developing its awareness of the group dynamics in the here-and-now.

In the following case, a specific group activity, a fishbowl process, was used in an attempt to enable executive board members to move between being participants in a conversation and observers of the process of the conversation.

> The group I am facilitating is the executive board of a financial services business whose activities range from high-street retail banking division to international corporate investment.
>
> The executive board of eight people is meeting to consider the scope of a leadership development initiative. Their motivation to have such a programme

is based on a concern for the rehabilitation of the sector's reputation in light of the financial crash of 2007–2008.

There is a commitment to 'doing something that is not simply cerebral but is also human and heartfelt' that is explicitly stated by the group head of Leadership Development and Organizational Development (OD). As evidence of this commitment, the group is willing to experiment with a different way of exploring the topic in this session. We are going to use a fishbowl method that allows conversation and observation to be taking place simultaneously. The author describes the concept of negative capability to the group and connects it to work on Bohmian Dialogue (Bohm, 1996), of which they have some experience in this organization.

We discuss the value of spending some time today, trying to just live together in the question of 'What leadership is being called for by our organization and our markets?' I also introduce how I think a fishbowl approach might help us.

The method is described to the group: three people volunteer from the eight to sit in an inner-circle of three chairs arranged together into a tight group – this is the fishbowl. The rest stand around the three who are in the centre and have pads of large post-it notes (A5) and marker pens (see Figure 12.1).

There are two specific roles. If you are one of the three people in the fishbowl in the middle then you are there to explore the topic in conversation with your two colleagues. If you are one of the observers around the outside of the fishbowl then you are making observations, one per post-it

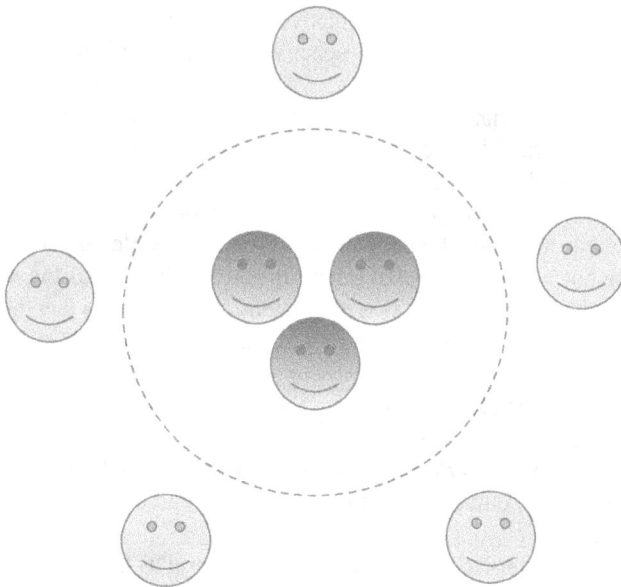

Figure 12.1 The fishbowl

note, on (a) what strikes you about the conversation in the bowl and (b) what you are noticing in yourself as you listen. If you are observing, you do not speak.

The final instruction is that if you are in the fishbowl and you are ready to leave it you can vacate your seat and join the observers outside the fishbowl. Someone else from outside the fishbowl can then occupy the vacant seat and join the conversation. As a result of this coming-and-going from the group in the middle, the composition of the participants in the fishbowl conversation is changing every few minutes.

After 30 minutes, the conversation is to be drawn to a close and all the post-it notes will be put upon a wall together, so that they can all be seen in a single sweep of an eye – a group of this size will typically produce 50 to 100 observations.

The group appears to find the instructions straightforward and after a couple of questions of clarification, the process begins and runs with a reasonable fluidity. It takes a minute or so for the group in the middle to overcome the self-consciousness of the situation. The first few hand-overs of seats in the middle are hesitant and slightly awkward. However, this settles down into more fluency with the process in the first eight to ten minutes. The group members seem to be both amused by, and enjoying, the novelty of the process. They build to a crescendo of coming-and-going from the 'hot-seats' in the middle. And then the time is up and we post our observations onto one wall of the meeting room.

The group is invited to review the observations with 'soft eyes' looking for any patterns, i.e., looking to let the patterns in the data make themselves known to them, not taking a reductive or analytical stance, allowing what strikes them to be significant irrespective of whether it is mentioned once or many times.

One direction that this review takes, as the group stands side-by-side in a huddle, is sparked by the recognition by one member of the group that the comments on the wall tend to be either about what *we* do as leaders or what *they* do as leaders. The conversation that just happened in the fishbowl was at times either judgmental, about another group of people who are leaders and who are not in this room, or at other times were about *us* as the leaders. The individual raising this point was most energized by the idea that the conversation has demonstrated a creation of a 'them' and 'us' in the way we conceive of leadership.

This reflection seems to polarize the group into two factions: those who want to uphold this potential splitting, i.e., the identification of a 'them' who need to develop *their* leadership, and a faction who can see the splitting *itself* as a group dynamic to explore, although they do not use the term 'splitting'.

'Splitting' refers to the perception of the world as having wholly good or wholly bad parts, groups or individuals. It is a consequence of the process by which we fail to accept both the positive and negative aspects of ourselves and project these 'split' parts of ourselves onto the external world resulting in a polarised view.

There is a conversation amongst the second faction exploring 'who are the leaders in the organization', 'has it ever been articulated' and 'to what degree do we uphold an ambiguous definition of who and what it is'? And 'if we do maintain that ambiguity, what are we trying to uphold or avoid by so doing?'

The first faction in contrast are saying that 'the real issue is still about how we get the leaders to simply comply with the behaviours required of them that have already been defined'. They are very confident that this is the most important issue.

As the facilitator of this workshop I am feeling ambivalent about the progress we have made. On the one hand there has been something that feels satisfyingly like a breakthrough for a sub-set of the board. They have been able to suspend their focus on defining a solution long enough to experience themselves at work as a group and reflect upon that experience. They have extracted from that experience an observation of themselves engaged in splitting. Based on their identification of this phenomenon, I am then able to provide them with a label for it, i.e., 'splitting', and describe something of the psychological basis. Given their ownership of the experience and identification of it, they seem genuinely interested in the concept.

On the other hand, another 3 or 4 people in the group have expressions and body-language that suggest to me feelings of being disheartened and sad-dened. They want to know what can be done about getting more uptake of the already existing and documented leadership behaviours.

The workshop is considered a success by the client and they would like to engage in further work with a wider population on this topic; the meaning of leadership for the organization. I am also feeling that the client is satisfied with the *approach* we have taken, and this is demonstrated by their strongly expressed request that further work maintains the spirit of inquiry and explo-ration that they have felt in this workshop.

At the time, at the end of the workshop, I would have described it as only a partial success – as the feelings of disheartenment and sadness I described above come to mind. Now with reflection I would simply say that it *was* a useful process.

In writing this description of the experience, I have become curious about the possibility that in shedding some light upon one form of splitting, it has created its own shadow. Could it be that those in the group that feel sad and who would like there to be a simple 'technical' solution for a 'them', are representing on behalf of the group our (I am including myself in this) *collective* sadness? And that the sadness is for our unacknowledged collective loss of some certainty, confidence and/or status?

As mentioned above, the method we applied appears to have been useful in providing a vehicle for at least a proportion of the group to create and experience a more reflective space. In this more reflective space they were 'able to be in uncertainties, mysteries and doubts without any irritable reaching after fact or reason'.

And perhaps for some to be in 'uncertainties, mysteries and doubts' *required* others to become more polarized in 'irritable reaching after fact or reason' – a necessary manifestation of our yin and yang.

13 The importance of not being earnest

The role of humour in the boardroom

Paula Wilson

Humour

Firstly, it might be useful to understand what is actually meant by humour. Beard M. (2014) describes how ancient theorists, such as Plato ('even the gods love jokes') and Aristotle described humour as an often 'cruel expression of superiority and derision', often mocking those less fortunate.

Carey and Freud (2014) introduces us to the topic of humour, and how jokes are related to unconscious mechanisms of the human mind. In Freud's (1982) view, jokes are the verbal and interpersonal expressions of humour, and that 'when the conscious allows the expression of thoughts that society usually suppresses or forbids, the superego allows the ego to generate humour', resulting in a light and comforting humour, while a harsh superego creates a biting and sarcastic type. A very harsh superego suppresses humour altogether. Freud (1921) cites two examples of varying styles of humour structure, including modification and word fusion, each with a different intention and delivery method.

Modern theorists refer more often to a 'theory of incongruity' with humour and laughter stemming from the inappropriate mixing of categories or registers of meaning. In *The Humour Code: A Global Search for What Makes Things Funny* a marketing and psychology professor and a journalist tested their theory that humour rests on 'benign violation i.e. laughter is provoked when it is "wrong, unsettling, or threatening" but also seems "okay, acceptable, or safe". This can include 'light teasing' or laughing at 'mix-ups'.

Executive coach Professor David Clutterbuck describes a 'five levels of laughter' model, ranging from "a polite smile, through to an engaged grin, up to full-on side-splitting hysterics". He asserts that, "incongruity is at the heart of humour", and explains how stories about incongruous situations are amusing not only because they are often ridiculous, but also because they remind us of something similar that has, or could have happened to us.

Humour can be illuminating and enlightening; it can raise awareness rather than be used as an attempt to fix and it can catalyze a learning process by building understanding and enabling insight. A good laugh can encourage creativity, engagement and collaboration. Through the vehicle of self-deprecation, we can often hear the voice of our colleagues more clearly – not just what they are saying, but also what they are not saying. Whether our role is that of chair or board member, or we are acting as consultants to the board we may also, where appropriate, use self-deprecation to share our own weaknesses to assure the client that fallibility affects us all. In a recent board meeting, I gently asked the CEO to playback a statement he had just made in relation to a request for the introduction of a performance management system – ('I'm far too busy running a business to worry about managing performance!'). He suddenly realized the ludicrousness of his own words and had a laugh at himself! He then saw the situation from a different perspective and viewed his company performance issues in a very new light. His board colleagues also respected his rare glimpse of vulnerability, humility and self-deprecation and saw him as being more human.

Humour enables understanding and creativity and creates a space where stories and metaphors can create a new reality. It values the 'here and now' and can create a stance of interested inquiry, allowing curiosity and play, untying knots and enabling new meanings. There is also simplicity around humour, which can engender straightforward 'clean' dialogue. It can also provide a tool to help us name and explore 'what's in the room', tell us something about what is going on unconsciously in the group, and enable the group to move on into the exploration of new territory and new discovery, rather than being 'stuck' in a place that is neither useful nor generative.

Humour can highlight invalid assumptions held about both self and the corporate context; or it can be employed in an attempt to disguise or discount a deeply held view. I recall the MD who gave a nervous laugh as he declared 'It's not like anyone actually does what I ask around here!' opening a door to allow genuine discovery around his confidence as a leader. Boardroom laughter can also signpost potential collusion and can be used as a divisive tool to engender allies or to encourage splitting or exclusion. An effective chair must be vigilant to these dynamics at play and intervene accordingly.

Humour can be provocative and evocative and laughter is often accompanied by a heightened emotional association with the story. One leader, wanting to rehearse with her executive coach for a forthcoming board meeting which she was approaching with dread and anxiety, launched spontaneously into a hilarious monologue of all the things she believed she 'shouldn't' say during the session. Subsequently, she described how she then entered the real-life board meeting scenario with greater confidence, as her associations with the issue were now of enjoyment and lightness, rather than those of fear and apprehension. Another board member who had, in their head, built an 'obstructive colleague' into a 'vicious and scary monster', took immense pleasure and joy through an executive coaching session in playfully downsizing the image into one of an innocuous rag doll, enabling them to no longer view the relationship nervously and to have real conversations from a more resourced state.

We lead best by showing our humanness. One chairperson perceived as ruthless in a rigorous 360 degree feedback review, had been trying to exercise greater emotional intelligence, sensitivity, compassion and empathy within his organization, and often hilariously described his patchy efforts in this area to his board. That approach, allowed him to talk about 'that soft stuff' safely, whilst he tried to develop further in this area.

Interestingly, there is some evidence suggesting significant differences between the use of humour by men and women in the boardroom and how humorous comments and jokes are received. Linguistics expert Dr Judith Baxter's research discovered that 'the majority of male humour (80%) in business meetings takes the form of flippant, off-the-cuff witticisms or 'banter' with about 90% of it receiving an instant, positive response, usually in the form of laughter'. However most female humour during the course of a meeting was 'self deprecatory in nature and more often than not received in silence'. Has the 'male gaze' extended into the male laugh?

Humour diffuses tension and builds rapport. Often leaders, particularly those new to the board, describe scenarios where they are a little anxious to use humour or to try out 'lighter' approaches or following their intuition and 'being real' for fear of appearing foolish. They describe how they worry that using humour might make them look 'lightweight' or irrelevant to the corporate challenges. However, once laughter enters the boardroom rapport actually heightens and anxiety and tensions subside. One study conducted by the University of Ottawa corroborates this belief, suggesting that 'humour provides a key mechanism for enacting a sense of community for group members'. Specifically, the study examined the process through which putdown humour helps foster group identity and cohesion in a temporary group. Putdowns followed a pattern of development that signaled increasing trust and inclusion, and was regulated by implicit rules that incubated the emergent solidarity. The meaning of certain humorous episodes was equivocal, but the act of laughing together glossed over the equivocality so that the sense of community was reaffirmed. The authors concluded that "shared 'putdown' humour and the implicit set of rules regarding its use may facilitate solidarity".

Laughter is incredibly cathartic – it is relational, binding people together, making connections and is a great social leveller. It makes us feel good and it can be remarkably therapeutic. Laughter in the workplace releases tension and is proven to reduce symptoms of stress and anxiety. It provides a mechanism for group anxieties to decompress and leave the boardroom 'lighter' and liberated and resulting in a more cohesive, team-minded, high-performing board.

Of course, this is not about being facetious or hurtful or alienating and excluding others. This is not about taking the stage, being entertaining to be liked, or saying or doing anything which would contravene professional values and code of ethics or governance. Running an organization is a serious business and the utmost sensitivity and respect for the issues raised for the board is critical.

It is about respectfully and empathetically using humour, where appropriate, and always in service of the individual, the board and the organization. Humour must be used skilfully, carefully and ethically and it must be relevant to the context and commensurate to the level of trust, rapport and empathy within the group.

Some suggested guidelines for board members on the use of humour in the board-room include:

1 Be yourself: Your humour will only pay off if it is congruent with who you are and how you are as a board member. Exercise your own unique brand of humour and be authentic.
2 Be realistic: You are unlikely to be the world's no 1 comedian and do not need to try to be one. This is not about having colleagues rolling in the aisles. However, to cite Clutterbuck (2010), you do hope to get 'beyond the intellectual approach of a polite smile'.
3 Be humble: Self-deprecation demonstrates your own humanity and openness and will encourage others to do likewise.
4 Be ethical: Clearly political, sexist, racist, religious, world disaster centric humour is out.
5 Be a role model: Demonstrating that despite the seniority and weightiness of the board role, you can bring lightness and creative energy through humour will set the tone for the rest of the board and the organization.
6 Be generic: Do not single out individuals as the focus of your jokes – unless it is yourself.
7 Be light: Contrary to frequently held opinion, we can be professional and light where appropriate in tandem. They are not mutually exclusive.
8 Be relevant: Contextually real humour, about real organizational issues, assists with bonding around shared experiences.
9 Be aware: Read the room and notice the impact of your efforts. If there is any disconnect between your intention and impact, stop! Likewise, notice when the mood needs easing.
10 Build trust: Humour will be best received and will flourish within an environment of trust. Engender trust through other strategies such as board building activities, strategy days with space for real conversations and creative activities. Thus, within an environment of trust, humour will find its place.

Humour is an under-used boardroom resource and we tend to forget its immense power to build understanding and insight within corporate relationships and the amazing conversations which it can initiate and enable. It exists, in all of us, awaiting use, amidst the myriad of boardroom tools we utilize by default, and it sits comfortably with professionalism, perception, presence, challenge and empathy.

Go on, have a laugh!

14 Narcissism and boards

George Fischer-Varvitsiotis

The myth of Narcissus

Freud (1914) introduced the term narcissism in reference to the myth of Narcissus, who became the victim of his self-love: when he bent down into a river to kiss his reflection, he fell into the water and drowned. Freud used the term primary narcissism to denote the pre-occupation of the infant with its own body imbued with libido, a state prior to the infant's ability to relate to other objects with libido: 'An original cathexis of the ego, from which some is later given-off to objects, but which fundamentally persists and is related to the object-cathexis much as the body of the amoeba is related to the pseudopodia which it puts out' (Freud, 1914, p. 75). Freud distinguished this primary state from secondary narcissism, in which libidinal impulses are withdrawn from the objects back to the ego, thus making the ego become its own love-object: 'The libido that has been withdrawn from the external world has been directed to the ego and thus gives rise to an attitude which may be called narcissism' (Freud, 1914, p. 75).

The structural concepts of ego-psychology suggests that narcissism is a regulatory function of the feeling states of the ego. They suggest 'an approach to narcissism and its disorders from the viewpoint of deviations from the ideal state of wellbeing' (Joffe & Sandler, 1967, p. 63). Kernberg (2001) influenced by the Kleinian school, differentiates pathological from normal narcissism and distinguishes three domains of pathological narcissistic manifestation – pathological self-love (grandiosity, superiority, omnipotence), pathological object-love (envy, devaluation of others, exploitative behaviour, lack of empathy, inability to depend on others) and a pathological superego (inability to express depression, dramatic mood oscillations, shame). Kernberg (2001) identifies pathological narcissism as unintegrated early rage, which causes the splitting and projection of a devalued self and object representations onto others.

Self-psychology defines self-disorders based on the level of self-cohesion vs self-fragmentation: states, in which the self is temporarily and reversibly fragmented, vs. states involving the person's entire self-experience:

> The patterns of ambitions, skills and goals; the tensions between them; the programme of action that they create; and the activities that strive towards the

realization of this programme are all experienced as continuous in space and time – they are the self, an independent centre of initiative, an independent recipient of impressions.

(Kohut & Wolf, 1978, p. 414)

Early in childhood, 'objects' supply the infant with mirroring, empathy and idealization, serving as self-objects and thus supplying cohesion to the early self. Kohut proposed five ways in which the individual aims to accomplish a cohesive self: (i) the mirror-hungry, seeking admiration from others; (ii) the ideal-hungry, seeking others to idealize; (iii) the alter-ego, seeking relationships with others as self-objects; (iv) the merger-hungry, seeking symbiotic relationships to maintain structure and (v) the contact-shunning, avoiding relationships in order to maintain a cohesive self.

Early experiences, composed of feelings, patterns of thoughts, social adjustments and behaviours consistently exhibited over time, strongly influence one's character shapes, self-perceptions, values and attitudes, as well as one's orientation towards the environment. For a successful development, supported by attention, appreciation and basic ideals, a personality with a healthy self-love, self-respect, but also with attention and respect to others, is established. These properties characterize a healthy narcissism; they form a 'field of gravity' that holds the self together. Drive, creative experimentation, the courage to make decisions and charisma are just some of the positive merits of narcissistic personality traits. Winnicott (1960, pp. 140–152) suggested that being seen in the eyes of others is a crucial aspect for the development of self-recognition and self-identification.

The opposite – inattention, insults and continued rejection – may result in a narcissistic mal-development. A narcissistically disturbed person experiences the fragmentation of his personality. Feelings of emptiness, loneliness and depressed mood, force such a person to take countermeasures. To compensate for the broken self, a shield of feelings and fantasies of grandeur, power and uniqueness is built. Not infrequently, this escalates into a grotesque need for admiration, criticism, intolerance and arrogance. Well-known are the talented personalities, whose brilliant public appearances belie inner self-doubt, emptiness, loneliness or discontinuity, while some unfortunately only find their escape via drugs or suicide in extreme cases.

Thus, clinically we differentiate narcissistic grandiosity from narcissistic vulnerability. The shape of narcissistic personality attributes ranges from functional normality to psychosis. The Diagnostic and Statistical Manual of Mental Disorders, commonly referred to as DSM-IV, classifies several traits of personality, which help to differentiate between personality trait and Narcissistic Personality Disorder (NPD). The latter is assumed if an agglomeration of five or more indicators are present:

1   Has a grandiose sense of self-importance;
2   Is preoccupied with fantasies of unlimited success, power, brilliance, beauty, or ideal love;
3   Believes that he or she is 'special' and unique;
4   Requires excessive admiration;

5   Has a sense of entitlement;
6   Is interpersonally exploitative;
7   Lacks empathy;
8   Is often envious of others or believes others are envious of him or her;
9   Shows arrogant, haughty behaviours or attitudes.

A central narcissistic character feature is the need for admiration. To accomplish great goals, narcissists have more courage than most to break new ground. Therefore, they contribute a high-level of creativity and are willing to take considerable risks. They show a special talent in empathizing with the expectations of their environment and meeting them with charm. They come with a well-groomed appearance and eloquence with a readiness of speech at a moment's notice. With this charisma, they are able to win and convince others of their projects. In the context of a rounded personality, good results may occur when people have a combination of strong narcissistic traits and developed skills and talent. A climate of substantial performance and success arises beyond the charismatic aura, may create an environment in which all participants can thrive.

However, the exaggeration of narcissistic attributes entails risks: by focusing on triumph, greatness and uniqueness, narcissists lose judgment on limits and realities. They overestimate themselves and indulge in haughty plans with more and more new ideas and dazzling projects, but without sustainable success. Since they are extremely vulnerable, they do not tolerate objections and opposition and often tend to pass responsibility to others. Since revising one's own behaviour is very difficult, the commitment to the course of action remains rigid; visible failures and timely counter-corrections are neglected. A paranoid thought system, in which others are seen as traitors or even enemies to the big idea, is often encountered.

Much has been written about the behaviour of narcissists, but there is not much discussion about how the people around them cope. To outsiders, the narcissist is rather a fascinating phenomenon. With their demand for adoration, they offer their followers a focal point for the followers' need to admire (think of celebrities and charismatic leadership personalities). However, the narcissist's feelings towards their entourage are ambivalent, because although they enjoy the adoration, they remain dependent on it and are ultimately at their mercy. If admiration is refused, he reacts with anger, hostility and demotion. In this spiral of admiration and dependence, any criticism is perceived by the narcissist as an insult and answered with a scarcely tolerable anger, vindictiveness and devaluation. The elimination of critics follows and thus a narcissistic monoculture of an entire leadership can be created. In such an isolated system, loss of reality is not far off. Once pursued, this path could lead the narcissists and their environments to complex disasters, as some examples from politics and business, leadership and executive boards demonstrate. A narcissist must dominate his surroundings. While he is very sensitive in his reaction to criticism, he is extremely harsh with his criticism and devaluation of others. And because his plans are always large, he accepts damage to people and businesses as collateral damage through the course of implementation.

The narcissist cannot tolerate even small differences of opinion, perceiving friendly feedback and advice as arrogance and over-bearance. Equal relationships, like partners, who can provide him with constructive criticism, are exceptional, as each bond carries a risk of emotional dependence and would thus be a gap in the character's armour that guarantees his autonomy. As a mentor, he is hardly suitable. He wants to influence others and not to contribute to their own development. On his side, he is a difficult target for mentoring as he rather seeks confirmation, not criticism. This explains why narcissists are not only resistant to advice, but do not even seek counselling and advice. Good outcomes may develop when a competent mentor, advisor or board member manages to establish an empathic, authentic and appreciative dialogue of equals.

When dealing with narcissistic personality attributes, we have to keep in mind beneficial and detrimental narcissistic characteristics and options that facilitate cooperation with and support of talented narcissistic personalities.

Two brief case studies[1] are described here.

William

William, CEO of his company, is a highly valued person because of his professional excellence, his strategic thinking, and his effectiveness and efficiency. He is charming, eloquent, and appealing. On the other hand, William can be arrogant, intimidating and devaluing of others. He demonstrates extremely high self-confidence, insists on his own opinion and neglects the perspectives of others. At times, he is sarcastic and insulting, not hesitating to offend others, overtly and publicly. William subdivides his environment into two groups: friends and foes. His friends enjoy his support, friendliness and advocacy, his enemies savour disgrace, obstruction and even unabashed harassment. His classification into friends and foes seems to be arbitrary and erratic. Some of his friends find themselves overnight on his enemy list.

I encountered William as the chair of a supervising board that entrusted me with consultation to the members of the executive board. The acute reason for this project was the impending failure of a crucial project, which threatened to split the board. At the beginning of this consultation, I conducted several interviews with the supervisory and executive board members and with direct reports to the board. One of the prevalent pieces of information I received was that many people were afraid of William and his 'famous fits of rage'. Many of them stated that they would avoid making "difficult statements". This was the jargon in William's environment for criticism, objection or pinpointing an impending risk. Instead, people would rather give positive feedback in order to 'live in safety'.

The consultation consisted mostly of group conversations. I conducted individual conversations with board members for personal issues that were too sensitive for group discussion. With William, I had several conversations. After he had made sure that I was impartial, that I treated him with respect and handled all personal information with the utmost confidentiality, we developed a trusting working basis. In spite of his heroic appearance, William was suffering from a severe fear of failure. He compensated for this fear through effort, tenacity and control and masked it by an impenetrable armour of grandeur. By splitting internally between 'William, the Great' and 'Deadbeat William', he could project the latter onto his environment, thus creating a mass of losers around him whom he could devalue and dominate and keep greatness for himself. In terms of group dynamics, 'William, the Great' was the condensation point of his board environment for heroism, invulnerability and greatness; William, the narcissist, was not 'The Problem', but a reflection of his organization's unconscious life in as much as William's fear of failure, mirrored his entire board's (and by extension his organization's) accumulated fear of failure.

During the course of the collaboration, which lasted two years, William managed to mitigate his fear and ameliorate his stance in the executive board, and the supervisory board, and as an organizational leader by tentatively seeking connection to colleagues and his direct reports, empowering his people, and creating an atmosphere of psychological safety around – and including – himself. Slowly, he experienced that this method was not only more effective with regard to his relationships and his leadership effectiveness, but it was also a relief with regard to his own fears and stress.

Paul

Paul, the new CEO of a company, said he wanted to develop his entire leadership team (six executive board members and their thirty direct reports). Paul presented with predominant narcissistic attributes. He stated that 'his board members were surprisingly successful, but actually incompetent' and that the entire 'leadership band, inherited by an old-school predecessor' (who had been his former boss, mentor and sponsor) had to "change radically or be thrown out". Paul said he wanted to change the culture of his company radically, from its hierarchical and paternalistic mind-set and towards a "collaborative culture of respect and openness".

My consultation proposal started with board conversations, individual conversations with board and leadership team members, then more group conversations with the leadership in a full group and in small groups. At the beginning of my presentation, Paul interrupts me brusquely. Two things seem 'weird' to him: Firstly, he said, he would sponsor the project. He would be willing to visit the group sessions for their latter part and let the participants report about the sessions. But he would definitely not be part of the project. Secondly, conversations with the entire board would be, "unnecessary and, for the time being, impossible, as the board members don´t communicate well". His idea was, "to concentrate on the leadership team and rally them behind my leadership concept". I respectfully proposed that my analysis of his findings were the strongest indication for involving the whole board. I said that the results he was aiming for would be best achieved by involving all members of the board and the leadership team. He answered with a sarcastic smile and gesture with the remark: "Just forget it. My way or no way. I imagine that you have your reasons for suggesting another method, but I don't want to hear them". Despite his narcissistic attitude, Paul had certain amicable facets. Without being intimidated, and regardless of his rejection, I explained my interpretation of the board situation and my conception of individual and group consultation. Paul and I decided not to work together; we separated not only politely, but in a friendly manner and with mutual respect.

Eleven months later, Paul invited me for a new conversation in which he asked me to support him personally as his coach and "perhaps also with ideas about board conversations". We explored the outline of a possible collaboration.

We can summarize that:

1   Narcissistic personality traits can be beneficial when it comes to entrepreneurial thinking and charismatic leadership.
2   If these characteristics occur excessively, they pose a risk of mistakes.
3   Not only are the characteristics of narcissistic leadership personalities important, but the systems in which they move need to be understood. Criticism-free affirmation on the part of the system may lead to uncontrolled and uncontrollable developments later on.
4   An intolerance of criticism is characteristic for narcissistic personalities.
5   Narcissistic character traits can affect the internal and external work of the board.

Those working alongside narcissists should aim to support their strengths without letting criticism-free zones arise. This requires a high level of expertise among colleagues in the board or from an external personal adviser. Colleagues and mentors need the integrity and courage to intervene at the very first indication of undesirable developments. Essential prerequisites for the success of an intervention are – more so with narcissists than other character structures – a principally tactful and appreciative handling that avoids any offense. Further, the intervention demands clear and firm positioning of boundaries so that the charismatic grandeur of narcissistic presentation cannot be allowed to corrupt mentoring or coaching.

Note

1 For confidentiality reasons, the names of people have been changed.

15 Competition, corruption and collusion

The quest for power

Tammy Noel

Background

The author worked with a board and helped it deliver and implement a much-needed new direction, keeping to a challenging pace. It was the most draining piece of work she had ever done and she explains this in the context of her former career as a teacher at a tough secondary school. Having noticed early on that the board did not work well, she realized that neither did she work well with the board. Noel asserts that the board was crippled by deadlines that it had set for itself and some of the processes that were implemented seemed to ignore the impact on staff. Noel left the board at the end of her 12 months, feeling wrung out, with her health negatively impacted. The board too was in a state of disarray with one member on long-term sick leave, another opting to take a career break and a third securing a new role in a different organization. Meanwhile, the director, the head of the board, felt the board had done some of its best work!

Noel describes her sense of disbelief about how this work was delivered, what it needed to deliver and the discrepancy between how she and the board director viewed the outcome. Noel ended up feeling exhausted whilst the board director thought the board had done very well. In hindsight, Noel saw that the board's dynamic as a whole was unhealthy as they struggled to break away from unhelpful patterns of behaviour. She hypothesized that the board members, including herself, were locked into a pattern of competition, corruption and collusion, driven by a desire to stay close to the director, who held the power. She defines this pattern as a holy trinity of unhelpful unconscious behaviours that the board members were unable to control or change.

Organizational context

The organization was five years old, with approximately 60 staff, all based in the same location. Its purpose was to design and source generic learning and development interventions for client organizations. It looked to reduce overall spend and create economies of scale. Feedback from clients showed some clear weaknesses in the organization's delivery model and capability to meet customers' needs. The board was relatively new, the director had been in post for six months, and had recruited six deputies who headed up teams. The director was clear that the board was meant to swiftly improve the reputation and performance of the organization. Members of the board had never worked in a learning and development environment before, but all had achieved high levels of success in previous organizations and were recruited because of their successful delivery histories.

The board consisted of a director and six board members in the roles of operations – IT, commercial, finance; generic curriculum development; leadership development curriculum; operations development curriculum; transformation – project management, communications and redesign. Noel was commissioned to support the board in re-designing the structure of the organization and supporting the implementation. The board was clear about its objective in all aspects of the organization's operations – to change and to do so as quickly as possible. There was a script operating within the board that the faster the pace of the restructuring, the more humane the process would be. This was vocalized in the board, but privately, board members said that they did not believe the rhetoric. The director had become a container for the feelings of board members around difficulties with working there and implementing a tough restructuring process and the effects this would have on staff. Words such as 'bullying' and 'ruthless' were heard to describe the director. Her own experience confirmed this. In addition, she noted that her own developing sense of personal ambition was mirrored in the members' seeking favour with the director. This helped to explain the boardroom dynamic of competition, corruption and collusion.

This case study is based on the author's observations and conversations with board members and staff in the organization, including the director, during her time as a member of the board and the three-month period after she had left the board.

How do competition, corruption and collusion show up?

When discussing competition, corruption and collusion in a board, the recent high profile case of BHS's board comes to mind.

> According to a parliamentary report into the failure of BHS, Green and (Dominic) Chappell had systematically plundered the retailer before it shut. Green controlled BHS for 15 years until he sold it to Chappell's company, Retail Acquisitions, for £1 in March 2015. During this period, the tycoon, his family and other shareholders collected more than £580m in dividends, rent and interest payments on debt. Retail Acquisitions, meanwhile, was paid at least £17m – despite having owned the chain for only 13 months before its demise.
>
> (Butler & Ruddick, 2016, p. 1).

Behind these decisions at BHS, a board, we presume, must have allowed such actions to take place, knowingly or unknowingly, over a period of time. This example raises questions about how easy it is to move away from the primary task of the board to oversee good governance.

Competition, corruption and collusion do not always lead to extreme shifts from the primary task to questionable business practices. All three are natural human behaviours and are present in every board in some form. Noel asserts that in successful boards, the extent to which these behaviours differ from the primary task is less amplified.

A strong connection existed between competition, corruption and collusion in the board (see Figure 15.1) in order to stay close to the director, which kept the informal board hierarchy intact. The director was a source of power; able to 'make or break' individuals and therefore worthy of impressing. The director, as the source of power, interacted with others in ways that drove more collusive and corrupt behaviours, mostly through creating competition.

Power is the ability to assert control over others. Power is defined as:

> Externally, power comes from what the individual controls – such as money, privileges, job references, promotion and the like – and from sanctions one can impose on others. Internally, power comes from individuals' knowledge and experience, strength of personality and their state of mind regarding the role: how powerful they feel and how they therefore present themselves to others.
>
> (Obholzer, 1994b, p. 42).

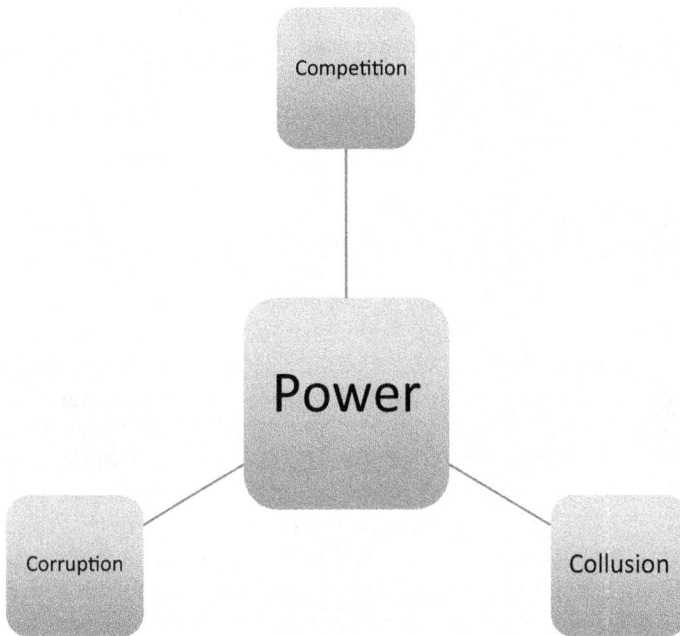

Figure 15.1 Power

The chief executive is frequently the source of power; they are given a formal position of power through the organizational structure and therefore become figures that people want to connect with, approve their decisions and ensure their part of the organization survives. Power is a mutual exchange – just as the CEO takes power, they are also given it by the rest of the board.

Competition is a dynamic that strives to gain something by defeating others or establishing superiority over them. Corruption is an activity that distorts from the primary task and results in a breakdown of ethical behaviour. Collusion serves a different purpose from the primary task. Competition, corruption and collusion are three elements that are undertaken to gain power or to get close to the source of power. The driver may not be personal gain, it may be about fear, loss or survival.

The board members were gripped by a desire to please the director and in so doing, handed power to the director and consequently, board members were content to collude with each other in order to avoid conflict. Noel both observed this behaviour and found herself falling into this pattern too. On the surface, it would have appeared to be a fairly normal board. However, Noel experienced feelings of stuckness and powerlessness, which she noted were related to the board members' subservience to the director, handing the director the sole responsibility for decision-making. The members in turn would not allow tasks to be completed without the director's input. Relationships in the board had greater or lesser strength with the director than with others, and on the whole, these preferred relationships were disliked by most of the members. The differences in these relationships stoked competition and increased the amount of collusion amongst the board members. Thus, the board's desire turned to pleasing the director and soon enough this became the board's unconscious primary task.

Three examples of where competition, corruption and collusion were unconsciously present are provided below:

Collusion

In one instance, following a recent employment selection process, the board were discussing how best to provide feedback to successful candidates. It was proposed that feedback should be provided over the phone, along with the message that their scores were adequate, but there was clear room for improvement. Most board members said they felt this was the right thing to do, but one member and Noel both said they were doubtful, expressing concern about the impact this type of messaging could have on the individuals and their future engagement. Both then said, that despite this, they agreed with the group consensus. Later, Noel spoke again to the doubtful member and they both wished they had stood their ground, but at the time they admitted that it felt like the right decision. Thus, they unconsciously were colluding with the rest of the group.

Competition

The director recruited people he felt could make a difference to a failing organization. Noel was appointed on this basis too. Each new board member in turn was told that they were to be elevated because of their skills and experience in leading to organizational success. Then within a few months, after failing to deliver, they were struck down, often publicly, by the director. This vignette suggests that as a group, Noel and the board members were exhibiting basic assumption pairing, a term coined by Bion (1961), in which people are held up as the saviours of the department and then blamed and rejected when they are unable to rescue. Board members said they had agreed to take on pieces of work for which they were not experienced, or would do work 'secretly', for example, a board member was made responsible for producing a new operating model for the organization. Noel was not involved in this, despite it being a piece of work that formed part of her role. The person who asked the board member to produce the operating model was a friend of Noel's, yet she excluded Noel from the process in order to be able to take sole credit for the job so as to impress the director.

Corruption

There was a shared view that a group of employees were not able to perform to the standard required in the new organization. Board members undertook a downsizing restructuring, making the under-performing group of employees apply for their own jobs. The recruitment panel set the standard excessively high so that only 15% of applicants succeeded. When these board members were challenged, they said they were simply carrying out the selection process according to regulations. However, many of those rejected were able to demonstrate that they had applied for jobs with the same skills and had passed other similar recruitment processes. The board was effectively corrupted because it had applied a process to conceal their motives in making staff redundant. On the other hand, staff actually knew what the board was up to.

As a board, there was a collective denial that there was anything wrong with the group, beyond their director being unreasonable. This group's actions seemed designed to please the director and implement the director's wishes at all costs because it served as a diversion from the board members' primary task of changing operations in the shortest possible time. The proposition is that the board members knew that the agreed objective was an unachievable primary task and they therefore tried to avoid the pain and shame associated with failing.

How should a board operate?

The elusive question of how to improve the performance of a board is a common one. Understanding what commonalities exist in successful boards is a good start. Sonnenfeld (2002, p. 106) sets out five key factors that are linked to the success of boards:

1   Create a climate of trust and candour
2   Foster a culture of open dissent
3   Ensure individual accountability
4   Utilise a fluid portfolio of roles
5   Evaluate the board's performance

This board did not display any of the attributes highlighted by Sonnenfeld. Individually, the board struggled to speak up against the voice of the group and provide a voice of dissent. People that spoke up often had their opinions ignored or were agreed with in the board meeting, but then outside of the meeting the director would take the action that went against the collective decision. As time went on, board members were speaking out less and less and where staff did raise concerns, they were often placed out of favour and excluded from future decision-making. Thus, Sonnenfeld's (2002, p. 106) recommendation that, "if you're a CEO, don't punish mavericks and dissenters, even if they're sometimes pains in the neck. Dissent is not the same thing as disloyalty" is particularly persuasive in this context.

This board tells us that achieving Sonnenfeld's key factors is not easy, but the more a board can foster these key attributes, the stronger it will be. Allowing people to be mavericks and dissenters takes trust, an ability to relinquish control and allow others to claim it. Noel at first aligned herself with the director as did everyone else, but she soon realized that responsibility had to be taken up by the board as a whole.

By allowing a different voice into the conversation, a board opens itself up to challenge and opportunity of exploring the task differently. This board had a holding pattern of working in Bion's basic assumption dependency. Although all board members said they disliked being treated like a child by the director, they ultimately kept returning to this pattern. The board members would not oppose the group or the director, which effectively made the board as a whole less effective.

Sonnenfeld (2002) suggests boards should ensure they create the right balance between process and behaviours to drive performance and success through having external challenge, where voice is given to the conscious and unconscious dynamics in the board, recognizing how difficult it is to receive and to hear critical challenge. However, whilst without critical challenge a board has a limited sense of their performance and impact; board members could easily collude with each other and convince themselves that they are performing as expected, which makes board evaluation even more critical. Self-evaluation can be problematic because boards tend to be "more lenient, less variable, more biased and show less agreement with the judgement of others" (Carcio, 2004, p. 100).

How should a practitioner work with competition, corruption and collusion?

Noel reflects on her time working with the board and wonders why she could not see what was happening. She recounts that she was present and was aware that something was not right, but simply did not have the knowledge of the unconscious life of the board to give it voice. Her keenness to ensure that she did a good job and her awareness that others had been rejected by the director resulted in a relationship of collusion with the director when she should have provided candid feedback. Board members too were unable to name the dynamics operating in the board or to work out a way of changing it. For some, the only option was to leave the board and retreat to a more familiar environment.

As the practitioner consultant, there is a need to build deep trust and candour in relationships quickly and that candour must also include speaking truth to those in positions of power. When operating in an organization, it is important to ensure that a strong anchor exists outside of the system where one can gain perspective and keep a professional distance. This will not only benefit the consultant, but also the client, as the consultant often is different, insightful and is meant to provide meaningful challenge.

There are four key areas of focus that will lead to a more balanced relationship with a client:

1   *Be present and name what you see early on in the process*

Being in the room, focusing on the process of the group is critical. However, as a consultant one must voice what they see. Psychodynamic theories about the unconscious processes at play provide a vocabulary to begin naming what is observed. It is important to get the balance right between building rapport and naming what one is seeing fairly early in the work one undertakes. By naming what is happening, rapport will be built and credibility would be demonstrated, therefore making future interventions easier.

2   *Anchor yourself outside of your client system*

Whilst undertaking work on this board, Noel was isolated. She did not have a strong connection to her professional group, who could help anchor her outside of the system she was working in. It was easy for her to lose her sense of impartiality whilst being so immersed in the client system, and thus she was able to hide the shame she felt of not being able to fully support the board. By connecting to other organizational practitioners, formally through a process such as supervision or informally through conversation with peers, the practitioner can gain insight from colleagues in order to receive an alternative view, provide reciprocal support and calibrate against other boards and systems.

3   *Build process consultation into the work you do with clients*

Noel had contracted to give the board feedback, but did not contract to undertake regular process consultation with it. This feature made it difficult for Noel to move into the 'feedback' role. This is an important point because when we learn, we often are subject to accompanying shame, and this is often a difficult emotion to deal with. However, it is vital that boards understand the importance of paying attention to behaviours. Helping board members to see the value in process consultation is vital to the health of a board. At the point of contracting, it is important to highlight the added value that process consultation offers.

4   *Work in partnership with your client*

It is an easy trap to fall into as a consultant to take responsibility for fixing the client's problems and to have a fully worked answer. It is often what the client wants and what they say they are paying for, but does it really create the best work? Interventions have the greatest longevity when they have been created by and are owned within the system. A shift is required to move to a relationship where neither the organisational practitioner nor client knows the answer but work in partnership. This relationship may help to create a different power dynamic and also build in a greater degree of ownership and agency.

Conclusion

Board interactions and behaviours are as important to its success as its ability to deliver its objectives. The primary task of a group can be seriously impacted by issues in the group dynamic, which can manifest itself in Bion's basic assumption behaviour as competition, corruption or collusion.

Focusing on the dynamics that operate below the surface is critical to the health of a board. However, giving voice to this can be uncomfortable and challenging for board members and consultants alike. The process can produce feelings of shame and vulnerability especially where learning is concerned. The role the organizational practitioner plays in supporting this process is paramount to the board's success. They need to build a trusting relationship and help them see the value of giving voice to unconscious dynamics. The practitioner's ability to stay independent of the client system and connected to their profession will ultimately help them provide a more objective view of the board.

To conclude, the board gave its director power and their behaviour ensured that board members did not challenge the director's position. Board members colluded with each other by remaining in denial that the board's problems were due to their own behaviour. The author's role as the board's organizational development practitioner was severely compromised by working in the client system and by being in the management hierarchy. This context made it hard for the author to be objective, to challenge without consequence and to separate herself from this unhealthy dynamic.

This chapter describes how competition, corruption and collusion present themselves in a group and how they are used to reinforce the power dynamic. Competition, corruption and collusion are worthwhile areas for further exploration in the service of improving board dynamics.

16 Board effectiveness

Learning to and from experience

Toya Lorch

On-task and off-task groups

Board members have a limited drive to overcome the challenges of working in groups for several reasons, including their level of seniority, diverse leadership styles, incompatible interests, and time-constraints. Arrogance (*'I know'*), insecurity (*'I should know'*), narcissism (*'I need to run the show'*), and fear of leaving their comfort zone (*'Why should I take risks'?*) are some of the thoughts and feelings impairing their ability to work effectively as a group. Conceptually, every group has two opposing and competing tendencies: one that contributes towards the accomplishment of what the group is supposed to do (stay on-task) and another that detracts the group from accomplishing what it is supposed to do (get off-task). These modes are referred to as *work group mentality* and *basic assumption mentality*, respectively (Bion, 1961).

To be effective, members must develop the emotional competencies required to operate as a *work group* for most of the time. As this is almost impossible, the group must also become aware of the moment when members are operating under the *basic assumption mentality* mode if the goal is to revert the group's dynamics whenever necessary. To illustrate this process, the following elements are discussed in this chapter:

1   A description of how unconscious dynamics influence effectiveness based on the concepts of the *basic assumption mentality* (Bion, 1961) and the *scheme of affective links, namely knowledge, love, and hate* (Bion, 1965);
2   An emphasis on the importance of *learning from experience* (Bion, 1961), which is the capacity to metabolise unpleasant, unprocessed affective experiences in order to restore collective performance and effectiveness;
3   Introduction to the concept of *learning to experience*, which represents the commitment to restore and/or increase the capacity of tolerating the anxiety that arises from not knowing at the cognitive (what one is thinking about – related to a business issue) and the emotional (how one is feeling about – related to a person and situation) levels; learning to experience is a pre-condition to learning from experience.

Most board members have reached a certain stage in their careers where they live in an environment that is not conducive to self-development. Therefore, the challenge consists of knowing how to *breakout from this developmental inertia* and *ignite the drive* needed to develop the emotional competencies required to be an effective board member.

Locked in underperformance by unconscious group dynamics

The focus of this chapter is to consider how members fulfil roles and interact with each other. It faces the challenge of opening the 'black box' of boards (Minichilli et al., 2007, p. 617). Two cases are used to illustrate the dynamics between board members and the impact it has on the board's capacity to add value to the business.

Mary, 49 years old, is a non-executive board member representing the private equity firm at a service provider company. She reports that, according to her and the shareholders assessment, the board is underperforming:

> During our board meeting, the trio of founders continue to behave like entrepreneurs instead of board members. They have no idea about their role as board members; don't have the necessary competencies to think strategically, and are not willing to learn.
>
> (Personal communication)

John, 44 years old, is an executive board member and CFO of a listed company operating in the infrastructure sector, facing critical financial and reputational crises. The controlling group is formed by three members of a leading private equity firm with successful track records in the financial market. John's case represents an example of how an ethical dilemma (the controlling group´s deliberate intention to "make-up" the financial results of a listed company) affects the group´s dynamics:

> Reflecting about my move as an investment banker to become an executive board member I conclude: when you earn a lot of money in the financial market, you can be misguided by the paradox of ignorance, and believe that your wealth reflects how knowledgeable you are, when, in reality, there are several things that you don't know.
>
> (Personal communication)

Mary's and John's examples illustrate two interconnected 'individual traps' into which, board members can fall. At the cognitive level, they underestimate the learning curve required to develop the necessary competencies to perform at board level (i.e., acquiring knowledge about the market, strategic vision, influencing without authority). At the emotional level, they can consciously or unconsciously cross the thin line that distinguishes those with a healthy amount of narcissism from those pseudo-stars with excessive narcissism:

> Usually un-healthy narcissists' drive, impulsiveness and defence mechanisms (i.e., denial, splitting, projection) leads to excellent short-term results. However, their maladaptive and rigid behaviour can lead to functional impairment and cause significant distress to others, which of course contributes to the board's underperformance
>
> (Kets de Vries, 2012, p. 177)

The 'group trap', into which members can fall consists of the *basic assumption mentality* (Bion, 1961), which is manifested when a group faces unpleasant (e.g., complex, risky, intimidating) realities. In order to avoid experiencing the uncomfortable feelings intrinsic to such situations (e.g., frustration, fear, aggression), members unconsciously engage in three counterproductive off-task behaviours, referred to as basic assumptions dependency (baD), fight/flight (baF) and pairing (baP). These assumptions hijack the group's capacity to reflect, act and interact – which can temporally or chronically impact the groups' effectiveness.

Mary describes her board's dynamics in the following way:

> The three male members constituting a majority in the controlling group display fairly regressed behaviour, acting almost like naughty teenagers ganging together, expecting money to simply be poured into their business. I am described as picky, especially when they arrive with a closed mind-set related to an issue that should be addressed by the board; they respect us (the private equity firm) as an institution, because we have the money but they don't respect our ideas and contributions.

It can be inferred from Mary's words that the board was operating under *basic assumption dependency* (baD), since part of the group seeks safety and protection (majority group) whilst another part provides it (private equity firm) in order to create an artificial sense of shared comfort. The three male members constituting a majority in the controlling group act as care-takers and Mary as care-giver. In this case, the unproductive level of interdependency is leading to disappointment, regret and resentment, as investors are realizing that the business is not viable and founders are realizing that money will not continue to be poured into the business as they were expecting.

John's description of his board's dynamics:

> We didn't know enough about the business and, despite my commitment to learn on the job, I would never be the right person to fulfil this role, and the lack of knowledge about how the business operates made it even more difficult to build trust between board members.

Our relationship was antagonistic, characterized by the controlling group on one side and us, executives (CEO and CFO), on the other side because we shared the same ethical values.

It can be inferred that John's board was either consciously or unconsciously determined to under-perform. This is a good example of a 'set-up for failure' situation that can be fairly common in a board's formation. According to John, the main characteristic of the group dynamics was that of splitting.

The split at the top level (controlling group versus the alliance between CFO and CEO) resulted in a collusion of primary tasks. The phenomenal primary task is the task that can be inferred from the members' behaviours (Roberts, 1994). For John, the way in which the phenomenal primary task was being carried out by the controlling group (lack of ethical values) became psychologically intolerable to him. The collusion of primary tasks is associated with the *basic assumption of fight and flight (BaF)*. The controlling group was flying away from reality by making-up results, focusing on the private equity's financial survival instead of implementing the best practices in corporate governance. The CEO and CFO were fighting for the long-term survival of the business, for their ethical values and professional reputation. Roberts (1994, p. 31) states that the primary task relates to the survival in relation to the demands of the external environment, while basic assumption activity is driven by demands of the internal environment and anxieties about psychological survival. The CFO and CEO engaged in a "fight" against the controlling group in order to survive psychologically from such a complex ethical dilemma.

Unlocking performance by *learning from experience*

At this point, hopefully, the reader might have recognized why it is important to be aware of how unconscious dynamics can prevent boards from fulfilling their primary task and therefore the need to act accordingly. The next step, then, is to ponder about how board members can process individually and collectively emotions 'in the here and now' so that they can make the best use of their distinctive experience and competencies and therefore fulfil their primary task and responsibilities.

In order to exert influence and negotiate conflicting interests, board members have to fulfil a complex leadership role, which involves various levels, types and intensities of interaction with executives and non-executive members (Van de Loo, 2013). The nuances of how to manage these boundaries can be represented by Schopenhauer's hedgehog's dilemma. Humans are like hedgehogs: if too close, their spikes can hurt each other; if too far apart, they can either be attacked by a predator or die from the cold (Kets de Vries, 2013).

When asked about how Mary felt during board meetings, she replied:

I feel excluded from the club (composed of the three members of the controlling group), in the passenger's seat. I don't feel valued by my background and competencies. I have a network that could help the business enormously but they just don't accept any help that I can offer. They can only see me as a "picky investor" rather than someone who can really contribute with my knowledge to our business.

Looking beyond present constraints, defining a new strategy, detecting long-term opportunities and identifying emergent risks require that board members elaborate complex hypotheses, build on existing knowledge and as a result, think about the unthinkable (what could not have been previously thought of and known about if that specific group of people were not together). The schema of affective links – knowledge (K), love (L) and hate (H) – clarifies why and how emotions such as love and hate have the potential to "contaminate" a group's urge to know (Fisher, 2011).

From Mary's example it can be inferred that disappointment and resentment at being dependent led 'the club' to rebel against what is, in their minds, the source of dependency, in this case, financial dependency was represented by Mary. This un-processed emotion left the board stuck, unable to process knowledge (K), and therefore unable to create the necessary conditions to implement relevant decisions.

Bion defines *beta elements* as un-metabolized and unprocessed affective experiences that cannot yet be thought, while *alpha elements* are metabolized and processed affective experiences that can already be thought. The *alpha-function* is what transforms *beta elements* into *alpha elements*, metabolizing and processing affective experiences to make them available for thought.

Conversely, as in Mary's case, boards with deficient *alpha function* are more likely to engage in *basic assumptions*. As a consequence, experiences and knowledge (what boards should be all about) cannot be accessed and processed collectively. This leads to a -K emotional state, represented by a desire to remain ignorant, actively avoiding available knowledge, or even destroying potential sources of new knowledge (e.g., an expert opinion person, a report, or an innovative concept). A -K state of mind is an attack on a +K state of mind: experiences of love (L) and hate (H) "contaminate" the urge to know (Fisher, 2011). This concept complements the idea of *basic assumption* since, as stated by Stokes (1994a, p. 26), "when operating under *basic assumption mentality*, the formation and continuance of the group becomes an end in itself . . . as members become more absorbed with their relationship to the group, than with their work task".

As stated by John:

> Despite the CEO's and my efforts to move forward with decisions, the controlling group's task was to only protect their personal assets and not to think on behalf of the entire business. The board meetings were unproductive as they kept searching for confirmation biases, expecting us (fellow board members) to say exactly what they (controlling group members) wanted to hear.
>
> The controlling group's continuous denial of reality (e.g., hiring an inexperienced CFO; not trying to understand the sector; disengaging from board

meetings and disempowering the CEO and CFO) prevented the board from making decisions that could have turned the business around.

John's board was operating under *basic assumption fight/flight (baF)*, characterized by splitting fuelled by love (L) and hate (H). The board was completely distracted from its primary task and as time and energy were invested on preserving alliances based on love (L) and spoiling relationships based on hate (H) leading to an unproductive -K state of mind.

In this context, exposure to truth and reality are vital elements for growth and development, and groups that are successful at applying the *alpha function* can tolerate the frustrations inherent in 'learning from experience in the here-and-now' Bion (2004).

Learning to experience as a pre-condition to learn from experience

Mary and John described how the group dynamics negatively impacted their performance and candidly acknowledged that they were also responsible for the overall underperformance of the boards they were part of. Both board members felt undervalued, prevented from contributing more, and disappointed with fellow board members' contributions, leading to either a passive attitude (Mary) or on the verge of a psychological breakdown (John). Translating their description of both group dynamics into Bion's language, it is implicit that the triad of emotional experiences – love (L), hate (H) and knowledge (K) – created a -K mind set. As a result of this -K state of mind, Mary and John refer to how they felt in relation to the group dynamics, that is: hesitant, disempowered, stuck and entangled, which is associated with *basic assumption mentality*.

Looking back, what could have helped Mary and John? Perhaps, if they had engaged in a process *of learning to experience* they could have been more equipped to *learn from experience*. *Learn to experience* is a term coined by the author associated with the one's disposition and commitment to the process of restoring and/ or increasing his capacity to tolerate anxiety associated with not knowing at cognitive (what one is thinking about – related to a business issue) and emotional (how one is feeling about – related to a person and situation) levels. Rilke (2000, p. 35) poetically describes how one feels while learning to experience:

> Do not now look for the answers. They cannot now be given to you because you could not live them. It is a question of experiencing everything. At present you need to live the question. Perhaps, you will gradually, without even noticing it, find yourself experiencing the answer some distant day.

Rilke's (2000) "invitation" has no appeal to the majority of board members, making the case that *learning to experience* requires self-awareness and humility. According to Van de Loo (2013), there are four crucial conditions that can enhance board effectiveness and integrity: building trust, having humility, having the courage to speak the truth (parrhêsia), and creating reflective space.

Learning to experience requires a conductive environment, *ambiance*, so when describing *reflective spaces*, Van de Loo (2013) highlights the distinction between thinking and reflecting. To implement the concept of *reflective spaces*, the *leitmotiv* of 'thinking + action = performance' needs to be challenged.

The adult development theory proposed by Kegan (1994) contributes to the understanding of the concept of *learning to experience*. The theory attributes different developmental stages that depend on an individuals' capacity to apprehend and interpret complexity. Each stage is characterized by a more complex process of taking and building unique perspectives, constructing and challenging knowledge, building and adapting complementary identities that serve distinctive networks and objectives. Ideally, at board level, *learning to experience* involves making a conscious effort to remain comfortable with complexity, which involves making a transition from a self-authoring mind to a self-transforming mind. This transition involves shifting from holding views and opinions of others exclusively to strengthen one's own argument and set of principles, to start reflecting on the limits of one's own ideology and authority, in order to continuously transform one's own system of arguments and principles. It also implies shifting from a perception that authority is found in the 'self' to coping with the fact that authority is fluid and contextual (Berger, 2011).

Conclusion

In this chapter, material from board members and consultants were used to illustrate how unconscious dynamics prevent board members from sharing and applying their experience. Bion's theory was applied to board members' interviews to show the mechanisms that hinder the capacity to reflect collectively.

To achieve their tasks, members need to face uncomfortable realities and feelings, and avoid engaging in unconscious, unproductive, *off-task* behaviours. Boards have to *learn from experience (in the-here-and-now)*, by tolerating the frustrations inherent to learning, so that members can share their knowledge and experience in a constructive way (work group), i.e., to challenge each other, reflect collectively, and apply their conclusions and decisions to address real-world business challenges. However, the interviews reveal that many of the board members are senior and successful professionals who are unwilling to leave their comfort zones. Based on this assessment, a previous stage of *learning to experience* was developed as a necessary step to *learn from experience*.

There are developmental interventions at process levels (i.e., governance models) and behavioural levels (i.e., assessment by third party, facilitation, coaching) that are based on different theories of management and psychology. The risk is that the majority of these methods are heavily based on rationality of human beings and on the naive belief that processes are flawless.

The concept of *learning to experience* seems highly relevant for consultants working with boards, and could be incorporated in board development initiatives. Interventions focused on deepening self-awareness, increasing humility and developing attitudes associated with the *self-transforming mind* can increase a boards' capacity to *learn from* experience, allowing members to contribute with their experience and knowledge, and to reflect collectively. When boards fulfil their potential, businesses have greater chances of realizing the full value of their boards.

Exercise to practice *learning to and from experience*

Step I: Reflecting on a specific situation and associated emotions:

1   Develop awareness of one's own emotions and the emotions of others in the group.

    a   What are these emotions and how are they used?
    b   What prevents you and others from being more aware of these emotions?

2   Reflect on how one's emotions (pleasant, unpleasant, revealed, disguised) impact other parties.

3   Over time, what positive or negative differences were observed in the way you and others

    a   exchanged information?
    b   negotiated conflicting interests?
    c   exerted authority and accepted compliance?
    d   took decisions?
    e   managed boundaries?
    f   committed to actions?

4   How did you and others, evaluate the end result (below or above what was expected; or totally unexpected)?

5   What did you learn about yourself and others, when acting under such conditions?

Step II: Evaluate your openness to learn *from experience* in this particular situation.

1   Do you recall reflecting together with others on the issues above whilst handling the rational, concrete aspects of the group's tasks?

    •   If yes, you are engaged in the process of learning from experience as you are processing the emotions that are present in the systems within which you are members;
    •   If not, you miss the opportunity of learning from this particular experience as are probably not processing emotions

When *learning from experience*, members are engaged *in a meta-conversation* about how individual emotions may be impacting the group's performance and vice versa. The content and level of disclosure depends upon the degree of trust among members, extent to which members are aligned and committed to a shared objective, what's at stake for whom, and how much time is available to address issues that are not considered rational. The necessity to become vigilant about when, why and how sweeping irrationality leads to underperformance can be perceived as a gift for some and as a curse for others.

Step III: Reflecting about your candidness *to learn to experience*

1   After answering these two questions above, how are you feeling about yourself (proud, happy, ashamed, regretful, competent, incompetent, better/worse)?
2   What would you like to do differently in the future? How do you plan to continue developing yourself?

Actually, how you feel is not that relevant. What is important is that you are able to realistically assess how you feel and reflect about the impact you had on others. In order to *learn to experience* you must have a predisposition to be a "healthy-constructive narcissist, with a proportionate and realistic appraisal of your own achievements, and who is committed to be lifelong learners, aware that they usually do not know what they do not know. When they receive feedback, they take note and act on it" (de Vries, 2012, p. 176). As mentioned above, the challenge is to breakout from a developmental inertia and ignite the drive needed to develop the emotional competencies required to be an effective board member.

Part IV

Case illustrations

This section contains six case studies in which the authors describe the application of their knowledge and practice derived from the Dynamics @ Board Level programme. The case study method forms a central pillar of the programme on the principle that direct consulting experience trumps theoretical and academic knowledge in the universe of the organizational development practitioner, and is a factor which gives Tavistock Institute-trained consultants the edge in working with complex systems.

David Strudley, in Chapter 17, points to evidence suggesting that in spite of the considerable challenges, many people sign up to become charity trustees. He asks why and considers the implications for their doing so in terms of their own roles and the impact they may have on the boards they join. Interesting insights emerge, including unconscious childhood influences that give meaning to their role. Strudley also addresses the processes associated with working in groups, both conscious and unconscious, that affect the functioning of boards, for good and ill. As a result of his analysis we are left with a sense that there is still much to do to understand the functioning of charity boards. There is certainly scope for further improvement, particularly through challenging the status quo and addressing gender and age imbalances. Additionally, the scope for further research is great and potentially far reaching so it is likely to become an area for much greater study and analysis in future.

In Chapter 18, Janette McCrae reviews the early development phase of a public sector board, highlighting challenges experienced on a journey towards enhanced board maturity. She provides two models through which public sector board behaviours may be understood and improved – the 'political' level, which incorporates parliament, ministers and civil servants with a focus on policy; and the 'societal' level of authority, where its raison d'etre is public service, and the focus is on a better society. McCrae describes a board holding a line of authority vertically between the 'political' and 'professional' levels within two organizations: the Police Service of Scotland and the Scottish Police Authority (with the added complexity of the CEO as accountable officer, directly responsible to parliament). McCrae describes transgressions of authority, which occur when a group or a person in one level crosses into a different level's area of responsibility, or a level is circumvented, resulting in a diminution of the relative authority of the distinct levels within the system.

Social housing is the next case in Chapter 19, in which Thomas Brull writes about conflict in the board of a family business on government contract to reduce the housing deficit in an east European country. The company was obliged to seek outside capitalization thereby experiencing a loss of power for the family and creating tensions between the board and the management team.

Anand Narasimhan writes in Chapter 20 about corruption, leader narcissism and the dynamics of board governance in the case of Marks & Spencer, using a psychodynamic perspective on corruption in order to provide a cogent account of corporate governance failure owing to narcissistic leadership. Corruption in the psychodynamic sense is understood as "a hostile turning away from internal objects . . . the erosion of values and standards through noxious processes that haven't been foreseen, haven't been predicted or worked with until it is too late" (Sher, 2013, p. 170). Corruption thus defined has fairly broad scope. Narasimhan describes narcissism as a form of self-regard that can lead to creativity and humour; and grandiose behaviours and a pathologically excessive need for recognition from others. This paper makes two significant contributions – a 'group-as-a-whole' conceptualization of narcissism and a more sociologically defined enactment based on the collective psychodynamics of the leader-follower relationship.

Anja Salmi's case study in Chapter 21 is a country – Finland – which she describes as part of a complex adaptive system of north eastern Europe. She examines the anxieties and social and political changes in Finland over six months in 2016, investigating the patterns of defences present in the work of the Finnish government. Salmi's study assumes that the government, as the country's ultimate board, reflects unconscious dynamics of the country, creating a unique matrix and complex system. National identity, culture, taboos, founding circumstances and history combine to influence defences that appear to be leading to fragmentation or stagnation. When a system takes the form of a country with geographical borders and national identity, its dynamics can be called 'national dynamics.' Finland is a part of the environmental system of north eastern Europe through its relationships with neighbouring countries. Salmi describes how the 'board', that is, government, uses interactive methods of emotional exchange based on primitive defences of projection and introjection, thus making national identity an important issue in postmodern times.

In Chapter 22, Paul Duggan considers a group of distribution businesses, with a record of success for over 60 years, whose viability was threatened by the economic crisis. He focuses on the dynamics and key decisions taken by the group board, although all the issues faced by the group board were also faced by the subsidiary boards. Duggan also explores the impact of the crisis on the group CEO: how he felt, how he managed himself and what strategies worked well. Before stabilizing, sales fell by more than 50% in two years. Although the operating environment remained fragile, dynamic stability was restored when the board moved from a paranoid-schizoid to a depressive state, which took the form of directors accepting that there was opportunity as well as threat and recognizing this by agreeing to a new primary task involving a new definition of what success would look like – survival, increasing market share and protecting employment. Sacrifices were required from all stakeholders. Shareholders agreed to accept trading losses, suspend dividends and subscribe for additional capital. The group's bankers agreed to significant renegotiation of the group's debt facilities. Employees agreed to make significant concessions in the form of reduced working hours, reduced rates of pay and other benefits (including pensions). Suppliers agreed to increase the support they provided to the group. This allowed the group to confidently engage with the market, at a time when competitors were in full retreat. It allowed investment in strategies which secured increases in market share and long-term job security for staff. It ensured survival.

17 Joining charity boards

Consequences for board performance and future improvement

David Strudley

Introduction

Evidence provided by a range of organizations suggests there are enormous benefits in getting involved in charities and in particular in becoming a trustee (Voluntary Sector Network, 2014). However, being a trustee or charity board member involves assuming a number of onerous responsibilities, including making decisions that may have an impact on people's lives. Trustees use their experience and skills, normally without payment, to support their charities and help them realize their aims and objectives. According to the Charity Commission (*What's Involved?* CC3a, 2015), the principal regulator of charities, in addition to an expectation that all trustees will work together as a team, they have in common six main duties, namely to:

1   Ensure the charity is carrying out its purposes for the public benefit;
2   Comply with its governing document and the law;
3   Act in the charity's best interest;
4   Manage the charity's resources responsibly;
5   Act with reasonable care and skill and
6   Ensure the charity is accountable.

Additionally, a record is to be kept of all significant decisions for future review and accountability.

   With such daunting demands being placed on individuals, it is tempting to wonder whether people may put off joining charity boards and it is true that numbers are not as high as many would wish (The Civil Society Almanac [CSA], 2012). Furthermore, research suggests that charities themselves should devote more effort to broadening the diversity of their boards, in particular by increasing the numbers of women (Third Sector May, 2012) and younger people (CAF Young People's Guide, 2015).

   Nevertheless, by current estimates, there are over 600,000 trustees (CAS, 2012) in the UK, many of whom serve on more than one charity board. Furthermore, 21 million people (Saxton & Kanemura, 2015) have volunteered at some stage in their lives and the current combined annual income for charities in the UK is around £39 billion.

So, why do people become charity trustees and what are the implications for their role and the performance of the board(s) that they have joined? This chapter seeks to address these questions, before also assessing the scope for future improvements. Tabulated examples to amplify the main text will be provided from course materials and other literature, as well as experiences over a number of years in a range of charities. However, the main source of experience and example is the children's hospice movement where further detailed research is being undertaken. There is a rich seam of minable material available to investigate and analyze in a network of charities that make up a small but vital and unique area within the Third Sector.

Why do people join charity boards and what are the consequences for their role?

Overview

In the opening section of this chapter, we will investigate the various reasons, both conscious and unconscious, that persuade people to give their time, skills and commitment voluntarily. Joining a charity is likely to include an obligation to support a number of often diverse aims and objectives and these may sometimes conflict, with uncertain consequences both for individuals and for the boards with which they affiliate.

Additionally, as is argued by Obholzer (1994b, p. 40), by the act of joining voluntarily, people implicitly delegate some of their own authority to those who are put in authority in the charity (e.g., chair, vice chair and committee chairs). This authority is within an approved system that is thereby confirmed.

So why do people seek to join charity boards and what are the consequences for the roles they undertake?

Conscious reasons

First, concerning what is entailed, in Guidance CC3a (ibid), the Charity Commission makes it clear that trustees are the people who lead their charity and decide how it is run. Being a trustee means making decisions that will impact on people's lives. Depending on what the charity does, trustees will be making a difference to their local community and/or to society as a whole. Trustees use their skills and experience to support their charities, helping them to achieve their aims. Trustees often learn new skills during their time on the board.

Conscious reasons abound for them to apply, including what they may feel they have to offer, in particular by putting something back, a chance to develop transferrable skills, participating in the setting of strategy as well as oversight of its implementation, adding to CVs, meeting other interesting people and broadening their experiences (Coalition for Efficiency Guide, 2015). Family tradition may also play a part. Whatever the reasons, at its heart, being a trustee puts someone at the centre of the action of a charity. By their contributing to the work of the board, the more effective a board may become and the greater the difference it can make.

However, in observing the work of charity boards, it is clear that underlying an undoubted enthusiasm for the role, there are also some individual unconscious meanings that cause people to apply to become trustees and continue to contribute their time and commitment. Why might this be? For some clues, we first turn to the work of Melanie Klein.

Unconscious meanings

The relationship between the conscious and unconscious:

In her work with children in the 1920s, Melanie Klein developed a conceptualization of an unconscious inner world that identified the processes of *splitting* emotions and *projecting* bad feelings onto others that enabled children to come to terms with the pain of their internal conflicts. This normal stage of infant development – she dubbed – the *paranoid-schizoid* (paranoid – bad and schizoid – split) position (Klein, 1957a).

Through play or normal maturation, previously separated emotions such as love and hate, hope and despair, sadness and joy, acceptance and rejection were eventually brought together into a more integrated whole. Klein referred to this integration as the *depressive* position, because as indicated by Halton (1994, p. 14), giving up the comforting simplicity of self-idealization and facing the complexity of external and internal reality inevitably gives rise to feelings of guilt, concern and sadness. These feelings subsequently engender a desire to make reparation for injuries caused by previous hatred and aggression. This often leads to seeking to become a "helping" person, one of the perceived reasons for becoming a trustee of a charity, especially in a care setting. The taking up of a role in a charity is felt to be the result of that unconscious process. However, it may not always turn out as expected.

Role-taking

Role taking is clearly evident in many nurses and carers working in the care arena but perhaps less obviously so in those wishing to become trustees. However, while also a trustee, it can additionally lead to a person taking a role in which he or she does more than anticipated and as a result assists others to develop or improve (Mead, 1967). In a local children's charity in the South of England, a national HR director was invited to become a trustee in order to assist with the recruitment of suitably qualified staff for the charity and to improve HR practices, a task for which he was clearly well qualified. However, another and most valuable contribution to the charity proved to be in his acting as a trusted friend and mentor to other trustees, the CEO and HR director. His empathic nature, not so evident when acting in a professional capacity, clearly shone through when he played the mentoring role.

Anxieties

On the other hand, through splitting and projection, charities may also provide people who have unconscious anxieties or conflicts not fully overcome in child-hood with a means to locate unwanted aspects of themselves in some 'other' (Obholzer, 1994b). Internal personal difficulties can be projected onto organiza-tions with compensating charitable purposes. It is therefore essential for poten-tial trustees to have an insight into why they have chosen a particular charity. For example, if the stated reason is to put something back, is it in fact an act of sublimation of personal ambition in favour of the charity or conversely is it more about self-healing? This is particularly important in a caring charity where "splitting off" can lead to rigidity. If rejection is denied in their clients, it has to be directed elsewhere. In charities that depend for at least part of their income on statutory funding, it is all too easy to project resentment onto the government either nationally or more locally rather than address environmental realities.

Trustees also need to be aware of potential blind spots and their 'valency' (Bion, 1959) for adopting certain kinds of defences, or their vulnerability to par-ticular kinds of projective identification and the resultant dysfunctional behav-iours. Bion identified an innate tendency of individuals to respond to groups and group pressures in their own highly specific way. He termed this *valency*, or the positive or negative value assigned by a person to another person, event, goal, job, outcome, etc., based on their attractiveness. Interestingly, these behaviours could also give clues (Obholzer, 1994b) about unconscious anxieties and the defences that could in themselves have given rise to dysfunctional task definition.

Valency

An accountant from a manufacturing background appointed as treasurer to a healthcare charity caused mounting frustration within the care teams with his often repeated demands for quantitative measures of every aspect of care provided. Reinforced by unconscious anxieties associated by many years of overseeing the work of production lines, and seeing his role as the guardian of the financial well-being of the organization, he acted as if the primary task of the charity was productivity. Thus, only by measuring its outputs could the charity be sure it was meeting its targets and be effective in the delivery of the care it was providing. However, when he was helped to understand the quali-tative and highly individualistic nature of the care on offer, and how it also contributed to the overall strength and well-being of the charity, he was able to contextualize and adapt his demands, though he continued to seek quantitative measures as well.

Summary

In this first section, we have scratched the surface of what may constitute some of the reasons, conscious and unconscious, for people becoming trustees and the implications for their role. In the next section we consider the implications for the performance of the board they have joined.

Board performance

Overview

In this section we first consider the function of trust in board performance, and how it should operate to achieve the board's aims and objectives. We will consider why trust is not always developed and posit that this is sometimes because of a misuse of power. We will also consider how unconscious processes operating in boards occasionally interfere with the stated purposes of the board and the charity it serves.

Trust – why it is necessary?

Trust appears in almost every analysis of board performance: trust between members; trust between the members and the board; and trust between the board and its organization. Additionally, in charities where stakeholders are particularly concerned to see that their support leads directly to improvement for the charity's beneficiaries, trust is also essential between them and the charity itself. A lack of trust can lead to withdrawal of support and funding. Sonnenfeld (2002) concurs by indicating the critical importance of creating a climate of trust and candour. Additionally, Kelleher et al. (2003), posit a number of benefits that ought to accrue from good performance, based on an assumption of building trust and an equitable distribution of costs and risks, all leading to improvements for members.

Power

Somewhat surprisingly, therefore, research at the Tavistock Institute of Human Relations (TIHR) implies that roles and tasks are assigned often unintentionally as part of the power play in direction-finding and decision-making. As a result, weaker board members may feel coerced and at times isolated and unable to express themselves, often to the detriment of organizational best interests. Lack of frequent contact (charity boards often only meet quarterly) probably makes things worse. We may deduce from this that power needs to be more equally spread, hopefully leading to greater cooperation among members (see the box below).

The misdirected use of power

Problems may arise when an over-powerful group of members, who perhaps have joined the charity at various stages in the charity's life, from a range of strategic or managerial backgrounds, perhaps, in commerce and manufacturing, or whose professional qualifications are centred in the world of financial management. Their background and experiences may lead to their joining the charity largely ignorant of the true nature of its primary task.

A lack of effective induction in the early stages of their membership further emphasizes their sense of not needing to account for the caring aspects, while seeing themselves as having a vital duty to contribute their financial skills to the organization's future. The common ground of their experiences further strengthens their burgeoning power as a group. Over time they assume the decision-making function on behalf of the board.

The caring trustees, or those with little understanding of financial management, conclude that their knowledge and power to influence are too weak to gainsay the stronger group and slowly become excluded from the decision-making process. They in turn fragment and split, rather than collaborate, because this feels more comfortable than simply being ignored. This in turn leads to a polarization of the board and a consequential reduction in effectiveness.

This phenomenon has been observed during the strategy making process in charities providing care when financial constraints overtake the need to decide the strategy based on the level and quality of care required.

Bion's experiences with groups

A further vital aspect concerns the business of operating in groups that is a necessary part of the collaborative relationship between trustees, whether socially, in committee or on the board itself. Bion's (1959) work in groups helps us to understand many of the dynamics of boards and the difficulties that emerge from time to time. Its importance lies in the difference between what he terms the work group and basic assumption mentality. French and Simpson (2010) extend this theme of work group and basic assumption mentality by explaining that work group mentality describes the disposition and dynamics that characterize the life of a group, to the extent that its members are able to manage their shared tensions, anxieties and relationships, in order to function effectively; the result is a capacity for realistic hard work.

By contrast, in basic assumption mentality, the group's behaviour is directed at attempting to meet the unconscious needs of its members by reducing anxiety and internal conflicts. In other words, the group has been taken over by strong emotions (anger, depression, anxiety, fear and hatred) and as a result, has lost touch with its core purpose. As Bion (1961) intimates, much of the irrational behaviour of groups can be seen as springing from basic assumptions common to all their members. He cites three such basic assumptions, *dependency, pairing* and *fight or flight*. For a brief analysis of these assumptions and their observed impact in regard to experiences gained in various organizations, see the box below. In the first two cases, reinstitution of a work group mentality led to a revitalization of the organization. In the third, the departure of the instrumental group allowed more task individuals to join the board and assume responsibility for governance.

Bion's basic assumptions

In *dependency*, the group seeks a leader who will relieve them of all anxiety. This leader is thus invested with omnipotence and is expected to be able to solve all problems. If this magical leader does not perform to perfection, then the leader will be attacked and a replacement sought. At a children's hospice, the director of care was seen as the protector of the care team until a sudden decline in the charity's fortunes led to a number of redundancies and his departure from post. Over the last five years, the current incumbent has developed a professional work group that sees itself as accountable in the delivery of an integrated model in the provision of care.

In *pairing*, the development of the group is frozen by a hope of being rescued by two members who will pair-off and somehow create an unborn leader. This was the case at the author's charity when he took over. Chairman and CEO had previously held in thrall the whole board, which had become incapable of acting without them. Sadly, as a result, the charity had lost its way; it had no strategy and its operational effort was extremely haphazard and directionless. The problem was resolved by strategic and operational restructuring; the development of effective board assurance committees and a board charged with the development and implementation of strategy.

Finally, in *fight or flight*, the group acts as if its main task is to fight or flee from some common enemy who may be found either within or outside the group. The board of a retraining and rehabilitation trust saw itself as defenders of their clients from the extremely adverse external environment to which they felt they had been exposed. Refusing any form of aid or advice, they accepted no other approach than that of constant combat, until slowly the key members retired or left, allowing a more task-focused board to assume responsibility for the organization's future.

However, one is left pondering whether the two mentality sets (work group and basic assumption) really are as distinct as these brief descriptions imply. For example, a current situation at a West Midlands charity concerning the need to push for more statutory funding was in danger of developing into basic assumption fight or flight because of a belief that the commissioners were simply not willing to respond to the acknowledged legitimate requests for increased funding. By approaching the situation with a work group mentality the charity is addressing the situation objectively, raising the level of challenge to meet the need for increased support. The key to maintaining balance in this situation would seem to be to avoid being drawn into an unconscious collusion when strong emotions like anxiety, anger, fear and depression vie for dominance. The CEO will need to contain the situation and maintain an equitable balance, while the battle rages.

Summary

In this section, we have considered the various conscious and unconscious processes that can help or hinder board functioning. Clearly, there is still much to do and so in the next section we will address the scope for possible improvement.

What improvements may be possible?

Overview

In light of what we have learned or observed and the examples we have been able to discover, what do we believe are the prospects for improvement? First, as emphasized by the National Council for Voluntary Organizations (*NCVO Knowhow*, 2014), there is a vital need for careful recruitment and induction. Induction is vital to provide a gateway for new trustees, helping them to catch up with the role, organization and their legal responsibilities. Induction ensures that trustees have an awareness and understanding of their role and key policies and procedures.

Secondly, as intimated by Sonnenfeld (2002), the chair should engender a climate that fosters open dissent, uses conflict to confront issues and sees individual accountability as superior to mute conformance. The chair must also maintain focus on the charity's core purpose and not allow unconscious anxieties to prevail. Rigid agendas allow reticent people to hide behind the details. From experience, this is best ameliorated by making the agenda more fluid and encouraging full participation during every important discussion. Separating decision-making from strategic thinking and discussion is also a powerful mechanism for wider involvement, potentially allowing the emergence of new solutions to old problems.

There should also be willingness among its members to assess and evaluate the performance of the board on an ongoing basis.

Challenge

Members need to feel able to challenge more. This vital aspect is best achieved through effective and constructive questioning (Kelleher et al., 2003). Becoming adept at challenging is one of the greatest contributions trustees can make to their charities. Furthermore, challenge through effective questioning is a test of cohesion of the members of a board. It is also a measure of the strength of the chair to what extent he or she invites dissent and ensures the full participation of each member. Gaining clarity, rather than seeking contest, appears to work best.

As is also further indicated by Sonnenfeld (2002), and borne out by experience, there is a danger in members becoming typecast in a role, for example, as the cost-cutter, big-picture merchant or peace-maker. It is essential that everyone including the CEO is pushed to challenge through being made to take alternative stances, not aggressively which evokes resistance, but authoritatively.

Equality and diversity

Next, gender and age balance are increasingly essential elements in mainstreaming equality and diversity. Another TIHR paper (Sher, 2015) gives us some helpful pointers through what is termed *positive action* as opposed to *positive discrimination*. Providing more opportunities for women to work on high profile projects and women acting as role models, are just two examples of this. As to young trustees, the Charities Aid Foundation (CAF) publication (*The Young Trustee's Guide*, 2015) challenges us to change our thinking and allow youth to have a voice in the furtherance of charity.

Anxiety

In charities, like other firms, we have seen that leadership, structure and organization are vital and that financial constraints are an unavoidable reality. However, what has also been emerging is the part played by social, group and psychological phenomena as well. Without taking these into account, both individually as trustees and collectively as boards, charities may risk the very enterprise they are seeking to nurture and improve. Thus, beyond the construction and implementation of strategy and financial management, they should also consider how to contain the inevitable anxiety (Obholzer, 1994a, p. 207) that accompanies the frequent occurrences of uncertainty, misfortune and fear of failure, common to many charitable organizations.

Drawing further on Bion's thinking about groups (1993) for the board as container to be effective in containing and even sublimating anxieties, it needs to be in what Melanie Klein termed the *depressive position*. Only thus can it face both the environmental and unconscious issues. To do this the chair and his or her officers need to stay focused on the charity's core purpose, sustain its vision and remain alert to the anxieties through detecting their projection onto the board. At all costs, these unconscious processes must not be blocked out of consideration, as is sadly often observed as a more normal defence in some charities.

Summary

In summary, while there is much to do and considerable progress still to be made in the way charity boards function, there is also much cause for optimism, not least because a fresh understanding has been gained through exposure to complexity theory as described by Aram (2015) and the value of "just talking" (Shaw, 2002, pp. 12–18).

Ongoing study

Attending this course has been of immense value both in learning and in the encouragement to go further. Future study and research could be undertaken to delve deeper into the governance and operations of charities, their leadership and the way they look after their people. Complexity Theory (Aram, 2015) has brought a new and very exciting dimension to future execution in charities. The possibility of moving from linear cause and effect decision-making to non-linear thinking is as exciting as it is scary. The inherent paradoxes in any part of life give rise to opportunities for entirely new ways of approaching strategic planning and implementation. Complexity will therefore be explored for the possibilities it presents, with a view to framing recommendations for the future governance and execution in charity boards.

18 Birth of a board – a public sector perspective

Janette McCrae

Background

On 1 April 2013, the Police and Fire Reform Scotland Act (2012) heralded the unprecedented amalgamation of eight police forces and two organizations to form the Police Service of Scotland (PSoS). The Scottish government proposed that the PSoS would ensure police reform, enhance services and generate savings of £1.1 billion by 2026.

The Act (Scotland, 2012) also created the Scottish Police Authority (SPA) and SPA Board, whose functions are to:

- *Maintain the Police Service,*
- *Promote the policing principles set out in section 32,*
- *Promote and support continuous improvement in the policing of Scotland,*
- *Keep under review the policing of Scotland,*
- *Hold the Chief Constable to account for the policing of Scotland" (1.2.1).*

The advent of the SPA dramatically changed lines of accountability and authority for policing – local governance through tripartite arrangements between police boards, chief constables and the minister shifted to a centralized, hierarchical line of authority designed to hold the sole chief constable to account.

The chief constable is accountable to the SPA and board, which in turn are vertically accountable to the cabinet secretary for justice (CSJ) and ultimately the Scottish parliament. The SPA chair and board members are appointed by the CSJ. The SPA CEO is the accountable officer to parliament. The Act states: "The Authority must comply with any direction (general or specific) given by the Scottish Ministers" (1.5.1). However, the CSJ cannot direct specific policing operations.

The SPA affords an arm's length separation between the state and the operational independence of the chief constable.

However, Heald and Steel (2015) indicate: "The formal justifications for establishing public bodies often include expectations of greater operational efficiency and of 'independence' that insulates decision making from political intervention. How secure that depoliticization is, can be uncertain". These arrangements can also provide "ample opportunities for blame-avoidance and blame-shifting tactics" (p. 258).

The SPA and the PSoS are subject to additional horizontal scrutiny through inspections, audits and investigations by Her Majesty's Inspectorate of Constabulary in Scotland (HMICS), Audit Scotland and the Police Investigations and Review Commissioner (PIRC). These agencies operate under statutory powers and are expected to cooperate and coordinate activities, preventing duplication.

Further complexity arises via the Parliamentary Justice Committee and Policing Sub-Committee in taking evidence from the chair and chief constable, as it holds the CSJ to account. The omnipresent fourth estate ensures an ongoing media spotlight.

Developments

By late 2015, significant changes were evident. However, anticipated transformational police reform might be more accurately described as police "consolidation and delivering operational stability" (HMICS, 2016, p. 4).

Changes in personnel included a new CSJ and a new SPA board chair, who subsequently appointed a new chief constable. The new chair has a better aligned board composition with his vision and specific skill-set requirements for members.

The PSoS executive has experienced structural reporting changes, realignment of areas of responsibility, addition of a civilian deputy chief officer and new appointees in several chief officer and director roles.

Recommendations in the chair's *Review of Governance in Policing* (Flanagan, 2016), prepared by the board chair in response to an urgent ministerial directive, are being implemented; a policing strategy for 2026 is developed; a second staff survey is completed after an initial *SPA/Police Scotland Opinion Survey* (2015) revealed numerous detrimental findings.

In December 2016, the auditor general (Audit Scotland, 2016), stated: "The Scottish Police Authority and Police Scotland are among the largest and most important public bodies in Scotland. I have reported to the Parliament on weak financial leadership and management in all three years of their existence" (p. 9).

She further commented that 'The SPA could have a cumulative deficit of almost £0.2 billion (circa £188 million) in real terms by the end of the current parliamentary session' (p. 7).

Concurrently, the HMICS (2016) indicated that "Urgent work is still needed to further strengthen the capability and capacity within the finance function and improve the overall governance" (p. 5). An HMICS inspection of the SPA is scheduled for 2017, with a focus on governance and oversight of transformational change.

In January 2017, *The Scotsman* carried the headline: "Those who police the police are failing". These developments paint an ominous overview of the policing organizational landscape.

The remainder of this chapter explores how perceptions and behaviours related to authority, role, group dynamics and leadership have impacted on the board.

Authority

Authority is a quality derived from one's role in a system and the shared task. Authority, according to Obholzer (1994b), is "the right to make an ultimate decision, and in an organization it refers to the right to make decisions which are binding on others" (p. 39).

Authority in policing is contingent upon delegation by the state through legislation of police powers (from 'above') and sanction (from 'below') by the public – upholding 'policing by consent'. According to Sher (2013), authority also requires internal authority within the mind of the leader. "Awareness of the presence and workings of unconscious personal, interpersonal, group, intergroup and intra-institutional processes among both leaders and followers is essential" (p. 190).

Police preserve the peace, protect life and property, and prevent and detect criminal offences. Policing's core function is to prevent civil unrest – in whatever form it manifests. Consequently, policing is regulating and constraining. The inaugural chief constable supported this position: "My view is policing doesn't solve problems. We are not a solution agency, we are a restraint agency" (Scott, 2014, p. 3).

Policing also provides, according to Stokes (1994a), a holding place for society's projection of attitudes towards authority:

> We need the police to be available, psychologically speaking, for the projection of certain of our attitudes towards authority. Indeed, accepting these projections, working them through, and handing them back to society at large is part of the task of police. If the police see themselves only as providing a service, and do not realize that psychological containment of tensions within society is also a central function, there is likely to be an increase in disorder rather than a reduction. If the police are no longer available in this way to society, they will not provide the necessary sense of authoritative containment.
>
> (p. 125)

Law, standard operating procedures and tradition are the cornerstones of policing; crisis is its realm of operation, and despite significant efforts to develop more transformational senior leaders, authority through command and control still predominates.

Clarity of authority

In addition to the conceptual complexity of authority, lack of clarity concerning the practical workings of levels and lines of authority, and role boundaries, between the constituents of the system, precipitate impediments which impact on effectiveness and legitimacy.

The *clarity of authority* model (Figure 18.1) proposed by Dame Ruth Silver (personal communication, June 1, 2015), identifies distinct levels of authority, a vertical line of accountability and signals disruptive transgressions of authority that arise when expectations of entitlement combine with illusions of power.

Political
↕
Loyal to Policy - Voted in to deliver policy

Societal
↕
BOARD in Public Service
Loyal to the Future - Focus for a better society

Professional
↕
Loyal to Practice - What the professionals do

Managerial
Loyal to Delivery - Operational deployment of resources

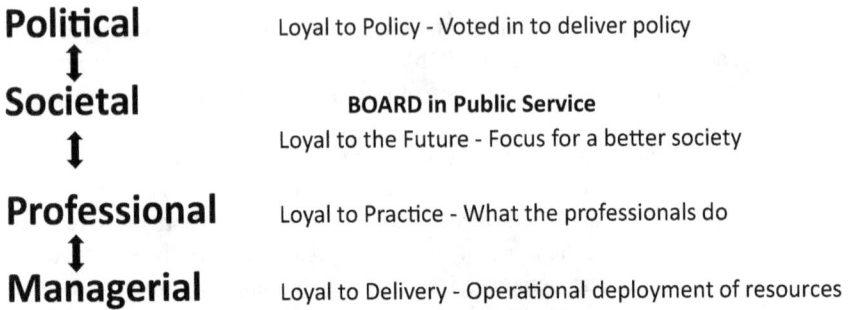

*Reference: **Dame Ruth Silver***

Figure 18.1 Clarity of authority

The 'political' level incorporates parliament, ministers and civil servants with a focus on policy. Public sector boards operate at, and are contained within, the 'societal' level of authority, where its raison d'etre is public service, focus is on a better society and loyalty is towards the future. The SPA board holds a line of authority vertically between the 'political' and 'professional' levels within two organizations: the PSoS and the SPA (with the added complexity of the CEO as accountable officer, directly responsible to parliament). Operational delivery in both organizations rests within the 'managerial' level.

Transgressions of authority occur when a group or person in one level crosses into a different level's area of responsibility, or a level is circumvented, resulting in a diminution of the relative authority of the distinct levels within the system. Heald and Steel (2015) highlight the potential for public bodies to be circumvented: "A recurrent fear on the part of the interviewed chairs and chief executives was of being excluded from decisions fundamental to their operations or even existence, without having access" (p. 262).

During significant system restructure, initially, boundaries may be tested and uncertainties potentially exploited. With maturity, however, boundaries should be understood and respected.

Transgressions may manifest as a consequence of continuing historical custom and practice, ambiguity, misinterpretation or even a perceived 'needs must' circumstance, for example,

- Pre-SPA, under tripartite governance structures, chief constables liaised directly with the CSJ and civil servants. Continuation of direct historical lines of communication sits uncomfortably within the SPA governance structure. When "authority from below, in the form of not sanctioning . . . occurs . . . full authority cannot be obtained, and . . . there is an increased risk of undermining and sabotage" (Obholzer & Roberts, 1994b, p. 40).

- Civil servants' direct influence on policing is truncated with the shift to the hierarchical structure.
- Early board membership carried historical patterns from legacy organizations. 'Carry-over' ensured maintenance of policing knowledge. However, it perhaps hindered the speed with which new governance structures were adopted.
- Media reports of struggles between the inaugural chair and chief constable, over ownership of staff and resources, necessitated further clarification of the legislation by the CSJ.
- Delays appointing permanent SPA executive directors, resulted in board members undertaking executive duties, making it subsequently difficult for board members to relinquish this level of engagement and maintain the boundary of 'societal' authority.

The chair's governance review (2016) states:

> The SPA has yet to be seen to be sufficiently separate from Government or to fully establish its role and authority. There is now a more linear relationship . . . This model needs to be more fully understood and followed by all stakeholders to allow the SPA to become more effective and credible in its statutory role.
>
> (p. 10)

As board composition changes and enhanced clarity ensues, lessons can be drawn by reflecting on early board experiences. Adherence to the distinct levels and lines of authority will evidence maturation within the board and the policing system.

Role

Edward Craft, well versed in corporate governance, stated that "boards forget what they are there to do!" (Personal communication, July 21, 2015).

Much theoretical direction offered to public sector boards is derived from private sector experiences. Heald and Steel (2015) offer caution against wholesale acceptance and transferability by highlighting differences within the public sector: multiple principals; the role of the accountable officer; additional horizontal accountability; difficulty in defining success.

Cornforth (2003), provides a summary of the multiple theoretical perspectives in relation to board roles. Two theories predominate: agency theory, focuses on ensuring management compliance; stewardship theory, promotes a partnership approach to improving performance through strategic endeavours.

These theories contain different assumptions, emphases and procedures: 'conformance' through management supervision, monitoring and controls, versus 'performance' through partnership, policy formulation and strategic thinking. (Cornforth & Chambers, 2010).

The functions of the SPA Board explicitly require these simultaneous dual roles. Undertaking these roles in tandem requires a masterful aptitude in divergent areas of capability – a challenge for any board.

The chair indicated that prior to his appointment, the board's focus on 'performance' elements was limited, as "strategic intent was put on the backburner" (Robertson, 2016, p. 3). This was amid controversies around operational issues – resulting in a disproportionate focus on 'conformance' issues.

Despite sustained 'conformance' focus on finances, a deteriorating situation, as per 2016 Audit Scotland and HMICS reports, remains. Financial competence aside, understanding systemic influences and held beliefs or the 'organization in the mind', which may contribute to the ongoing financial challenges, is important.

Hypotheses might include: the police reform business-case lacked accurate initial analyses; policing reform could not be achieved within budget, given constraints of political manifesto promises of constant police numbers and no compulsory redundancies; police reform, a political flagship policy, cannot be allowed to fail, consequently budget deficits will be covered; if containment of civil unrest is a core function of policing, additional funding will always be found.

Strategic focus – lacking historically – is underway with the 2026 police strategy. The board should be mindful that " the maintenance of openness, proactiveness, and a focus on joint value creation are important antecedents of the board's contribution to the strategic decision-making process" (Pugliese et al., 2009, p. 310).

As the board matures and revised governance practices are implemented, an improved balance in board roles between 'conformance' and 'performance' should result.

Group dynamics

Board success in 'conformance' and 'performance' roles is dependent on individual and collective knowledge, skills, attitudes and behaviours inherent within the membership. Awareness of the dynamic interplay between these capabilities and a wider appreciation of the components underpinning group relations are often areas for development. The author offers a model (Figure 18.2), which is simple in design and provides a means of exploring what is, should and should not be occurring in group interactions.

Content, process and relationships, constitute a readily-recallable acronym (CPR). Impedance in any of these elements affects progression towards task completion with less than optimum impact. Spirit "has the potentiality to contain that which has yet to be brought into being . . . a container for a new idea . . . It is a function of the connectedness of the people who are there, why they are there, and the primary task" (Bain & Bain, 2002, pp. 3–4).

'Team spirit', a familiar term in sport, appears rarely in relation to 'group spirit' or 'board spirit'. Creative strategic planning, foresight and optimal impact,

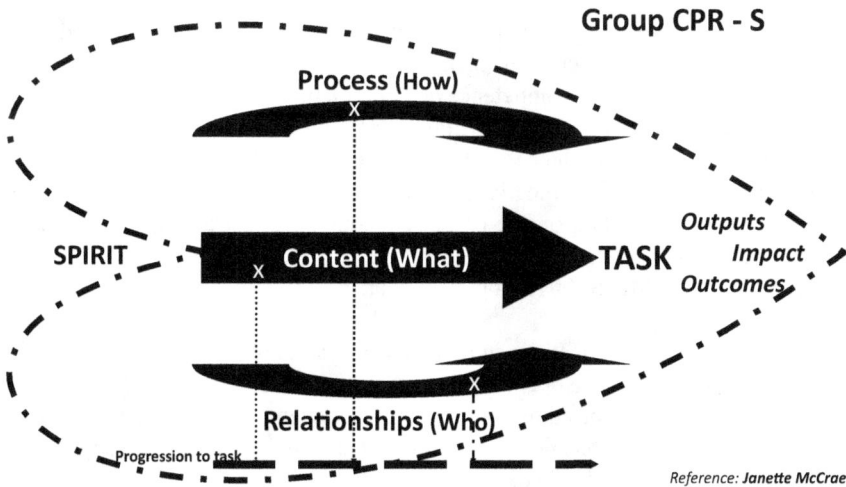

Figure 18.2 Elements of group dynamics

generated collaboratively by a group, can only manifest when group spirit is present.

Creative partnership working (a key board responsibility), is predicated on the harmonious interaction of these elements within each partnership group – maximizing the potential for significant congruence between partners.

Content

Poor transparency and lack of rigour in PSoS documentation submitted to the board is noted in the chair's governance review. Sonnenfeld (2002) states that:

> destructive and dangerous pattern(s) happens all the time . . . a phone-book sized report . . . with important information . . . buried in a thicket of sub-clauses and footnotes . . . it is impossible for a board to monitor performance and oversee a company if complete, timely information isn't available to the board.
>
> (p. 5)

Dick (1991) reminds us that "information not heard or not understood is of little use in decision making" (p 21). He offers the FIDO model (feelings, information, decision, outcomes), which highlights that information shared is often underpinned by undisclosed feelings arising from beliefs, relationship history or solely from the present situation. Unacknowledged, this distorts the information and subsequent decision-making processes.

Process

Process varies, depending on context, participants and audience. SPA board public meetings are formally chaired, agenda-led, highly choreographed, and do little to enhance perceptions of competence and confidence in board members.

Committee contributions to decision-making processes are addressed in the governance review. The chair views committees as undertaking assessments of issues and making recommendations to the board for final decisions – not making decisions that are binding on the board. He concludes that committee meetings should be held in private.

However, the HMICS (2016) indicated that:

> to hold committee meetings in private seems at odds with the SPA's commitment that it should be open and transparent and operate to the highest standards of public sector administration and management. . . . I would question the benefit of their business being conducted solely in private and supporting papers not being published.
>
> (p. 5)

Relationships

Media headlines, such as "*Scottish Police Authority board 'fractured'* " (Scottish Legal News, 2015), have reported the ebb and flow of board relationships over time.

The chair's governance review stated that the SPA "*has to govern essentially through its relationships and influence rather than having a direct ability to instruct*" (p. 16).

Quality relationships, founded on shared values, are essential for collaboration, cohesion and effectiveness. Sher (2015) states that a board should be a "steward for the primary purpose and values of the organization" (p. 191) and further comments that "Encouraging the board to commit to a consistent set of values, can be a potent way to encourage a board to work around social pressures and norms" (p. 6).

The SPA and the PSoS have publicly stated values with 'respect' and 'integrity' common to both. Disappointingly, the initial opinion survey revealed that only 19% of police officers and 26% of staff believed that senior management's behaviours are consistent with the SPA/PSoS values. Congruence between organizational leaders' behaviours and stated values is critical.

Trust is paramount in ensuring quality relationships, be they personal or organizational. Trust is personal, requires vulnerability and manifests as a bond of interdependence. In relation to boards, "developing and maintaining trust is a goal in its own right" (Sher, 2015, p. 6).

Sonnenfeld (2002) places trust at the centre of a virtuous cycle of respect, trust and candour – a feature of an effective team and a successful board. Maintaining this virtuous cycle, generates "bonds among board members that are strong enough to withstand clashing viewpoints and challenging questions" (p. 6).

The chair is key in fostering trust and nurturing appropriate and effective challenge. Board members need to:

> express themselves with confidence and without feelings of inadequacy or rivalry interrupting the flow. The Chair must encourage attention and listening with respect, appreciation and encouragement of other's ideas and allowing sufficient emotional release to restore rational thought and finally incisive and purposeful questions

> (Sher, 2015, p. 5)

Trusted leaders, according to Hope-Hailey et al. (2012), demonstrate ability, benevolence, integrity (encompassing fairness and honesty) and predictability of behaviour over time. Taking stock of the level of trust in board relationships, internal and external, would be highly informative.

Spirit

Board spirit cannot manifest where weaknesses exist in content, process or relationships. Historical constraints need to be acknowledged and improved. Achieving and maintaining Board spirit is an on-going aspiration for all boards.

Leadership

Widely reported power struggles arose between the various leaders and respective organizations in the early stages of police reform. In response to this turbulent beginning, Audit Scotland (2013) stated: "Considerable work is now required by the SPA board, the SPA senior management team, Police Scotland and the Scottish Government to build mutual confidence, trust and respect" (p. 17).

As Sher (2013) indicates:

> Power is personal and has little to do with authority. If personal power is exercised in a punitive, dictatorial or rigid manner, it provokes either submission or conformity . . . or rage, rebellion and sabotage, in which case the system becomes unstable and moves towards disintegration . . . destructive of creativity

> (p. 189)

The early dynamics displayed by the SPA, board and the PSoS were akin to Bion's fight-flight basic assumption group where action is essential, casualties are to be expected, and self-reflection or self-knowledge is considered nonsense (Rioch, 1970). Casualties were experienced – organizational values, employee goodwill and effectiveness.

By the time the new chair and chief constable were appointed, a system-wide expectation of 'salvation', as opposed to an intent for 'revelation' in order to address the underlying debilitating causes, was apparent. An air of 'If only X, then all will be well!' (where 'X' equals a new chair, a new chief constable, a new governance structure or a balanced budget) pervaded the system.

This linear thinking falls far short of a mature understanding of complex systemic issues. Herington and Colvin (2016) indicate, "Because complexity is multidimensional and is characterized by ambiguity, as complexity increases so the chances of any one person having all the answers – or even being able to make sense of the problem – decreases" (p. 2).

During this leadership transition, both the SPA board and the PSoS executive appeared to be paralleling Bion's dependency basic assumption group – where security is sought from an omnipotent, omniscient leader (Rioch, 1970).

Messianic salvation is not within the gift of either the chair or chief constable. However, each may contribute a distinctive, transformational leadership style.

Conclusion

Only time will attest as to whether the new chair and chief constable exemplify leadership which is conducive to genuine, transformational police reform. In congruence with the board, they will need to demonstrate the capability to uncover and address complex systemic flaws, the creativity to employ a range of insightful approaches and quality improvement strategies, and the vision to engage and re-energize the policing system.

Governance is about values and relationships coupled with personal and collective responsibility. Edward Craft (personal communication, July 21, 2015) stressed that, 'Good governance is not about documents, it is about behaviours'. Governance won't deal with a lack of trust.

All boards face challenges. Progression towards maturity and effectiveness demands honest reflection, commitment to values and a collective, creative vision.

19 The Caspian Sea housing company

The role of board member in a two-family business

Thomas Brull

The conflict

The CEO voiced strong dissatisfaction with the board:

> "They are always asking for new reports without analyzing the present ones"
> "The board does not contribute"
> "They don't understand the business"
> "They meet without me and give me 'dry' orders"
> "The board does not care about strategic issues and concentrates on topics that are the responsibility of the management team"

These complaints have been made known to the families and to this author in separate meetings, following difficult conversations with members of the board. The complaints were made to me in the presence of the chairman-owner. He listened, without replying.

The context

The Caspian Sea Housing Company is a real estate company in the business of developing social housing under a government programme directed to reduce the housing deficit in an eastern European country. Caspian Sea Housing is owned by two families, and managed by a professional team. The company is in a growth phase. The CEO and his professional team of executive directors, who are aligned with him, have been in post for several years.

Two years ago the company received a capital injection from an international cash-rich sovereign fund, representing a minority stake in the business but changing important governance issues, giving itself veto powers relating to investments and loan decisions and creating a new board with seven members: five chosen by the two families who still hold more than 70% of the controlling shares, one independent and one Brazilian representative of the overseas fund. Of the five members representing the two families, three are new and chosen by the families, and two – the CEO and myself – were already members of the former board that existed before the funders joined the company. At that time the board comprised only the executive directors and myself. There were no external members.

This group of five, representing the two families on the board, met monthly with other family members in a meeting named the Previous Board Meeting, with the declared objective of aligning and preparing its representative members for the official board meeting. It is in this environment that the afore-mentioned conflict arose.

Before the fund's capital injection, the CEO complained of excessive interference by the two families and their limited competence. The company had a negative image in the market and many on the board thought that the dynamic of a new shareholder and new members on the board would provide a solution to this problem. Complaints about the two families were known to the top executives, who sympathized with the CEO.

After the founders retired, many years ago, each founding family chose two members who follow the business very closely. I began working for the holding company three years ago. In addition to Caspian Housing, the families had other businesses, all of which were in difficulty. In 2008, the group almost became bankrupt. Although the group survived, the business units are still fragile and in a dangerous position. The housing business is the only successful one and it sustains the families and these other businesses, mainly from its high dividends. In fact, the group has become a burden to the housing company, because it has to distribute its total profits as dividends and because it must devote its resources and talents to help the other family businesses.

A relevant recent development: excellent business opportunities became available recently since competitors are cash-strapped and are willing to sell assets that are synergetic with Caspian Sea's strategy. To buy these assets, the company would have to reduce the current level of distribution of dividends and increase its capital base. Management sees the existing minority shareholder as the solution: it can inject more capital in the company and buy some of the shares from the families that could help support their other fragile businesses. There is a stalled negotiation in progress about a claim by the fund on excessive dividend distribution.

The families are hesitant about this big leap because as controlling shareholders, they do not wish to be diluted. Whereas in a classical conflict between owners and managers, the professional management of the company wants to do business and grow as much as possible. A larger company would also mean that the families would have less influence and management would be less constrained in their decisions.

The governance structure – basic organs

The family council focuses on the education of the third generation (now aged between 20 and 30 years), and where major problems should be resolved. In fact, in the case of relevant decisions, the families work in their individual family meetings and then the representatives of each family try to come to a consensus, with excruciating difficulties.

> The board of directors comprises seven members, besides the five representatives of the controlling family members and the fund representative, plus one independent member. This board meets quarterly.
>
> The 'previous board meeting' comprises five representatives of the families at the board and four representatives of the two families. It meets monthly.

Formal committees exist comprising board members, executive directors and outsider experts (finance, business development, human resources, regulation). There are also monthly informal groups created by the families covering the following areas: finance, taxation and auditing matters in order to maintain control of the business.

Real management

Critical issues are debated in the previous board meetings, formal committees, the above-mentioned informal groups and also informal meetings between the families, and the families with the CEO. The fund gains control via the membership of the finance committee and a monthly performance review with the CEO and the CFO. Consequently, the official board meeting has little to discuss.

The previous board meeting has existed for about a year, since the entry of the fund and it has become the main board.

The four family members meet almost every day in their family office but they are not able to handle important conflicts and they do not have an approved conflict-resolution document. Some important conflicts are: they do not agree what business to keep and what to sell; they have different perceptions about the solutions they need, and they do not have a common view about their risk appetite for growth.

Hypotheses

The conflict reflects a clear combination of anxieties and consequent unconscious defences together with poor structure design.

The main anxiety is related to the owners' fear of losing control of the business. Being second generation, they received a healthy and booming business from their fathers and they almost bankrupted it a few years later. It is possible that this recent episode is the reason for their difficulty in taking decisions. An important psychological reason for this could be that the two families, although enjoying good relations on the surface, are antagonistic and rivalrous towards each other. Indeed, the two founding widows told me that the most important thing for them is to keep intra and inter-family harmony.

Could it be that by not reaching a decision, they are keeping the business from growing in order to prevent any major bankruptcy risk? Is it possible that non-decision making is an unconscious way of preserving harmony?

Also, the present CEO led the successful recovery of the business and was key to the fund's decision to acquire a minority stake in the company. That also may have created envy. This is realized through constant attacks on the CEO and the stalling of decision -making. 'In professional settings, the envious attack may take the form of a debate about general principles, or technical issues or technique, and is presented as if it were in the pursuit of progress, if not ultimate truth' (Obholzer, 1994b, p. 44). Obholzer comments that these attacks not only gratify unconscious wishes, but also prevents the pursuit of the primary task (Obholzer, 1994b, p. 44); this is precisely the way the CEO perceives events.

The CEO's narcissistic traits may add to the envy and confusion on the family's' side. According to Kets de Vries (2006, p. 24), a certain degree of narcissistic behaviours is required for leadership success. There are strong narcissistic features in our CEO; particularly his dislike of being challenged or his low tolerance of negative feedback. As a typical defence mechanism pointed out by Kets de Vries (no date available), he is prone to splitting by claiming that the owners are "bad", his management team is "good", the minority shareholders are "good", and the five representatives of the families are "bad".

These psychological aspects led to the creation of a dysfunctional structure, in particular, the previous board meeting. Once the fund came in as a minority shareholder, new governance changes were introduced, e.g., the creation of the board of directors as described before. Thus, it was a logical step to create the previous board meeting as a tool to align the decisions to be made in the board. The idea came from the CEO and his hidden objective (as he told me) was to defend himself and the company from the owners. The agenda in these previous board meetings was quite extensive covering many relevant topics even if they were not to be discussed at the next official meeting of the full board. Also, these official full board meetings were held every three months, whereas the previous board meetings were held monthly.

The owners liked the idea and their objective was to use the previous board meetings, not to align the topics but as a way to express their demands and attempt to keep control of the CEO. It is also quite comforting as it serves as splitting and projection mechanisms, as described: "The painful conflict between love and hate for the mother, for instance, can be relieved by splitting the mother image into a good fairy and a bad witch. Projection often accompanies splitting and involves locating feelings in others" (Halton, 1994, p. 13).

In this case, the previous board meetings lead on the 'bad', by criticizing the CEO, asking difficult questions, changing decisions, while the owners, individually and collectively, lead on the good, often taking the side of the CEO outside the meetings!

In brief, the previous board meetings, formally created to align decisions before board meetings, became a battleground where the owners tried to impose their will and control their envy and anxiety. The CEO, on the other hand, is frustrated because the previous board meetings, instead of protecting him from the owners, became another source of attack and he finds himself defending himself and the company.

With a formal task and two hidden tasks, the new members of the previous board meetings felt confused about what they should do and decide.

I felt the same confusion when I first joined the organization. It began at the very first selection interview I had with them. Then we agreed what needed to be done, but once I joined, the task became blurred, neither the family nor the CEO knew what they wanted.

At that time, I suppressed my feelings, but after the Tavistock experience I learned to take my feelings seriously, and use them as a diagnostic tool. It is a product of the psychoanalytic concept of countertransference: "The state of mind in which other people's feelings are experienced as one's own" (Halton, 1994, p. 17).

Confusion is a characteristic of this company and is a consequence of old and new conflicts already described.

As a result, an anti-task organizational design was developed. As stated by Stapley (2006, p. 277), "that the way things are done around here is not appropriate to the performance of the primary task". By this design the board is not the centre of the governance structure, but the previous board meetings, which do not have a clear primary task, are used to hide the real intentions of the family-owners and the CEO.

Thus, new members of the previous board meeting felt confused too. Being hired by the owners, I observed that we became a type of basic assumption fight-flight group as defined:

> In the fight-flight state, a leader of the group with a valency to fight or flight leads the group into a collusive functioning that seeks to present itself by fighting someone or something . . . The fight leader may lead the group in an attack on senior management.
>
> (Stapley, 2006, p. 210)

In our case this is predominantly done by two members in alternate positions against the CEO. Interestingly, the CEO has presented to the owners one of the RPC members as the trouble-making figure. It is clear to me that this member is a spokesperson for the group. The group anxiety is caused not only by the general confusion described above but also because they see the CEO's explanations as not clear enough and holding insufficient data. It is the battle between the narcissistic CEO refusing to submit and a board that doesn't trust him and feels confused by the owner's expectations. I am afraid the two families will see the problem as something individual and not address the systemic and psychological issues present in the situation. As perfectly described:

> The difference in the two approaches [individual or institutional] to the situation is of major consequence. To treat it as one person's misbehaviour allows everyone else to continue disowning and projecting aspects of themselves into the targeted individual and the process will continue unabated, to the cost of both the individual and the institution.
>
> (Obholzer & Roberts, 1994a, p. 133)

I can even sense some retreat from the member as he becomes less active during the debates and even stays mute for long periods, a pattern related to subjective boundaries. As Hirschhorn (1988, p. 33) says, "In retreating from a task boundary and creating an imaginary world, people are frequently retreating from the imagined consequences of either injuring another or being injured in turn."

The future

We, the five representatives of the families are focusing on how to solve the decision-making issue and redesigning the structure in order to define the board meeting as central to the governance structure and no more to the previous board meeting.

I believe we have three basic issues to resolve:

- The owner's inability to decide – this is a very difficult obstacle and I think it requires a special coach.
- The animosity between the members of the previous board meeting and the CEO which I think we can solve through evaluation meetings and maybe coaching with the CEO. As beautifully stated, questions boards have to address: their ability to explore in depth the internal workings of the board and the areas they find particularly challenging, building trust and finding a common purpose (Kelleher et al., 2003).
- The redesign where the board takes the protagonist role, already offered to the owners by us, their board representatives.

My feelings

In the beginning of the new governance structure, when the three outsiders came in I felt insecure and less valued, maybe because of a sense of failure, since there was a need to bring new people in.

As I understood better what was happening, I tried a more active role by meeting the new members and attempting to be in contact with each other outside the boardroom. As I felt more confident I also used the Tavistock course as an excuse to begin a more personal contact with the CEO and now we meet for breakfast once a month. While this gives me new insights and understanding of board dynamics, it enables the CEO to test his feelings and ideas. I have to take care to not disclose inside information of the board and also not to be co-opted by him.

I feel like being inside a laboratory. I am happy and hope to be part of the solution. I also feel more confident. It has been a privilege to take the course and have this true and live experience at the same time, which is continuing.

20 Corruption, leader narcissism and the dynamics of board governance

The case of Marks & Spencer, 1999–2000

Anand Narasimhan

Narcissism

Narcissism is a form of self-regard that is understood to engender both upsides and downsides in interpersonal interaction. Upsides of the trait include positive self-appraisal that can lead to creativity and humour in social situations (Kohut, 1966; Kets de Vries & Miller, 1985). Downsides include grandiose behaviours and a pathologically excessive need for recognition from others (Kernberg, 1967; Rosenthal & Pittinksy, 2006). The literature on organizational leadership does acknowledge the impact of both aspects of narcissism (Maccoby, 2000).

This chapter makes two significant contributions. The first contribution is a 'group-as-a-whole' conceptualization of narcissism (Bion, 1961). I submit that narcissism is usefully presented as more of a sociological enactment, that is, as a 'valence' that is expressed as a consequence of collective psychodynamics of the leader-follower relationship, and less of a trait, that is, a consistent individual disposition that is unvarying across situations.

The second contribution is to provide a multi-level perspective on the psychodynamics of corporate governance failures. The extant literature on corporate governance failure from a psychodynamic perspective has focused on explanations centred on corruption of the individual narcissistic leader (Stein, 2013) or to an enchantment of an amorphous collective of leaders (Tuckett & Taffler, 2008). This author submits that corporations are organizationally sophisticated: to guard against the leadership risk owing to individuals, there are mechanisms of governance in the form of executive leadership teams and boards of directors (Garratt, 1996).

How, then, does governance failure occur? In this chapter, I provide an empirical study of the enactment of narcissism, as a form of psychodynamic corruption that engenders corporate governance failure.

Approach taken

One key problem in the empirical study of board dynamics is the lack of reliable data. Board meetings and top teams are not easily observable for research purposes, and therefore data on behavioural dynamics in such contexts is hard to come by. To make up for this omission, researchers often take an "upper echelons" view to count the countable indirectly in order to theorize dynamics (e.g., Hambrick & Mason, 1984; Peterson et al., 2003). Whilst such theorizing is useful, the empirical basis on which conclusions are drawn are contestable (Hollenbeck et al., 2006).

I adopt a novel approach to get closer to the analysis of governance dynamics – the use of data from a retrospective television documentary that incorporates multiple sources of recounting organizational events from different perspectives. The corpus of data that I have used in this study comes from an episode of the *Money Programme* broadcast on BBC2 on 1 November, 2000. The half-hour programme, entitled "Sparks at Marks" looks into causes of the then recent and surprising decline of the UK-listed company Marks & Spencer PLC.

The context of this study is the end of Richard Greenbury's reign as chairman and CEO of Marks & Spencer in 1999–2000. Greenbury had enjoyed a five-year run of success from 1993 until 1998: turnover was up 39% (from 5950 million to 8243 million GBP), profits up 59% (from 736 to 1168 million GBP), earnings per share up 62% (from 18 to 29 p a share), and dividends up 77% (from 8.1 to 14.3 p a share). Then, without much warning, profits plunged by 44% to 512 million GBP in 1999, and in 2000, Richard Greenbury departed from the company.

These years were extremely turbulent for the M&S board. In 1998, at the peak of Richard Greenbury's financial performance, the board was 22 strong, comprising 16 executive directors and 6 non-executives. After Greenbury's departure from the board in 2000, the board had been slimmed down to 11, with 4 executive directors and 7 non-executives. A net of 23 directors departed between 1998 and 2001, and in these years Marks & Spencer was often portrayed by the media as a 'basket case' in corporate governance (Bevan, 2000).

The *Money Programme* documentary is a unique source, in that it paints a picture of how Richard Greenbury led the board and the company, based on unusually candid interviews of Greenbury himself and those who worked for him. Hearing both sides – the leader and the followers – allows us to make some conjectures about the dynamics of situations across different levels of the organization, allowing us to make psychodynamic inferences, which are typically lacking in governance scandals, because one or the other party in the leader-follower relationship is bound to confidentiality and non-disclosure agreements.

Methods of analysis

In this study I analyze three incidents from the documentary that present the points of view of both Richard Greenbury and one or more of his former subordinates. The analysis aims to uncover the behaviour of Greenbury, the board, and his executive team members in these three situations; thereby allowing us to draw some conclusions about the collective dynamics that can be seen as contributing to evolving trajectory towards the failure of governance. The three incidents were picked to illustrate the collusion required to invoke the tendency for narcissism in the individual leader at varying levels of the organization.

I compiled the complete transcript of the three incidents that reveal the impact of a leader's narcissistic behaviour enactment at three levels: board, executive team and company followers at large. I used multimodal lexical analysis (Machin & Mayr, 2012) to code each unit of the transcript for evidence of narcissistic behaviour that could be attributed to Richard Greenbury, based on information revealed in the interviews. A unit of text is a sequence of words conveying a coherent point that incorporates visual cues visible on the television documentary to the viewer (Weber, 1990). Codes were assigned based on positive and negative trait markers of a leader's narcissistic behaviour.

In assigning codes, I made a distinction between attributions made to the leader in this situation, i.e., coding of words spoken by his subordinates versus the coding of Greenbury's own words. This distinction in the analysis allowed us to construct separate images of narcissistic behaviour – those projected onto Greenbury by his followers versus those projected outward by Greenbury. The author then used the empirically observed codes to iterate back to the tripartite theoretical framework, in order to make a grounded psychodynamic interpretation of the corruption of corporate governance, at the three levels of analysis.

Empirical findings and psychodynamic interpretations

Incident 1 – board level: children's clothing

The first incident concerns the restriction of children's clothes in the stores. It appears that after the company reported record profits of more than 1 billion GBP in 1997, Richard Greenbury focused on stocking the stores with high-margin items and correspondingly removing items that delivered lower margin regardless of their value to the customer. Many of Greenbury's more distant subordinates were of the view that indiscriminate reduction in the range of children's clothing, a low margin item, would hurt the economic performance of the company because such clothing served as 'loss leaders' – mothers that walked into the store attracted by the offer of low prices for children's clothing went on to buy higher margin items such as baby-food. However, when his subordinates wanted to put this point across to him, they were blocked from doing so by more immediate sycophants that feared Greenbury's wrath for daring to disagree with his directive.

Narcissism enactment data (board level): Coding of the transcript revealed that M&S employees seem to have experienced the board chair's behaviour comprising the following trait markers: *inflexibility, omnipotence, tolerates only sycophants, enraged by criticism,* and *vengefulness*. The board seems to have set a target of continuing billion-pound profitability through higher operating margins and this directive informed what could and could not be stocked in the store, despite the best local knowledge of the appropriate pattern of merchandising. When the interviewer revealed the claim of this pattern of board behaviour emerging from the views of his employees, Greenbury projected the following markers: *anger, lack of empathy, coldness, contempt, use of scapegoats,* and *hypersensitivity*. As chair, he is complicit in leading a board that fails to create psychological safety required for good governance (Nembhard & Edmondson, 2006).

Psychodynamic interpretation of board-level corruption: Marks & Spencer made a profit of over 1 billion GBP in 1997, and followed it up with higher profits in 1998. Given the ambition of its narcissistic chair, the board moves to a position of expecting more profit in the following year. This dynamic on the part of the board contributes to the enactment of both the devouring boss whose desire for ever-increasing surplus is impossible to satisfy (Cremin, 2009) and the bounty hunter that seeks exclusive and limitless access to the source of what is good (Levine, 2005). This incident is extremely revealing of the tendency toward greed on the part of the board of directors – the enchantment of the goose that lays golden eggs (Bettelheim, 1976). Fed on repeated helpings of extraordinary surplus, the board of directors make a corrupted movement from the reality principle to the pleasure principle (Tuckett & Taffler, 2008).

A board inhabiting the reality principle is one that incorporates the characteristics of a Kleinian depressive state (Halton, 1994). In this state, there is acknowledgement and tolerance of anxiety, uncertainty, ambivalence, imperfection, and conflict. As the analysis of the first incident reveals, the movement to the pleasure principle is accompanied by the need for perfection, defences against the attainment of desire and the suppression of conflict. This creates a pathological dynamic between the board and the company – the narcissistic leader of the board is increasingly enchanted by impossible achievements and the followers are put in a bind in which they are supressed from revealing that the goose no longer lays golden eggs. The board then shows a hatred of the knowledge that the impossible cannot be achieved (Bion, 1961). When the fallout occurs, it proves to be catastrophic: it would take Marks & Spencer over a decade to return to the billion GBP-profitability mark.

Incident 2 – executive team level: wearable fashion

The second incident concerns the extent to which Greenbury's executive team members showed him the entire range of fabric purchased ahead of a season. The executive subordinates showed concern that M&S was increasingly being conservative in its offer of colour and style, and as a result, was lagging behind its competitors. Greenbury was known to have conservative tastes, and so the buying team of his executive subordinates coped by showing him only a limited range of what was bought that corresponded to his tastes rather a more representative sample of their purchases.

Narcissism enactment data (executive team level): In this incident, executive team members paint a picture of a narcissistic leader that has *a sense of omniscience, consults no one, is a poor listener*, and *tolerates only sycophants*. When Greenbury is informed by the interviewer of this ruse, he responds with *anger* and *contempt*, and reveals that his behaviour as a leader might have comprised both *a sense of entitlement* as well as *feelings of inferiority*.

Psychodynamic interpretation of executive team-level corruption: The psychodynamic view of groups theorizes two levels of activity: one at the 'work group' level that is rational and conscious, and another at a deeper level of 'basic assumptions' that is dominated by emotions and is mostly unconscious (Bion, 1961; Foulkes & Anthony, 1957).

What we find in the case of Marks & Spencer based on this incident is evidence of the stark transmutation of the executive team from a 'rational' work group (that ought to be focused on the duty of care and openness in critical thinking) to a basic assumption dependency group (that is concerned with feeling safe and stops thinking critically). There is collusive enactment between the narcissistic leader and the executive team in moving towards an unconscious state of dependency. When the 'bubble bursts' so to speak, the leader disavows any knowledge of dependency in which he himself was complicit in engendering and then engages in a "hostile turning away from internal objects" (Sher, 2013, p. 170).

Incident 3 – company followers' level: 'Potemkin Village' staffing

The third incident in the BBC Marks and Sparks documentary that provides 'both sides of the picture' data, concerns the desired staffing levels at the stores in 1999. Richard Greenbury issued a directive that the staffing levels should be kept lean at the reduced level deployed during the economic recession of 1998. At the same time, he ordered stores to provide excellent customer services to shoppers through the presence of staff on hand. These two orders were contradictory. Greenbury's followers responded by keeping staffing levels lean and boosting levels temporarily in the area that he was known to visit at any given time.

Greenbury prided himself on being close to the customer through his store visits; he claimed to have spent two days a week visiting stores. The schedule of his store visits was known in advance and so it was easy for his followers to enact a 'Potemkin village' ruse to dissemble on the level of staffing when he was visiting the area.

Narcissism enactment data: Coding revealed that followers expressed being subject to *inflexibility, ignoring of their needs, grandiosity, their leaders' insatiable need for recognition*, and *his tolerance for sycophants*. Followers are caught between a rock and hard place, and they are forced to engage in duplicity that has nothing to do with the work task as such. Greenbury seems to have been consciously unaware of his followers' 'Potemkin village' ruse until this was revealed to him by the *Money Programme* interviewer. He seemed to acknowledge his *grandiosity*, while being *paranoid* and *contemptuous of others* as he looked to *scapegoat others*.

Psychodynamic interpretation of company-follower level corruption: This incident clearly revealed the movement of the leader as the constructive narcissist (one that is mindful of other people's needs), into the reactive narcissist (dominated by feelings of omnipotence, delusion and hypocrisy) in relation to his followers. The continued encouragement of narcissism in their leader eventually created a perverse set of expectations for followers that was impossible to sustain. Although Greenbury was, at a conscious level, surprised at the 'Potemkin village' ruse, at an unconscious level, he was complicit in setting it up as a game to be played between his followers and himself (Berne, 1964). Narcissistic corruption includes the effort to mask unacceptable realities (Levine, 2005). When the spell is broken, the reactive aspects of narcissism completely overwhelms the constructive aspects (Sher, 2013; Stein, 2013). The corruption is complete and then the divide between the 'disavowed' leader and his 'perfidious' followers cannot be bridged.

Conclusion

The key contribution of this chapter is to demonstrate a comprehensive, empirically-grounded psychodynamic model of the narcissistic corruption of corporate governance. I argue that it is useful to view narcissism as a valence or tendency rather than a trait. Furthermore, for a large and complex organization to unravel, it takes more than a mere trait of narcissism on the part of the leader. I concur with Sher (2013, p. 173) in viewing the phenomenon as 'gathering up of individual intrapsychic dynamics and linking them to one person, where they are coordinated' with the one person being the leader given to narcissistic tendencies. From this perspective then, narcissistic leaders are simply embodying the tendencies for narcissism immanent in an organization.

What of the governance antidote then? Data from the corporate governance failure that surfaced at Marks & Spencer in 1999–2000 suggests that narcissism has fractal properties. The phenomenon is not merely centred on a singular leader, but is a collusive enactment occurring at several levels of the organization simultaneously: at the board level (from the reality principle to the pleasure principle), at the executive team level (from work group to basic assumption dependency group), and at the individual leader level (from constructive to reactive narcissism). Therefore, merely decoupling from a leader labelled as a narcissist may not be enough. What needs to be checked is the entire complex organization's tendency toward narcissistic corruption.

21 The Finnish tango

A study of boards in north eastern Europe

Anja Salmi

Theory, methods and materials

In Finland today, the patterns of inter-subjective narrative themes contain processes that organize the experiences of being together (Stacey, 2001, p. 235). The narrative defences neutralize the underlining anxieties. Frequent small changes made incrementally may accumulate into rapid radical strategic innovations (Anderson, 1999, p. 224). This process of evolution may turn into stagnation or fragmentation due to the usage of paranoid or manic social defences in the face of anxiety. Change therefore involves restructuring the social defence system. It implies freeing the underlying anxieties into the system until new defences are developed (Jaques, 1955).

Klein (1975) introduced the concept of human defence system as two states of the infant mind: the paranoid-schizoid position and the depressive position. Institutions may also be understood in terms of these two basic processes that operate at a most primitive level, writes Bion (1980). He continues: "All change is felt as catastrophic even when it is rationally recognized for the better and more threatening when the social institution has greater underlying anxieties". Menzies Lyth (1982) recognized derivatives from the psychoanalytic method in work with institutions and explains how this illuminates our understanding of their content and dynamics.

Two boards

This chapter assumes that the boards of two institutions – the Voluntary Association and the Government of Finland – are used by their members to reinforce the defensive mechanisms that are associated with paranoid anxiety and guilt. The defence mechanisms of individuals (Jaques, 1955, p. 425) against paranoid and depressive anxiety meet up with the defence mechanisms of the institutions of which they are members. Projective and introjective mechanisms of individuals are processes for creating interdependent relationships; similar processes apply in forming relationships between neighbouring countries. For Finland, these processes have been hugely influential in the social field (Emery, 1974) of north eastern Europe.

Defence mechanisms

Melanie Klein's work on social defence mechanisms, which was further developed by Jaques (1955; Kernberg, 1994), offers specific tools to understand complex adaptive systems through the use of defences. Defences against *paranoid anxiety* involve projecting internal bad objects and impulses onto particular members of an institution who *introject* them, either by *absorbing* or *deflecting* them (Jaques, 1953, p. 426).

Defences that are characteristic of the *depressive position* are called *manic defences*. Their important feature is *denial* of psychic pain, which is accompanied by attempts at *omnipotent control* in order to avoid feelings of persecution. *Omnipotence* is followed by *idealization* (of the good part of the original whole object) and *splitting*, together with *projective identification*. The manic defence system may *regress into the paranoid position* intensifying the fear of persecution and increasing omnipotence. The recognition of both the good and bad aspects of the object creates anxiety of losing the good object through *sadistic attacks* on the bad aspects of the object (Jaques, 1953).

Starting conditions

Finland was given independence in 1917 by Lenin as a sign of friendship. The country had been part of the Kingdom of Sweden until 1809 and thereafter it became part of Tsarist Russia. The starting conditions of social systems inevitably influence future environmental relations (Emery, 1974, p. 292).

Like Russia, Finland too was split into upper and lower social classes – the Reds and the Whites. It led to a bloody civil war in 1918. After their defeat, many Reds in the Finnish territory fled and migrated to the now 'idealized' Soviet Union, but Stalin ordered them to be executed or transferred to concentration camps. The Finnish territory, Karelia, was surrendered to Russia after World War II, but the area remained a nucleus of Finnish identity. Those Karelian people who refused to be evacuated to Finland were transferred to Siberia. Karelia of today is deserted because the resettlement of Russian people into Karelia failed. The ancient poems collected from this region form the basis of Finnish mythology, the Kalevala (Anon., 2004). After the Second World War Russia forced Finland to pay it war reparations, which established large industries in Russia and paradoxically laid the ground for future Finnish economic success.

Relationship with Baltic countries

The occupation of Baltic countries evoked fear and guilt in Finland. The bilateral Finno-Soviet Treaty, also containing a ban criticizing the Soviet Union, was signed in 1948. During the Cold War, Finland forged relationships with Sweden and the West. The introjected identification with the Soviet Union partly explains Finland abandoning the Baltic countries during their struggle to secede. Finland's identification with the Baltic countries was one of its weaknesses that brought about a new sense of guilt and shame. Omnipotence and denial of interdependency are still palpable in Finland's relationship with the Baltic countries.

Relationship with Russia

Today, Finland's geographical location and its national identity leaves the country alone in the middle of a struggle between the East and the West. The culture, history and interconnectedness that form Finland's identity is the result of primitive defences. The introjected combination of the melancholy of the Slavic soul (from Russia) and the brightness of the Scandinavian mind (from Sweden) are about to re-combine and trade places: Finns will think like the former and feel like the latter.

After the Soviet Union collapsed, laws relating to dual nationality and ownership of land in one another's territories were quickly legislated. Demands were made to change Finland's compulsory second language from Swedish to Russian. After the Crimean crisis, the Russian state required all of its citizens, including Russians with dual nationality in Finland, to support Russia.

During this study, the West was concerned about Finland's 'naivety' because of:

- the President's idea of playing 'two cards' during the Crimean crisis (separate cards for Russia and EU);
- the second Russian gas pipeline in the Baltic Sea is considered as an environmental issue only by the Finns;
- the Finnish president's proposal for the use of transponders in aviation security.

Finland's *fear, guilt, shame* and *gratitude*, coupled together with its introjective identification with Russia, forms elements of its current 'naivety'. These elements can be named as Finland's *gratitude for its independence* which was later cooled by its *fear of Stalin*. The *guilt* felt by allowing Hitler to lead Finland resulted in a *manic omnipotence* of the political slogan of 'opening the route to Asia' and the *shame* that came from failing in this effort. Subsequently, the end of the cold war and collapse of the Soviet Union became a wellspring of joy. Despite Finland's denial of its association with Hitler, it soon became apparent that Russia would not develop into a democracy, thus placing Finland under the influence of another tyrannical regime. The loss of the notion of the 'idealized neighbour' did not sink into the Finnish unconscious, despite Russia's exploitation and despoilment of Karelia.

A case study: June 2016 to December 2016

Sadism

Life next to a feared neighbour led the boards of the Finnish government and the Voluntary Association to rely primarily on defences against paranoid anxiety. *Sadistic impulses* can be denied by attributing the government's aggressiveness to the performance of its duties (Jaques, 1955, p. 426). The Finnish government cut funding for essential services, such as transport and education. Paranoid anxieties towards an outside enemy were rarely expressed. These anxieties towards the outsider Russians were suppressed and instead they were expressed by bullying, sadistic decisions and a 'culture of exclusion' towards the 'enemy within the system' – the Finnish people themselves.

In the case of the Voluntary Association, despite a lack of sufficient numbers of active members, the Association consciously excluded many people from its membership. This heartless behaviour on the part of the board of the Voluntary Association could be seen as a repetitive re-enactment of Finland's cultural isolation. The Association avoided encountering its inability to change direction in the face of its serious decline. At the same time, the board acted out *paranoid defences* by identifying and bullying one particular member, using *projective identification* processes to deal with its feelings of incapability and helplessness.

The boards of both the Government and the Voluntary Association approved exploitative financial measures that were deeply controversial and undermined any sense of national honesty. Both boards defended themselves against discontinuity. To sort out their numerous thefts and frauds would mean facing paranoid anxieties.

Introjective and projective identification

Klein (1945) explains how "object relations are moulded by an interaction between introjection and projection, between internal and external objects and situations". Identification of the ego with an object is identification by introjection. Thus, Jaques (1955, p. 424) notes that soldiers who take their leader for their ego-ideal, are projectively identifying with him.

Finland's *introjective identification* with Russia could be regarded as an interacting mechanism in the geopolitical environment that determined the interdependence between the two countries: the *paranoid defences* seemed to work against the West rather than the East when bad objects and sadistic impulses were positioned by the Government onto the commonly shared external enemy. Similarly, the board of the Voluntary Association referred positively to its former exploiting president.

The Finnish government actively suppressed the occasional paranoid flare-ups in relation to Russia. On a recent occasion a random shooting occurred on the street. In order to stimulate hostility between Finland and Russia, trolls spread rumours that the victims were Russian women. Russian media did not check their information – the victims were actually Finnish women. The result was that many Russians cancelled their trips to Finland.

In another example of mirrored social enactment between the Government and Finnish social institutions, the Western world was investing in renewable energy while the Government of Finland pushed through a political decision to allow the Russian company Rosatom to construct a nuclear power plant on Finnish soil. Construction was started and continues without the necessary security guarantees and licenses being agreed.

Likewise, decisions made by the Voluntary Association seemed to follow a similar pattern – the Association made arrangements with a private company to provide services to the Association's members so that the Association's finances could be circulated through this company. Finland and Russia, as well as the Association and the company, formed two systems but were joined together like Siamese twins. Two heads, two bodies and a joint circulation system prevented both from developing as successful independent entities.

Denial and interdependence

Replicating cultural taboos of not criticizing Russia led to denial combined with omnipotence. Critical political discussions were discouraged and television and radio programmes were shelved. The taboo extended to other controversial subjects, such as Brexit and refugees. Debates were considered 'threats to Finland's future'. Serious concerns were sadistically silenced by criminal charges. However, rebellion rose when the prime minister almost succeeded in preventing public discussion of his financial corruption.

Similarly, the Voluntary Association silenced discussions about its finances by the membership. The chair denied publishing the notes proposing discussions of the Association's primary task. This prevention of discussion created a split atmosphere in the organization where people worked in separate silos so that the meaning of joint membership of one organization was lost. Menzies Lyth (1982, pp. 463–464) suggests that more important than content are the dynamic psycho-social processes that go on in institutions at both conscious and unconscious levels. Of particular significance are the defences developed to deal with anxiety-provoking content and with the difficulties in collaborating to accomplish a common task. These defences appear in the structure of the institution itself and permeate its whole way of functioning.

Omnipotence

The Finnish government used the manic defence of *omnipotence* to oppose and deny its interdependence on the Western world by making decisions in favour of Russia. It was as if important national features of boldness and bravery were being demonstrated by a false sense of courage and arrogance by betraying Finland's commitments and loyalties to the West. Similar patterns of defence against anxiety and guilt were repeated in the Voluntary Association and elsewhere in Finnish society.

In a second case a Finnish right-wing demonstrator murdered a young man outside a railway station in September 2016 (Wikipedia, Helsingin Asema-aukion pahoinpitely). Finns were shocked and demonstrated against racism (Helsingin Sanomat 26.9.2016). After four days, the Prime Minister's response and that of the Minister of Finance was to condemn racism loudly (Helsingin Sanomat 19.9.2016). This delay perhaps reflects Finland's state of helplessness, denial or neglect. The Prime Minister and the Minister of Finance demanded of the right-wing liberal Minister of Foreign Affairs a list of his party members who had right wing fascist connections (Iltalehti 26.9.2016) in order to create 'control over' racist activities among Parliament Members and extending to the whole population (Helsingin Sanomat 26.9.2016). By controlling a small part of the totality, it was believed, control could be extended to cover all.

Racism was condemned, while the increasing levels of violence in Finnish society were left unattended (Helsingin Sanomat 20.9.2016). The murder was committed by a man with a long criminal record. Both the murderer and his victim were white Finnish males. After 10 days, the Prime Minister cancelled the legislation of new laws (Helsingin Sanomat 27.9.2016). Later, the municipal court failed to find any racist elements in the assault.

(Helsingin Sanomat 30.12.2016)

The social defensive pattern was the sense of shock, denial and omnipotence of the power of the law, splitting the arguments into racism and non-racism and the projective identification of ascribing responsibility for the problem into 'right wing liberals'. The unusual part of this episode was the prime minister and the minister of finance demonstrating on the streets, together with the people, making the foreign minister the target for paranoid projection.

Ambivalence

The warning voices of helplessness and fear seldom influenced the government's decisions. For example:

* The Institute of Foreign Policy released a report on the role of Russia and identified ten areas of economic life that Finland ought to be watchful in regard to Russia's intentions.
* The Nobel Laureate issued a statement cautioning against cuts in higher education funding.
* The secret police alerted the government that Russians had recently bought major land areas that were critical to Finland's defence.

These warnings created a sudden cloud of anxiety that was quickly turned into a denial of dependency and helplessness. The role of information war was central for upholding denial and preventing ambivalence. The Russian trolls destabilized reality by blaming the Finns for their 'russophobia'.

Omnipotent control

Similar to the ministers who became involved in anti-racist demonstrations, the chair of the board of the Voluntary Association lost his understanding of his position in unofficial meetings. The board had lost its connection with the members. Any constructive discussion with the membership over the primary task was not possible.

The Government of Finland planned legislation in order to trace memberships in fascist organizations. Similarly, the board of the Voluntary Association concentrated on studying the CVs of applicants for honorific positions. It is as if by badging these titles, the Government hoped to *control* the field and hence the whole country.

Slipping

The Voluntary Association's board did not respect the time boundaries of its meetings or its authorizations. The Association had invited a lecturer to Finland.

The invitation was authorized at the board meeting, but four days later, the authorization was reversed due to accusations of incapability and foot-dragging. This happened after a general post-meeting discussion over email. The Voluntary Association's reversed decision consistently mirrored the Government's behaviour: what is decided one day can be reversed the next. The country's main newspaper, *Helsingin Sanomat*, listed ten central Government's decisions that had been made and later cancelled. All the cancellations were decided in unofficial meetings.

The Government legislated laws that went against the constitution. When this was discovered, the laws had to be reversed. The Councillor of Justice reacted strongly to this pattern and proposed Government's mandatory consultation with the Commission of the Constitution. In a similar vein, the Voluntary Association's decisions were withdrawn via emails that did not reach all members and failed to appear in official documents, thus undermining any legitimacy the decision-makers might have had. Similarly, when insufficient numbers of members were present for voting, the board moved to conducting meetings over the Internet.

Splitting

Bion (1961) explains that understanding the nature of splitting helps to understand group dynamics, the challenges of the group's existence, how it finds security, purpose and hope. Splitting by the Government was considered negative and threatening. There was little understanding of how the processes of national dynamics get shaped by controversies that ought to be integrated rather than disapproved of. In the event, arguing through contrasting positions increased fragmentation and debate was subsequently silenced. The prime minister of a neighbouring country said, in relation to the events in the Finnish parliament that a people could never be ruled by denying discussion. The group process of *splitting* was used by the Finnish government and by the board of the Voluntary Association as a defence against anxiety. Healthy debate had essentially vanished from national and organizational dynamics and its denial has left the country and the members of the Voluntary Association with a feeling of suffocation, which had led to a state of *stagnation*.

Solutions

Throughout its history, Finland has lived, been occupied and survived the turmoil in neighbouring countries. Hard living conditions are reflected in a tune in a minor key that mothers sing in their lullabies to their children, wishing them a safe journey across the river of death. Loss, sorrow and mourning appear in Finnish art and literature. The Finnish tango is a locally composed melancholic music of longing, loneliness and despair. It was played in the 1950s with accordions, by the lakes on midsummer nights. Likewise, the Finnish tango is stiff and slow to dance. Finnish pop music developed in the 1980s on tango's foundations and was echoed in Finnish discotheques until the late 90s.

Mourning

Depressive anxieties, comprising persecution and guilt, may be dealt with by mourning. The feelings of loss, guilt and love are experienced and tolerated by successful restoration and reparation of the lost object. Internal chaos is reduced through social idealizing and manic denial in the mourning ceremony (Jaques, 1953, p. 429).

By increased usage of hypomanic defences, ceremonies of sorrow and mourning have gradually vanished from Finnish society. Failure to mourn provokes feelings of guilt (Jaques, 1953, p. 429). When the young man was murdered outside the railway station in September 2016 the president publically condemned racism but did not express his condolences.

Menzies Lyth (1988, pp. 463–464) writes that the institutional setting reflects the unconscious thoughts and feelings that one needs to understand, as well as the implicit thoughts and feelings that are not being said. This requires recognition of the defences that are making the content unconscious or implicit.

While death is dealt with in hospitals, funerals in Finland have, in many cases, become battlefields for domestic disputes where people are excluded or abstain from attending. The ones left behind increasingly have no place, no culture or no customs to mourn.

Jaques writes that participation in group idealization may alleviate depressive anxiety and reinforce good impulses that have been destroyed by manic denial (Jaques, 1955, p. 428). He continues, "All those associated in the mourning ceremony can further their internal mourning and continue the life-long process of unresolved conflicts". Sher (2013, p. xliv) states, "Psychoanalysis is increasingly illuminating core issues within the social sciences such as the role of loss and mourning". Klein (1957a, p. 194) informs us of the essential role of mourning to all reparation, how omnipotence is decreased by greater confidence and how the depressive position is conquered by mourning and experiencing feelings of gratitude towards the good object.

Conclusions

Finnish national dynamics are based not only on general implementations of large group dynamics (Giraldo, 2012) focusing on trust, hope, continuity and inclusion, they also include identity based historical, socio-anthropological, geopolitical and cultural ways of reacting and reflecting on life phenomena. Identity is formed by projective and introjective identifications to neighbouring countries. These defences in their turn are selected and used by national groups. Ways of coping with anxieties and their defences permeate all systems in the country; they appear in the structures of social institutions and influence their functioning, producing absurd outcomes and stagnation. Manic defences are prominent, identifying the 'enemy outside' as part of national paranoid phantasies. The country cannot hold out with continual praising of its excellence while denying the need to mourn and to face its fear and anxiety.

Complex adaptive systems need continuous reparation and working through of grief and mourning in which the struggle to preserve the good is faced and contained.

22 A view from the top

A CEO's reflections

Paul Duggan

This chapter is organized into six sections:

- The first sets the context and background.
- The second briefly introduces selected theories of group dynamics.
- The third discusses the application of these theories at the group board.
- The fourth discusses their application in the operating companies.
- The fifth focuses on the impact on the group CEO and how he responded to what was a mortal threat, starting with a brief introduction to a set of organizing ideas and human dynamics that offer a framework for understanding how individuals and groups function.
- The sixth draws some broad conclusions, which are intended to be provocative rather than definitive.

Context

The business is a group of five distribution companies of which the author is the chief executive and a significant shareholder. A business partner is also an executive and shareholder in the group and there are two external investors. The investors regard themselves as long-term owners.

The group board has a breadth of experience and comprises five directors: the business partner and the author, one of the investors, a representative of the second investor and an experienced non-executive director. The board works through the subsidiary boards (which the author chairs) and the subsidiary managing directors.

The group can be thought of as a system comprising five significant stakeholder groups:

- customers
- suppliers
- employees
- banks
- shareholders

Sales fell by more than 50% in less than 24 months, as a result of the economic collapse. The businesses have now stabilized and are beginning to recover, although the operating environment remains very fragile. Consequently they are susceptible to external shocks such as the imminence of Brexit and movements in exchange rates.

Selected theories of group dynamics

Psychodynamic

A broad spectrum of interlinked ideas rooted in psychodynamic theories offer reference points from which to explore group dynamics. Freudian thinking is based on the idea that the subject expresses thoughts (which include dreams and fantasy) from which it is possible to identify unconscious conflicts. These conflicts act as catalysts for specific behaviours.

Kleinian thought is rooted in the fundamental assumptions of psychoanalysis. Klein worked directly with children and developed a model of the psyche which proposed two states: the paranoid-schizoid state, which polarizes experiences as all good or all bad and the depressive state in which the good and bad can be seen as different aspects of the same experience.

Bion (1961, p. 98) proposed that groups fall into two categories: the work group (WG), which is concerned with the real task of the group and the basic assumption group (BaG), which is concerned with the emotional state of the group and tends to avoid work on the primary task.

Characteristics of a WG include the capacity to define its task and to structure itself to achieve the task. Membership is voluntary and members operate as individuals. However, an individual's self-interest is aligned to the interests of the group. The group tests its conclusions, learning and adapting to best achieve its goals.

The main characteristics of a BaG are a pre-occupation with the emotions and security of the group and seeking to "meet the unconscious needs of its members by reducing anxiety and internal conflicts" (Stokes, 1994a, p. 19).

Bion (1961) proposed that the behaviour of BaGs are rooted in basic assumptions of the members and he proposed three of these:

- Dependency, where the group task is subordinated to provide for the needs and wishes of the group members;
- Fight-flight, where there is a clear danger or enemy that the group can fight or run from;
- Pairing, where the group believes some unknown future event will rescue the group and this will be achieved by the pairing of group members or between the leader and some external person.

Building on Bion's ideas, theorists have proposed additional BaGs.

Systems approach

Miller and Rice (1967, p. 251) used their experience in research and consultancy to explore work systems. They proposed that every system or team has a primary task that the group or system must perform to survive. They proposed that systems have two orientations (requiring members of the system to operate simultaneously in each): a task system (focused on the primary task) and a sentient system (which relates to the interaction within the system and of the system with its environment). Flowing from this, they argue that every organization and/or group requires three forms: one to control specific task performance, one to ensure commitment to the enterprise and a third to regulate relations between the task and sentient systems.

Increasingly, theories and approaches used to describe complex physical, chemical and biological systems are being found to have relevance in understanding group dynamics. Many of these theories were developed to explain systems such as weather, where patterns emerge driven by interdependent forces of pressure, temperature, humidity and wind speed – all of whose interdependencies are defined by non-linear relationships. These systems can be dynamically stable or unstable, and at the boundaries of these states stability and instability can exist simultaneously. A physical example of this is boundary layer fluid dynamics (fundamental to the study of aerodynamics) where fluidic behaviour is unstable. In this space the dynamic system can be viewed as spontaneous, adaptive and alive. Small variations can have disproportionate impacts, destabilizing the system and creating conditions for the emergence of a new stability. Behavioural scientists see these theories and ideas as applicable to human behaviour, because they share the same characteristics. These theories can be used to model and predict outcomes in human groups operating in changing environments, in groups where there is competition and rivalry, in groups where success (or even survival) requires the group to adapt. These complex adaptive systems are capable of self-organization when operating at the boundary of dynamic stability and dynamic instability. This results in transformative behaviour.

Application at group board

> When the economic downturn hit in earnest in 2008, the group found itself operating at the edge of chaos where there was great instability and the group's very survival was threatened. This demanded adaptive behaviour from the board, the starting point of which was to accept that failure was a real possibility – this reality was the catalyst to adapt.

The prospect of failure represented a new vista for the board. Along with the financial loss, the directors were compelled to consider the consequences of failure on their professional reputations, their relationships with other providers of finance (particularly banks) and their responsibilities to other stakeholders in the business. This unappealing vista struck at their professional core, their sense of self, and resulted in the first instance in a paranoid-schizoid state.

The primary task, which had been generation of profit, was no longer viable and what had been a WG shifted to a BaG. To varying degrees, the three main BaGs were evident:

- Dependency: in this case the directors representing the interests of the investors made it clear that it was the executive director's responsibility to find adaptations that would restore dynamic stability.
- Pairing and fight-or-flight: in the beginning, when there was no obvious way to restore dynamic stability, pairing became evident.

    - The executive directors quickly moved into fight mode, and were supported by the independent non-executive director.
    - The non-executive directors representing the investors were in flight mode, and were supported by the group's bankers.

Dynamic stability was restored when the board moved from a paranoid-schizoid to a depressive state. Directors accepted that there was opportunity as well as threat and recognized this by agreeing to a new primary task. This was in the form of a new definition of what success would look like:

- survival
- increasing market share
- protecting employment (for those who wanted to retain their jobs)

Sacrifices were required from all stakeholders. Shareholders agreed to accept trading losses, suspend dividends and subscribe for additional capital. The group's bankers agreed to significant renegotiation of the group's debt facilities. Employees agreed to make significant concessions in the form of reduced working hours, reduced rates of pay and other benefits (including pensions). Suppliers agreed to increase the support they provided to the group. This allowed the group to confidently engage with the market, at a time when our competitors were in full retreat. It allowed investment in strategies, which secured increases in market share and long-term job security for staff. It ensured their survival.

Implementation in the operating companies

The boards and management teams of the operating companies understood the seriousness of the situation facing the group, and the consequences for them. They understood there had been a systematic change, which had shifted the balance from dynamic stability to dynamic instability. They understood the primary task of making a profit was no longer realistic and what had been WGs were rapidly adapting to BaGs. There was evidence of

- Dependency: abdication of responsibility for their own destiny and an expectation that someone would rescue them;
- Fight or flight: some staff hunkered down for a battle, others volunteered for redundancy and some resigned;

- Throughout the operating, companies' pairings emerged, each with their own independent purpose.

The redefinition of the primary task was cathartic; the operating companies (through their boards and management teams) grasped the new primary task with enthusiasm (despite the personal sacrifice it required) and assumed responsibility to develop plans to achieve the new primary task.

The principal modality used to execute these plans were cross-functional high performance teams (HPT). HPTs comprised various subsidiary directors as well as members of management and staff in the subsidiaries. The teams were constructed to be self-regulating systems, accountable to themselves. The HPTs adopted an Action Learning System approach.

The modality chosen was rooted in ideas and research that the author had carried out for an MBA thesis (Duggan, 1986). The research studied the use of small teams or boards or board subcommittees to enable changes in behaviour required to effect changes in strategy to accelerate company development. Strong correlations between successful outcomes and the presence of key human processes were identified. These processes were derived from the work of Lewin et al. (1939) on group dynamics, White and Lippit (1953) and Bales (1950) on group processes, Bradford and Gibb (1964) on group training and Dalton (1959) on group and interpersonal relations.

These include:

- Agreed group norms;
- Agreed member roles and functions in the context of group building and maintenance and the work of the group (Benne & Sheats, 1948);
- A leadership style tending towards subordinate-centred leadership (Tannenbaum & Schmidt, 1958);
- Effective communication;
- Processes to recognize and manage conflict and tensions;
- A structured approach to problem-solving and decision-making.

The research concluded that the groups who achieved successful outcomes had created the conditions that strongly supported and encouraged group learning and development.

Katzenbach and Smith (2005), in their study of the dynamics of small teams further sharpened these ideas by identifying conditions for effectiveness in groups. They concluded that the following characteristics were necessary, all of which were present in the HPTs:

- A small number of people – more than four, but less than ten;
- With complementary relevant skills – which validates their membership of the team;
- Committed to a common purpose – the primary task;
- Committed to a set of performance goals – increased market share and preservation of employment;

- Committed to a shared approach – proposed by Hawkins and Smith (2013, p. 25):

  - the team's ability to have effective meetings and internal communications;
  - the team's ability to work individually and collectively in representing the team and all its major stakeholders in a way which successfully engages the stakeholders and has impact;
  - the team's ability to increase the capacity and capability of each of its members, as well as continually develop its own performance and collective capacity and capability;
  - the team's ability to act as an emotional container that addresses and resolves conflict, aligns the work of all members, provides emotional support across the team and increases morale and commitment.

- For which they hold themselves accountable – the HPTs reported to themselves, and the hierarchy and responsibility for leadership within each HPT was shared.

The presence of these conditions greatly increases the valency towards a working group and away from a basic assumption group.

A corollary of the approach adopted was a decision to operate in the persuasive area of the spectrum of interventions – rather than directive – proposed by Bentley (1994, p. 64). Duggan's research also found that there was a correlation between non-directive interventions and successful outcomes. This is consistent with the principles Lao Tzu in Tao Teh Ching defines (Heider, 1985, p. 73):

It puzzles people at first, to see how little the able leader actually does, and yet how much he gets done. But the leader knows that is how things work. After all, Tao does nothing at all, yet everything gets done. When the leader gets too busy, the time has come to return to selfless silence. Selflessness gives one centre. Centre creates order. When there is order, there is little to do.

The approach adopted towards the various stakeholder groups, particularly to the employee group, contributed significantly to ensuring that the needs of each (as individual or a collective) were met in balance, at a time when there was an elevated level of risk and uncertainty. This created the environment that allowed them to access their thinking brains, thus ensuring that the HPTs were able to operate as WGs.

A critical characteristic of the HPTs was the fact that they were accountable, not to the hierarchy, but to themselves. This philosophy is entirely aligned to the ideas that underpin WGs and self-regulating systems. The process of self-review adopted and used consistently was iterative and simple. It comprised four questions which were designed to ensure that the WGs would remain focused on the primary task and the risk of becoming diverted into a BaG was minimized. The language used was specific and designed to focus on the positive and prioritize the future – recognizing that the past is what it is and the team could only impact what happened next. The questions were:

* What was the plan?
* What worked well?
* What could or should have worked better?
* What change in behaviour and performance is required to deliver a better outcome?

When considering what could/should have worked better the HPTs used subsidiary questions that were designed to encourage the team to consider its role in enabling improved outcomes:

* Did the HPT select the right person or people?
* Was the HPT clear in explaining what was required?
* Did the HPT ensure the tools and support necessary for a successful outcome were provided?
* Did the HPT review and provide feedback?

Impact on CEO:

> When you have quieted your mind
> Enough
> And transcended your ego
> Enough
> You can hear how it really is.
> So when
> You ARE with the candle flame, you ARE the candle flame
> And when
> You ARE with another Being's mind, you ARE the other Being's mind
> When
> There is a task to do, you ARE the task
> The mindless quality of Total involvement
> That comes only when the Ego is quiet
> And there is no attachment

(Alpert, 1971, p. 5)

Despite my experience across a number of industries in a number of countries, the financial crisis of 2008 was unlike anything I previously have been faced with. The collapse was deeper and more prolonged than anyone had predicted.

I began to think about how those around me were dealing with what was a never-ending tidal-wave of bad news, particularly after a period of unprecedented prosperity. I wondered where they found resilience and how they motivated themselves when they and those around them were facing job insecurity, reduced pay, increased taxes, mortgage default and their children emigrating.

To find answers and to begin to formulate strategies and tactics to cope, I looked into my personal experience of previous crises. I reached for past experiences that might offer insights. I looked for theories that might have some relevance.

Some years back, out of the blue, I had a life-threatening encounter with cancer. I confronted the challenge in the only way I know how – head on, with an open mind and curiosity. I accepted that my life was threatened by the illness but I decided to do everything I could to take control of my future. I refused to be corralled and blindly accept the experts' instructions. I questioned the treatments proposed. Supported by and together with my wife, we found better options that were not available in Ireland. We regained control, we fought, we won. I choose to recall this brush with mortality as an experience that has strengthened me, and one which, with hindsight, I would never trade. I choose not to dwell on the bad luck of getting the illness. I choose to remember the luck that it was diagnosed early, that the type of cancer was treatable, that the surgery was successful, that we found better options for treatment after surgery than the usual treatment normally available in Ireland. I choose to be grateful that while receiving this treatment, I found a new mentor who has played a large role in setting off on the journey I am currently on. It is an experience I would never trade – regardless of how difficult it was at times.

I realized that adopting this approach was how I found the energy I needed and what created the resilience and strength. I decided to use this experience and other similar ones to assist me in the new challenge I was facing.

I thought about the Stockdale Paradox (Collins, 2014):

> You must retain faith that you will prevail in the end, regardless of the difficulties and at the same time you must confront the brutal facts of your current reality, whatever they might be.

I thought about the genius of the "and" (Collins, 2005) – preserve the core values *and* stimulate progress in everything else. Only the most exceptional leaders embrace the entire continuum. They create conditions in which there is continuity and change, urgency and long term, creativity and discipline, humility and will, brutal and accommodating.

I also thought about 'Human Givens.' These ideas were first presented in *Human Givens: The New Approach to Emotional Health and Clear Thinking* (Griffin & Tyrell, 2013). The foundation of the theory is the idea that human beings have emotional needs as well as physical needs, which are every bit as important for good health.

Human Givens theory is interested in self-actualization needs and refers to these as emotional or innate needs:

- Meaning and purpose
- Achievement
- Emotional connection
- Community

- Attention exchange
- Privacy
- Status
- Autonomy
- Security

Unlike Maslow who proposes a hierarchy, the Human Givens argues that humans seek to have their emotional needs met in balance – Griffin and Tyrell argue the nature of this balance is dynamic depending on circumstances at any particular time. The theory also argues that when one emotional need is not being met, humans maintain an overall balance by securing over satisfaction of one or other of the other needs. The theory argues that the drivers of all human behaviour (including motivation) can be understood by analyzing the manner in which an individual is ensuring their emotional needs are being met in balance.

These were some of the experiences and ideas that informed the personal tactics and strategies I adopted during the downturn. Because we survived, because I am here, because I am sane, I believe they worked well, and struggle to identify what (which was in my control) could or should have worked better.

- Considering the ideas of 'human givens' and the 'brutal facts', I chose to ensure that my life had balance. I accepted that my needs in a business context were unlikely to be met, but resolved to ensure they were met in other axes of my life. I selfishly planned and protected personal time. I travelled extensively with my wife to places we would not have previously considered; I trekked and skied at a level I did not previously believe was possible for me; I actively began to work to prepare for the next phase of my life – a distinguishing feature of this was the decision to return to formal education after more than 25 years.
- I adopted the principal of the Stockdale Paradox. I chose to retain faith that we would prevail in the end. I chose to focus on what I could control and chose not to waste time or energy on what was outside of my control (which included the past). Collins describes this as the '20 mile march'; he explains that you cannot control weather, you cannot control the terrain, you cannot control what might aid or hinder you – but you can decide how far you consistently will walk every day, regardless of the conditions. I embarked on a trek of unknown distance or difficulty and resolved to complete 20 miles per day every day, regardless.
- I chose to follow the idea that almost everyone wants to do a decent job and if they know the parameters for the measure of a 'decent job' along with being equipped with the support they need to be successful and if they get timely and honest feedback, they are likely to succeed. I chose to treat adults like adults – and never to apologize when asking for 'the genius of and'. I frequently asked for (and often demanded) 'the genius of and'. I was rarely disappointed.

- I chose to separate what I was feeling from what I projected, while remaining realistic and never shying from the brutal facts. I recognized that those around me had an acute sensitivity to and could be influenced positively or negatively by my demeanour. When the days were darkest I never concealed the truth – but never showed my insecurity and fear.
- I became aware that I had always been expected to prescribe solutions and to direct. My leadership style was dissonant; I chose to become resonant. I resolved to develop a new habit of asking challenging questions, standing back and allowing those around me to develop their own answers.

I can see that my behaviour, which endures, has changed the system. The team with whom I interact regularly are flourishing. They have autonomy, they have control. They have permission to be creative and take measured risks. They are expected to defend our values, even when it hurts to do so and are allowed to change anything else. They are expected to deliver the short-term objectives and to always look to the long term. In challenging situations they are expected to be brutal but also accommodating. They know they are trusted. They feel encouraged to access and use their brains, rather than implement what the top end of the hierarchy prescribed in the past.

I am more effective as a leader and together we get more done. I choose to work on the things that will make a material difference to the group and eschew issues where, in truth, I have nothing to add.

I am an enthusiastic amateur cook and study world class chefs, their ideas, the technologies they use and their philosophies. One such chef, Daniel Patterson, directs the restaurant 'Coi' in San Francisco. It is not an easy place to work unless you meet Daniel's exacting standard. In his book (2013, p. 43), Patterson gives a vignette which, for me, perfectly describes the effect of great leadership:

> A few months ago, we got our pile of wiping napkins and distributed them around the kitchen, there was a funny silence and then the kitchen erupted.
>
> "What the fuck is this?"
> "Who rolled these?"
>
> And the entire kitchen, in unison, started re-rolling their napkins, grumbling under their breath. In that moment, I was proud. The staff understood one basic thing: details matter.

Reflection

The downturn was deeper and more prolonged than had been anticipated. Consequently, we were unable to avoid compulsory redundancies when the shareholders subscribed to the second capital call and the group's banks agreed to write off a portion of the group's debt. However the compulsory redundancies were in one of the group's five businesses and accounted for less than about 7% of the total group employment.

As the economic conditions improve, we can say that all five businesses in the group have survived, are profitable again and are growing. All five businesses have increased their market share.

The use of HPTs is now embedded in the group's businesses, which represents a fundamental change in the management style within the group. Decisionmaking is delegated and more inclusive, and it is difficult to see the wider body of staff tolerating a return to a more interventionist approach to the management of day to day operations. The role of the senior management team has fundamentally (perhaps irreversibly changed) changed; they are (for the most part) operating more strategically. Their main role is one of oversight, boundary management and looking over the horizon to anticipate and develop responses for future challenges and opportunities.

In two of the five businesses, the conversation quickly went beyond issues of pure survival. These two businesses decided to enter the UK market and in the last three years have built up sales which now approach €4m from a standing start. It had long been an objective of the leaders in these businesses to enter the UK market, but it was only when the organizations coalesced around this idea, from the ground up, that the impossible became possible.

In another two of the businesses, a major strategic initiative was successfully launched, which fundamentally changed the relationship with their largest customers from adversarial to one of partnership. By applying technology to the relationship the conversation moved from the traditional territory of product and price to value-added services (on the back of which product is sold). It is difficult to explain the extent of this transformation and its impact on every member of staff.

Through the introduction of HPTs, we involved staff in the process of developing the actions required to survive. Together we took on a mutual responsibility to each other for a shared future. This reduced the elevation of emotions, which is a primitive response to a crisis. Drawing on Schutz's work (Forsyth, 2009, p. 93), the approach we chose addressed the staff's underlying needs for inclusion, control and openness.

For me, as a leader, much of my work is through groups – and increasingly, I regard my role as a facilitator for these groups. I made a conscious decision to change my style of management and leadership within the group from dissonant (which to date, has served me well) to a more resonant approach. This change has systematically changed the culture of the business. I am no longer the provider of solutions; I help to create the conditions within which those individuals and teams charged with responsibility for the business can find their own solutions. To be effective this has required me to become more aware of what is happening within the HPTs and the forces which drive behaviour. The Canadian astronaut, Chris Hadfield puts it well:

> Over the years, I've realized that in any new situation, whether it involves an elevator or a rocket ship, you will almost certainly be viewed in one of three

ways. As a minus one: actively harmful, someone who creates problems. Or as a zero: your impact is neutral and doesn't tip the balance one way or the other. Or you'll be seen as plus one: someone who actively adds value. Everyone wants to be a plus one, of course. But proclaiming your plus-one-ness at the outset almost guarantees you'll be seen as a minus one, regardless of the skills you bring to the table or how you actually perform. This might seem self-evident, but it can't be, because so many people do it.

(Hadfield, 2013, p. 181).

The greatest challenge I see is to ensure that the group board and the senior management team do not revert to what had been their default behaviour. After all, when there was a mortal threat, there was an incentive to change, no matter how uncomfortable it felt. Now that the dragon has been slayed, and as memories of the crisis fade, underlying valencies begin to assert themselves again.

The anthropologist Gregory Bateson was intrigued by the complex and interconnected systems that comprise our world; he spent a lifetime trying to reach a level of comprehension:

What pattern connects the crab to the lobster and the orchid to the primrose and all four of them to me. And me to you. And all six of us to the amoeba in one direction and to the backward schizophrenic in the other.

(Bateson, 1979, p. 7)

As he approached the end of his life he felt he had come to a reconciliation, a truth within himself.

And so I feel it is for me: my journey has led me to a new truth, but this is far from a definitive or an ending; it is merely the starting point for a new exploration to find what can never be found.

References

Accenture. (2005). *Driving High Performance in Government: Maximising the Value of Public Sector Shared Services*. London: Accenture.

Ainsworth, M. (1969). Object relations, dependency, and attachment: A theoretical review of the infant-mother relationship. *Child Development*, 40: 969–1025.

Almaas, A. (1986). *Essence: The Diamond Approach to Inner Realization*. York Beach: Samuel Weiser, Inc.

Alpert, R. (1971). *The Transformation Journey*. San Cristobel: Lama Foundation

Anderson, P. (1999). Complexity theory and organization science. *Organization Science*, 10(3): 216–232.

Anon. (2004). *Kalevala, the Finnish Mythology*. Juva: WS Bookwell Oy.

Aram, E. (2012). *Complexity: An Introduction*. TIHR Lunchtime Talk Series. Available from: https://vimeo.com/28718956.

Aram, E. (2015). Complexity and boards: Course reading. *Dynamics at Board Level*. Tavistock Institute of Human Relations. Unpublished.

Aram, E. (2016). *An Introduction to Complexity Theory*. Available from: www.tavinstitute. org/projects/an-introduction-to-complexity-theory/ [Accessed: 27 December 2015].

Argyris, C. (1990). *Overcoming Organizational Defences: Facilitating Organizational Learning*. Boston, MA: Allyn and Bacon.

Audit Scotland. (2013). *Police Reform Progress Update 2013*. Available from: www. audit-scotland.gov.uk/docs/central/2013/nr_131114_police_reform.pdf [Accessed: December 2015].

Audit Scotland. (2016). *The 2015/16 audit of the Scottish Police Authority*. Available from: www.audit-scotland.gov.uk/report/the-201516-audit-of-the-scottish-police-authority [Accessed: December 2016].

Bain, A. (1998). Social defences against organizational learning. *Human Relations*, 51(3): 413–429.

Bain, A., & Bain, J. (2002). A note on primary spirit. *Socio-Analysis*, 4: 98–111.

Bales, R. (1950). *Interaction Process Analysis Reading*. Boston, MA: Addison Wesley.

Banet, Jr., A.G., & Hayden, C. (1977). *A Tavistock Primer in the 1977 Handbook for Group Facilitators*. La Jolla, CA: University Associates Inc., p. 156.

Barnard, C.I. (1938). *The Functions of the Executive*. Cambridge, MA: Harvard University Press.

Barrett, R. (1998). *Liberating the Corporate Soul: Building a Values Driven Organization*. London: Routledge.

Barta, T., Kleiner, M., & Neumann, T. (April 2012). Is there a pay off from top team diversity? *McKinsey Quarterly*, 1–3. Available at: http://www.mckinsey.com/insights/ organization/is_there_a_payoff_from_top-team_diversity.

Bateson, G. (1979). *Mind and Nature*. New York: Hampton Press

Beard, A. (May 2014). Leading with humour. *Harvard Business Review*. Available from: https://hbr.org/2014/05/leading-with-humor?autocomplete=true [Accessed: 14 January 2016].

Beard, M. (2014). *Laughter in Ancient Rome: On Joking, Tickling and Cracking Up*. Berkeley, CA: University of California Press.

Behan, B.A. (2006). Board assessment. In: Nadler, D.A. (Ed.), *Building Better Boards: A Blueprint for Effective Governance*. San Francisco: Jossey-Bass.

Benne, K., & Sheats, P. (1948). Functional roles of group members. *Journal of Social Issues*, 4(2): 41–42.

Bentley, T. (1994). *Facilitation: Providing Opportunities for Learning*. Gloucestershire: The Space Between Publishing.

Berger, J.G. (2011). *Changing on the Job: Developing Leaders for a Complex World*. Louisville, KY: Stanford Business Books.

Berne, E. (1964). *Games People Play: The Psychology of Human Relationships*. New York: Grove.

Bettelheim, B. (1976). *The Uses of Enchantment*. London: Penguin Books.

Bevan, J. (2000). *The Rise and Fall of Marks & Spencer*. London: Profile.

Bion, W. (1959). Attacks on linking. *The International Journal of Psychoanalysis*, 30: 308–315; republished in *Second Thoughts*. London: Heinemann, 1967, pp. 93–109.

Bion, W. (1961). *Experiences in Groups and Other Papers*. London: Tavistock.

Bion, W. (1965). *Transformations*. London: Karnac Books.

Bion, W. (1980). *Bion in New York and São Paulo*, Bion, F. (Ed.). Perthshire: Clunie Press.

Bion, W. (1993). *Attention and Interpretation*. London: Karnac Books.

Bion, W. (2004). *Experiences in Groups: And Other Papers*. New York: Taylor & Francis.

Bloomberg. (2017). *Executive Profile & Biography* [online]. Available from: www.bloomberg.com [Accessed: 23 January 2017].

Bohm, D. (1996). *On Dialogue*. New York: Routledge.

Bowlby, J. (2005). *A Secure Base*. London: Routledge.

Bradford, L., & Gibb, J. (1964). *Group Theory and Laboratory Method*. New York: John Wiley & Sons Inc.

Bresser Consulting. (2012). *ICF Global Coaching Study*. Lexington: International Coach Federation.

Brissett, L., & Sher, M. (2010). *Hidden Complexity*. London: ICGN, pp. 70–71.

Brissett, L., & Sher, M. (2015). Certificate in dynamics at board level introductory reading. *Dynamics at Board Level*. Tavistock Institute of Human Relations. Unpublished.

Brown, R. (2000). *Group Processes: Dynamics Within and Between Groups*. Oxford: Blackwell.

Burgoon, J., Guerrero, L., & Floyd, K. (2009). *Nonverbal Communication*. Boston, MA: Allyn and Bacon.

Butler, S. (December 9, 2012). Fresh, but not so easy: Tesco joins a long list of British failure in America. *The Guardian*. London. Available from: www.theguardian.com/business/2012/dec/09/fresh-not-easy-tesco-british-failure-america.

Butler, S., & Ruddick, G. (July 25, 2016). Sir Philip Green's reputation ripped apart in damning report on BHS demise. *The Guardian*. Available from: www.theguardian.com/business/2016/jul/25/bhs-demise-sir-philip-green-reputation-torn-apart-in-damning-report [Accessed: 25 July 2016].

Byrne, J.A. (July 28, 2002). No excuses for Enron's board. *Business Week Magazine*. Available from: www.businessweek.com/stories/2002-07-28/commentary-no-excuses-for-enrons-board.

Cairns, M. (2003). *Boardrooms That Work: A Guide to Board Dynamics*. Sydney: Australian Institute of Company Directors.

Caldwell, R. (2011). HR directors in UK boardrooms: A search for strategic influence or symbolic capital? *Employee Relations*, 33(1): 40–63.

Cappelli, P. (July/August 2015). Why we love to hate HR . . . and what HR can do about it. *Harvard Business Review*. Available from: https://hbr.org/2015/07/why-we-love-to-hate-hr-and-what-hr-can-do-about-it [Accessed: 3 December 2016].

Carcio, W. (2004). Board governance: A social systems perspective. *Academy of Management Executive*, 18: 100.

Carey, J., & Freud, S. (2014). *The Joke and Its Relation to the Unconscious*. New York: Penguin Books.

Carlyle, J. (2010). Destructive processes in analytic groups. In: Garland, C. (Ed.), *The Groups Book. Psychoanalytic Group Therapy: Principles and Practice Including the Groups Manual. A Treatment Manual with Clinical Vignettes*. London: Karnac Books, pp. 60–77.

Carney, D.R., & Hall, J.A. (2005). Beliefs about the nonverbal expression of social power. *Journal of Nonverbal Behavior*, 29(2): 105–123.

Cartwright, D., & Zander, A.F. (1968). *Group Dynamics: Research and Theory*. New York: Harper & Row, p. 19.

Casti, J. (1994). *Complexification: Explaining a Paradoxical World Through the Science of Surprise*. New York: HarperCollins.

Cavanagh, M., & Lane, D. (2012). Coaching psychology coming of age: The challenges we face in the messy world of complexity. *International Coaching Psychology Review*, 7(1): 84.

Chapman, R., & O'Toole, B. (2009). Leadership in the British civil service: An interpretation. *Public Policy and Administration*, 25(2): 123–136.

Charan, R. (2005). *Boards That Deliver: Advancing Corporate Governance from Compliance to Competitive Advantage*. San Francisco: Jossey-Bass.

Charas, S. (2014). *The Impact of Board Dynamics on Shareholder Value Creation*. The Conference Board Governance Center.

Charities Aid Foundation. (2015). *The Young Trustee's Guide: Developing the Next Generation of Charity Leaders* [Online]. Available from: https://collectionstrust.org.uk/resource/young-trustees-guide-developing-the-next-generation-of-charity-leaders/ [Accessed: 28 September 2015].

Charity Commission. (2015). *Charity Trustee: What's Involved (CC3a)* [Online]. Available from: www.gov.uk/guidance/charity-trustee-what's-involved [Accessed: 29 September 2015].

Chaskalson, M. (2011). *The Mindful Workplace Developing Resilient Individuals and Resonant Organizations with MBSR*. Oxford: Wiley–Blackwell.

Cherry, K. (2017). *What Is Groupthink? How to Recognize It and Avoid It* [online]. Available from: www.verywell.com/what-is-groupthink-2795213 [Accessed: 15 January 2018].

Civil Society Almanac (2012) [Online] Available from: https://fundraising.co.uk/2013/04/07/civil-society-almanac-2012-ncvo-almanac.

Clutterbuck, D. (2010). *Five Levels of Laughter*. London: Chartered Institute of Personnel and Development.

Coalition for Efficiency. (2015). *Trustee Guide* [Online]. Available from: www.cfefficiency.org.uk/trustee-guide/ [Accessed: 25 September 2015].

Collins, J. (2014). *The Stockdale Paradox. The Brutal Facts*. New York: Random House.

Collins, J.C., & Porras, J.I. (2005). *Built to Last: Successful Habits of Visionary Companies*. London: Random House.

Committee on the Financial Aspects of Corporate Governance. (December 1992). *The Financial Aspects of Corporate Governance*. London: Gee, p. 19.

Cornforth, C. (Ed.) (2003). *The Governance of Public and Non-Profit Organizations: What Do Boards Do?* London: Routledge.

Cornforth, C., & Chambers, N. (2010). The role of corporate governance and boards in organizational performance. In: Walsh, K., Harvey, G., & Jas, P. (Eds.), *Connecting Knowledge and Performance in Public Services: From Knowing to Doing*. Cambridge: Cambridge University Press, pp. 99–127.

Craft, E. (July 21, 2015). Personal interview.

Creelman, D., & Lambert, A. (July 2011). *The Board and HR: How Board Oversight of Human Capital Works*. Available from: www.womenboardmembers.co.uk/downloads/lambert-creelman-summary.pdf [Accessed: 3 December 2016].

Cremin, C. (2009). Never employable enough: The (im)possibility of satisfying's the boss's desire. *Organization*, 17: 131–149.

Daft, R.L., & Lewin, A.Y. (1990). Can organization studies begin to break out of the normal science straightjacket: An editorial essay. *Organization Science*, 1(1).

Dalton, M. (1959). *Men Who Manage*. New York: John Wiley & Sons Inc.

Davies Review. (February 2011). *Women on Boards*. Available from: www.gov.uk/government/uploads/system/uploads/attachment_data/file/31480/11-745-women-on-boards.pdf [Accessed: 12 December 2016].

de Board, R. (1978). *The Psychoanalysis of Organisations*. London: Routledge.

de Waal, A. (2011). *The Characteristics of a High Performance Organization*. Maastricht School of Management.

Dick, R. (1991). *Helping Groups to Be Effective: Skills, Processes and Concepts for Group Facilitation*. Brisbane: Interchange.

Diversity UK Editor. (December 19, 2014). Vince cable welcomes plans to increase ethnic diversity on FTSE 100 boards. *Diversity UK*. Available from: https://diversityuk.org/vince-cable-welcomes-plans-increase-ethnic-diversity-ftse-100-boards/ [Accessed: 16 December 2016].

Duggan, P. (1986). *The IDA Company Development Program: An Application of Catalytic Consultancy*. MBA thesis, University College Dublin.

Dutra, A. (November 5, 2012). A more effective board of directors. *HBR Blog Network*. Available from: http://blogs.hbr.org/2012/11/a-more-effective-board-of-dire/.

Effron, M., & Ort, M. (August 2015). The unsexy fundamentals of great HR. *Harvard Business Review*. Available from: https://hbr.org/2015/08/the-unsexy-fundamentals-of-great-hr [Accessed: 3 December 2016].

Emery, F. (1974). Methodological premises of social forecasting. *Annals of the American Academy of Political and Social Science*, 4(2): 97–115.

FCA & PRA. (2015). *The Failure of HBOS plc (HBOS): A Report by the Financial Conduct Authority (FCA) and the Prudential Regulation Authority (PRA)* [online]. Available from: www.bankofengland.co.uk/pra/Documents/publications/reports/hbos.pdf [Accessed: 23 January 2017].

Financial Reporting Council. (March 2011). *Guidance on Board Effectiveness*. London: FRC, p. 2.

Financial Reporting Council. (September 2012). *UK Corporate Governance Code*. London: FRC.

Financial Reporting Council. (July 2016). *Corporate Culture and the Role of Boards*. London: FRC.

Financial Reporting Council. (2016). *UK Corporate Governance Code*. London: FRC.

Financial Services Authority. (December 2011). *The Failure of the Royal Bank of Scotland.* London: FSA.

Fisher, J. (2011). The emotional experience of K. In Mawson, C. (Ed.), *Bion Today.* London: Routledge, pp. 42–63.

Flanagan, A. (2016). *Review of Governance in Policing – To Cabinet Secretary for Justice.* Available from: www.spa.police.uk/assets/128635/337350/337362 [Accessed: March 2016].

Forbes, D.P., & Milliken, F.J. (1999). Cognition and corporate governance: Understanding boards of directors as strategic decision-making groups. *Academy of Management Review*, 24(3): 489–505.

Forsyth, D. (2009). *Group Dynamics.* Belmont: Wadsworth Cengage Learning.

Foulkes, S.H., & Anthony, E.J. (1957). *Group Psychotherapy: The Psychodynamic Approach.* Harmondsworth: Penguin Books.

Franz, T.M. (2012). *Group Dynamics and Team Interventions: Understanding and Improving Team Performance.* Chichester: Wiley–Blackwell.

French, R., & Simpson, P. (2015). *Attention, Cooperation, Purpose: An Approach to Working in Groups Using Insights from Wilfred Bion.* London: Karnac Books.

French, R., & Simpson, P. (2010). 'The work group' redressing the balance in Bion's experiences in groups. *Human Relations*, 63(12): 1859–1878.

Freud, S. (1914). *On Narcissism: An Introduction.* The Standard Edition of the Complete Psychological Works of Sigmund Freud, Vol. XIV (1914–1916): On the History of the Psycho-Analytic Movement, Papers on Metapsychology and Other Works. London: The Hogarth Press, pp. 67–102.

Freud, S. (1921). *Group Psychology and the Analysis of the Ego.* Penguin Freud Library, Vol. 12. Harmondsworth: Penguin Books, 1984.

Freud, S. (1925). *Inhibitions, Symptoms and Anxiety. The Standard Edition of the Complete Psychological Works of Sigmund Freud, Volume XX (1925–1926).* London: The Hogarth Press, p. 66.

Freud, S. (1982). *Jokes and Their Relation to the Unconscious*, Vol. 6. London: Pelican Books.

Furnham, A., & Petrova, E. (2010). *Body Language in Business: Decoding the Signals.* New York: Palgrave Macmillan.

Gabriel, Y. (1999). *Organisations in Depth.* London: Sage, p. 192.

Garland, C. (2010). What is psychoanalytic about group therapy? In: Garland, C. (Ed.), *The Groups Book. Psychoanalytic Group Therapy: Principles and Practice Including the Groups Manual. A Treatment Manual with Clinical Vignettes.* London: Karnac Books, pp. 19–36.

Garratt, B. (1996). *The Fish Rots From the Head: Crisis in Our Boardrooms.* London: Profile.

George, W. (2012). Board governance depends on where you sit. In: Lorsch, J.W. (Ed.), *The Future of Boards: Meeting the Governance Challenges of the Twenty-First Century.* Boston, MA: Harvard Business Review Press.

Gill, A., & Sher, M. (2009). Psychological and behavioural elements in board performance. In: Walker, D. (Ed.), *A Review of Corporate Governance in UK Banks and Other Financial Industry Entities.* Final Recommendations: 26 November 2009. London: Walker Review Secretariat, pp. 139–146.

Giraldo, M. (2012). *The Dialogues in the Group.* London: Karnac Books.

Glennie, A. (August 29, 2013). *Daily Mail.* Available from: www.dailymail.co.uk/news/article-2405852/BBCs-head-HR-quits-scandal-severance-pay-wont-golden-goodbye.html [Accessed: 10 December 2016].

Global Investment Watch. (2008). *America's Most Wanted: The Lehman Brothers Board of Directors* [online]. Available from: http://globalinvestmentwatch.com/americas-most-wanted-the-lehman-brothers-board-of-directors-2/ [Accessed: 23 January 2017].

Goff, S., & Jacobs, E. (January 28, 2014). Psychometric tests led Co-op Bank to make Paul Flowers chairman. *Financial Times*.

Goldenberg, A., Saguy, T., & Halperin, E. (2014). How group-based emotions are shaped by collective emotions: Evidence for emotional transfer and emotional burden. *Journal of Personality and Social Psychology*, 107(4): 581–596.

Goleman, D. (2005). *Emotional Intelligence: Why It Can Matter More Than IQ*. London: Bantam Books.

Gosling, J. (April 2004). Leadership Development in Management Education. *Business Leadership Review*, I:I. Available from: www.Mbaworld.Com/Blr.

Green Park. (2016). *Diversity – A Ten-Minute Guide for the Busy Executive*. Available from: https://green-park.co.uk/wp-content/uploads/2016/11/GP-10-Minute-Diversity-Guide.pdf [Accessed: 31 December 2016].

Griffin, J., & Tyrell, I. (2013). *Human Givens*. Chalvington: Human Givens Publishing Ltd.

Grotstein, J.S., & Symington, N. (1993). *Narcissism, a New Theory*. London: Karnac Books.

Gudykunst, W.B. (2005). *Theorizing About Intercultural Communication*. Thousand Oaks, CA: Sage.

Hadfield, C. (2013). *An Astronauts Guide to Life on Earth*. London: Palgrave Macmillan.

Halton, W. (1994). Some unconscious aspects of organizational life: Contributions from psychoanalysis. In: Obholzer, A., & Roberts, V.Z. (Eds.), *The Unconscious at Work*. London: Routledge, pp. 11–18.

Hambrick, D.C., & Mason, P.A. (1984). Upper echelons: The organization as a reflection of its top managers. *Academy of Management Review*, 9: 193–206.

Harris Williams, M. (2010). *The Aesthetic Development: The Poetic Spirit of Psychoanalysis: Essays on Bion, Meltzer, Keats*. London: Karnac Books.

Harvard Business Review. (July/August 2015). 'Blow up HR' front cover. Available from: https://hbr.org/product/harvard-business-review-july-august-2015/BR1507-MAG-ENG [Accessed: 3 December 2016].

Harvey Nash HR Survey. (2016). Available from: www.harveynash.com/hrsurvey/ [Accessed: 14 December 2016].

Hawkins, P., & Smith, N. (2013). *Coaching Mentoring and Organisational Consultancy*. Berkshire: Open University Press.

Heald, D., & Steel, D. (2015). Making the governance of public bodies work: Chair-chief executive relationships in practice. *Public Money & Management*, 35(4): 257–264.

Heider, J. (1985). *The Tao of Leadership*. Atlanta: Humanics New Age.

Heidrick & Struggles. (2014). *Towards Dynamic Governance 2014: European Corporate Governance Report*. Available from: http://usatoday30.usatoday.com/money/industries/telecom/2003-06-09-board_x.htm.

Heifetz, R., Grashow, A., & Linsky, M. (2009). *The Practice of Adaptive Leadership*. Boston, MA: Harvard Business Press.

Helsingin Sanomat. (June 15–December 15, 2016): Sanoma Media Finland Oy.

Herington, V., & Colvin, A. (2016). Police leadership for complex times. *Policing: A Journal of Policy and Practice*, 10(1): 7–16. Available from: http://policing.oxfordjournals.org/content/10/1/7 [Accessed: February 2016].

Hirschhorn, L. (1988). *The Workplace Within*. Cambridge, MA: MIT Press.

HMICS. (2016). *Annual Report 2015/16*. Edinburgh. Available from: www.hmics.org/sites/default/files/publications/HMICS%20%20Annual%20Report%202015-16.pdf [Accessed: December 2016].

Hollenbeck, J.R., DeRue, D.S., & Mannor, M. (2006). Statistical power and parameter stability when subjects are few and tests too many. *Journal of Applied Psychology*, 91: 1–5.

Hope-Hailey, V., Searle, R., & Dietz, G. (2012). Where has all the trust gone? *CIPD Research Report*. Available from: www.cipd.co.uk/hr-resources/research/where-trust-gone.aspx [Accessed: November 2015].

Hopkins, J. (July 9, 2003). Report: WorldCom board passive. *USA Today*.

Hume, F. (2010). Bion and Group psychotherapy: Bion and Foulkes at the Tavistock. In: Garland, C. (Ed.), *The Groups Book. Psychoanalytic Group Therapy: Principles and Practice Including the Groups Manual. A Treatment Manual with Clinical Vignettes*. London: Karnac Books, pp. 101–128.

ICGN International Corporate Governance Network. (2017). *ICGN Global Governance Principles*. London: ICGN.

IFC International Finance Corporation. (2009). *Practical Guide to Corporate Governance: Experience from Latin American Companies Circle*. Washington, DC: IFC.

Janis, I. (1972). *Victims of Groupthink*. Boston, MA: Houghton Mifflin, p. 9.

Janis, I. (1982). *Groupthink*, 2nd ed. Boston, MA: Houghton Miffin.

Jaques, E. (1953). On the dynamics of social structure. *Human Relations*, 6: 3–24.

Jaques, E. (1955). Social systems as a defence against persecutory and depressive anxiety. In: Klein, M. (Ed.), *New Directions in Psycho-Analysis: The Significance of Infant Conflicts in the Patterns of Adult Behaviour*. Tavistock; reprinted Karnac Books: Maresfield Reprints, 1977, pp. 478–498.

Jaques, E. (1957). *The Changing Culture of a Factory: A Study of Authority and Participation in an Industrial Setting*. London: Tavistock Publications, Ltd. Third impression.

Joffe, W., Sandler, J., Baker, S., Edgcumbe, R., Kawenoka, M., Kennedy, H., & Neurath, L. (1967). Some conceptual problems involved in the consideration of disorders of narcissism. *Journal of Child Psychotherapy*, 2(1): 56–66.

John, S., & Björkman, I. (2015). In the eyes of the beholder: The HRM capabilities of the HR function as perceived by managers and professionals. *Human Resource Management Journal*, 25(4): 424–442.

Johnson, G. (2009). Humanistic Hakomi and its interface with non-linear science. *Hakomi Forum*, 22: 28–41.

Jung, C.G. (1969). *Archetypes and the Collective Unconscious*. Collected Works of C.G. Jung, Vol. 9, Part 1. Princeton, NJ: Princeton University Press.

Kabat-Zinn, J. (1996). *Full Catastrophic Living*. London: Paitkus.

Katz, D., & Kahn, R.L. (1966). *The Social Psychology of Organisations*. New York: John Wiley & Sons Inc.

Katzenbach, J.R., & Smith, D.K. (1999). *The Wisdom of Teams*. New York: Harper Perennial, p. 45.

Katzenbach, J.R., & Smith, D.K. (July–August 2005). The discipline of teams. *Harvard Business Review*.

Kauffman, S.A. (1993). *The Origins of Order: Self Organization and Selection in Evolution*. New York: Oxford University Press.

Keeley, B., & Love, P. (2011). *Crisis to Recovery: The Causes, Course and Consequences of the Great Recession*. Paris: OECD.

Kegan, R. (1994). *In Over Our Heads: The Mental Demands of Modern Life*, 6th ed. Cambridge, MA: Harvard University Press.

Kelleher, J., Sher, M., & Stern, E. (April 15, 2003). *'An Analysis of Board Performance'*, *Conference*. Improving Board Behaviour. Tavistock Institute of Human Relations, London.

Kernberg, O.F. (1967). Borderline personality organization. *Journal of the American Psychodynamic Association*, 15: 641–685.

Kernberg, O.F. (2001). Object relations, affects and drives: Towards a new synthesis. *Psychoanalytic Inquiry*, 21: 604–619.

Kernberg, P. (1994). Mechanism of defence development and research perspectives. *Bulletin of the Menninger Clinic*, 58(1): 55–87.

Kets de Vries, M.F.R. (2006). *The Leader on the Couch*. London: John Wiley & Sons Inc.

Kets de Vries, M.F.R. (2012). Star performers: Paradoxes wrapped up in enigmas. *Organizational Dynamics*, 41(3): 173–182.

Kets de Vries, M.F.R., Florent-Treacy, E., & Korotov, K. (2013). Psychodynamic issues in organizational leadership. In: Skipton Leonard, H., Lewis, R., Freedman, A.M., & Passmore, J. (Eds.), *The Wiley-Blackwell Handbook of the Psychology of Leadership, Change, and Organizational Development*. West Sussex: John Wiley & Sons Inc.

Kets de Vries, M.F.R., & Miller, D. (1985). Narcissism and leadership: An object relations perspective. *Human Relations*, 38: 583–601.

Klein, M. (1945). The Oedipus complex in the light of early anxieties. *International Journal of Psychoanalysis*, 26: 11–33.

Klein, M. (1957a). *Envy and Gratitude. A Study of Unconscious Sources*. New York: Basic Books, pp. 176–235.

Klein, M. (1957b). *Envy and Gratitude*. The Writings of Melanie Klein, Vol. III: Envy and Gratitude and Other Works 1946–1963. New York: The Free Press and Palgrave Macmillan, 1975.

Klein, M. (May, 1959a). *Our Adult World and Its Roots in Infancy*. Available from: Sagepub.com Social Science Collections at the Tavistock Institute [Accessed: 15 September 2016].

Klein, M. (1959b). Our adult world and its roots in infancy. In: Klein, M. (Ed.), *Envy and Gratitude and Other Works 1946–1953*. London: The Hogarth Press. Also in: Klein, M. (1959). Our adult world and its roots in infancy. In: Colman, A.D., & Geller, M.H. (Eds.), *Group Relations Reader 2*. A.K. Rice Institute Series. Washington, DC: A.K. Rice Institute, 1985.

Klein, M. (1975). *Love, Guilt and Reparation: And Other Works 1921–1945*. New York. In: New Directions in Psychoanalysis. London: Tavistock Publications.

Kohut, H. (1966). Forms and transformations of narcissism. *Journal of the American Psychodynamic Association*, 14: 243–272.

Kohut, H. (1996). *The Restoration of the Self*. Madison, CT: International Universities Press.

Kohut, H., & Wolf, E. (1978). The disorders of the self and their treatment: An outline. *International Journal of Psychoanalysis*, 59: 413–425.

Kotter, J.P. (2012). *Accelerate: Building Strategic Agility for a Faster-Moving World*. Cambridge, MA: Harvard University Press.

Levine, D. (2005). The corrupt organization. *Human Relations*, 58: 723–740.

Lewin, K. (1947). Frontiers in group dynamics. *Human Relations*, 1(1).

Lewin, K., Lippit, R., & White, R. (1939). Patterns of aggressive behaviour in experimentally created social climates. *Journal of Social Psychology*, 10: 271–229.

Lorsch, J.W. (2012). Introduction. In: Lorsch, J.W. (Ed.), *The Future of Boards: Meeting the Governance Challenges of the Twenty-First Century*. Boston, MA: Harvard Business Review Press.

Maccoby, M. (2000). Narcissistic leaders: The incredible pros, the inevitable cons. *Harvard Business Review*, 78(January–February): 69–77.

Machin, D., & Mayr, A. (2012). *How to Do Critical Discourse Analysis: A Multimodal Introduction*. London: Sage.

Mead, G., & Morris, C. (1967). *Mind, Self, and Society*. Chicago: University of Chicago Press.

Menzies Lyth, I. (1988). Psychoanalytical perspective on Social Institutions. In: *The Containing Anxiety in Institutions*. London: Free Association Books, pp. 43–98.

Menzies, I.E.P. (1960). Social systems as a defence against anxiety. *Human Relations*, 13: 95–121.

Menzies, I.E.P. (1961). *The Functioning of Social Systems as a Defense Against Anxiety*. Pamphlet, November 3. Tavistock Institute of Human Relations. London. In: Kets de Vries, M. (Ed.), *The Irrational Executive*. New York: International Universities Press, 1984.

Merchant, K.A., & Pick, K. (2010). *Blind Spots, Biases, and Other Pathologies in the Boardroom*. New York: Business Expert Press.

Miller, E., & Rice, K. (1967). *Systems of Organisation: The Control of Task and Sentient* London: Tavistock Publications.

Minichilli, A., Gabrielsson, J., & Huse, M. (2007). Board evaluations: Making a fit between the purpose and the system. *Corporate Governance: An International Review*, 15(4): 609–622. doi: 10.1111/j.1467-8683.2007.00591.x.

Muir, I. (October 2012). *Board Evaluation: Research into the Effectiveness of UK Board Evaluations*. London: Keeldeep Associates Limited, p. 6.

National Audit Office. (2009). *Unlocking Your Board's Full Potential: Board Evaluation Questionnaire*. London: National Audit Office.

National Council for Voluntary Organisations. (2014). *NCVO Knowhow: Guidelines on Recruitment and Induction 2014 on behalf of the Big Lottery Fund* [Online]. Available from: https://digitalpeople.blog.gov.uk/2014/01/21/the-basics-of-the-recruitment-process/ [Accessed: 25 September 2015]

Nembhard, I.M., & Edmondson, A.C. (2006). Making it safe: The effects of leader inclusiveness and professional status on psychological safety and improvement efforts in health care teams. *Journal of Organizational Behavior*, 27: 941–966.

Nevis, S., Backman, S., & Nevis, E. (2003). Connecting strategy and intimate interactions: The need for balance. *Gestalt Review*, 7(2): 134–146.

Northern Rock. (2007). *Annual Report and Accounts 2006: Northern Rock plc* [online]. Available from: www.n-ram.co.uk/~/media/Files/N/NRAM-PLC/documents/corporate-reports/res2006pr-annualreportandaccounts.pdf [Accessed: 23 January 2017].

Obholzer, A. (1994a). Afterword. In: Obholzer, A., & Roberts, V. (Eds.), *The Unconscious at Work*. Hove: Routledge, pp. 206–210.

Obholzer, A. (1994b). Authority, power and leadership. In: Obholzer, A., & Roberts, V. (Eds.), *The Unconscious at Work*. Hove: Routledge.

Obholzer, A., & Miller, S. (2004). Leadership, followership, and facilitating the creative workplace (Chap. 2). In: Huffington, C., Halton, W., Armstrong, D., & Pooley, J. (Eds.), *Working Below the Surface*. Tavistock Clinic Series. London: Karnac Books.

Obholzer, A., & Roberts, V. (1994a). The troublesome individual and the troubled institution. In: Obholzer, A., & Roberts, V. (Eds.), *The Unconscious at Work*. Hove: Routledge.

Obholzer, A., & Roberts, V. (1994b). Towards healthier organisations (Chaps. 18–21). In: Obholzer, A., & Roberts, V. (Eds.), *The Unconscious at Work*. Hove: Routledge.

Obholzer, A., & Roberts, V. (Eds.) (1994c). *The Unconscious at Work: Individual and Organizational Stress in the Human Services*. London: Routledge.

OECD. (2015). *G20/OECD Principles of Corporate Governance*. Paris: OECD.

Parliamentary Commission on Banking Standards. (March. 2013). *'An Accident Waiting to Happen': The Failure of HBOS, Fourth Report of Session 2012–13*. London: The Stationery Office Limited, p. 29.

Patterson, D. (2013). *Coi*. London: Phaidon.

Permanent Subcommittee on Investigations of the Committee on Governmental Affairs US Senate. (July 8, 2002). *The Role of the Board of Directors in Enron's Collapse*. Washington, DC: U.S. Government Publishing Office.

Peterson, R.S., Smith, D.B., Matorana, P.V., & Owens, P.D. (2003). The impact of chief executive officer personality on top team dynamics: One mechanism by which leadership affects organizational performance. *Journal of Applied Psychology*, 88: 795–808.

Petriglieri, G. (2017). *Psychoanalyzing the World's Problems Won't Solve Them*. Available from: https://hbr.org/2017/01/psychoanalyzing-the-worlds-problems-wont-help-us-solve-them [Accessed: 24 January 2017).

Prigogine, I. (1997). *The End of Certainty*. New York: The Free Press, pp. 30–31.

Prigogine, I., & Stengers, I. (1984). *Order out of Chaos: Man's New Dialog with Nature*. New York: Bantam Books.

Pugliese, A., Bezemer, P-J., Alessandro, Z., Huse, M., Van Den Bosch, F., & Volberda, W. (2009). Boards of directors' contributions to strategy: A literature review and research agenda. *Corporate Governance: An International Review*, 17(3): 292–306.

Puwar, N. (2004). *Space Invaders: Race, Gender and Bodies out of Place*. Oxford: Berg, pp. 129–132.

Rilke, R.M. (2000). *Letters to a Young Poet*. Novato, CA: New World Library.

Rioch, M. (1970). The work of Wilfred Bion on groups. *Psychiatry: Journal of the Study of Interpersonal Processes*, 33(1): 56–66. Also in: *British Journal of Medical Psychology*, 33: 56–66.

Robertson, A. (2016). *Edinburgh: Holyrood*. Available from: www.holyrood.com/articles/news/chair-police-scotland-oversight-body-labels-police-officer-target-%E2%80%9Cvery-inflexible [Accessed: February 2016].

Rosenthal, S.A., & Pittinksy, T.L. (2006). Narcissistic leadership. *Leadership Quarterly*, 17: 617–633.

Ryan, R., Weinstein, N., Bernstein, J., Brown, K.W., Mistretta, L., & Gagné, M. (2010). Vitalizing effects of being outdoors and in nature. *Journal of Environmental Psychology*, 30(2): 159–168.

Saxton, J., & Kanemura, R. (2015). [Online]. Available from: www.vcas.org.uk

Schanzer, L. (1990). *Does Meditation-Relaxation Potentiate Psychotherapy?* Psy.D. Diss., Massachusetts School of Professional Psychology.

Schwartz, R. (1995). *Internal Family Systems Therapy*. New York: Guilford Press.

Scotland. Police and Fire Reform Scotland Act. Chapter 1. (2012). *Edinburgh*. Available from: www.legislation.gov.uk/asp/2012/8/section/2/enacted [Accessed: December 2015].

Scott, K. (2014). *The Conversation*. Available from: http://theconversation.com/scotlands-single-police-force-has-had-teething-troubles-but-theres-progress-too-25177 [Accessed: November 2015].

Scottish Legal News. (2015). Scottish Police Authority 'fractured' after board members raise concerns about outgoing chairman. Available from: www.scottishlegal.com/2015/07/20/scottish-police-authority-board-fractured-after-board-members-raise-concerns-about-outgoing-chairman/ [Accessed: December 2015].

Sealy, R., Doldor, E., & Vinnicombe, S. (2016). *The Female FTSE Board Report 2016: Women on Boards: Taking Stock of Where We Are*. Cranfield University School of Management. Available from: www.cranfield.ac.uk/press/news-2016/women-on-boards-ftse-100-company-has-full-gender-balance-for-first-time [Accessed: 11 December 2016].

Shaw, P. (2003). *Changing Conversations in Organisations: A Complexity Approach to Change*. London and New York: Routledge.

Sher, M. (2011) Challenge in the Boardroom, The BVALCO 'Food For Thought Forum' Discussion & Debate For Chairmen, Board Directors And Company Secretariat, p. 8.

Sher, M. (2012). *Gender and the Boardroom. Handout 2.4 of Certificate in Board Dynamics Course*. London: Tavistock Institute of Human Relations.

Sher, M. (2013). *Dynamics of Change: Tavistock Approaches to Improving Social Systems*. London: Karnac Books.

Silver, R. (June 1, 2015). Telephone interview.

Simpson, P., French, R., & Harvey, C. (2002). Leadership and negative capability. *Human Relations*, 55(10): 1209–1226.

Sonnenfeld, J. (September 2002). What makes great boards great. *Harvard Business Review*, pp. 1–10. Available from: https://hbr.org/2002/09/what-makes-great-boards-great [Accessed: 5 December 2016].

SPA/Police Scotland. (2015). *Opinion Survey*. Available from: www.scotland.police.uk/assets/pdf/138327/307421/spa-police-scotland-opinion-survey-2015?view=Standard [Accessed: November 2016].

Spencer Stuart. (2017). *Spencer Stuart U.S. Board Index*. Available from: www.spencerstuart.com/~/media/ssbi2017/ssbi_2017_final.pdf [Accessed: 16 December 2016].

Stacey, R. (2001). Complexity and the group matrix. In: *Group Analysis*. London and Thousand Oaks, CA: Sage, pp. 222–239.

Stapley, L. (2006). *Individuals, Groups and Organizations: Beneath the Surface*. London: Karnac Books.

Stein, M. (2013). When does narcissistic leadership become problematic? Dick Fuld at Lehmann Brothers. *Journal of Management Inquiry*, 22: 282–293.

Stokes, J. (1994a). The unconscious at work in groups and teams: Contributions from the work of Wilfred Bion. In: Obholzer, A., & Roberts, V.Z. (Eds.), *The Unconscious at Work*. London: Routledge, pp. 19–27.

Stokes, J. (1994b). The unconscious at work. The unconscious at work in groups and teams: Contributions from the work of Wilfred Bion. In: Obholzer, A., & Roberts, V.Z. (Eds.), *The Unconscious at Work*. London: Routledge, pp. 56–66.

Stokes, J. (1994c). Institutional chaos and personal stress. In: Obholzer, A., & Roberts, V. (Eds.), *The Unconscious at Work: Individual and Organizational Stress in the Human Services*. London: Routledge, pp. 121–128.

Swiercz, P.M., & Lydon, S.R. (2002). Entrepreneurial leadership in high-tech firms: A field study. *Leadership & Organization Development Journal*, 23(7): 380–389.

Tannenbaum, R., & Schmidt, W. (1958). How to choose a leadership pattern. *Harvard Business Review*, 36.

The Code Steering Group. (October 2010). *Good Governance: A Code for the Voluntary and Community Sector*. London: The Code Founding Group, p. 10.

The Guardian. (2002). Enron's board of directors: Full list of Enron's key decision makers [online]. Available from: www.theguardian.com/business/2002/feb/01/corporatefraud.enron3 [Accessed: 23 January 2017].

The Scotsman. (2017). Those who police the police are failing. Available from: www.scotsman.com/news/opinion/chris-marshall-those-who-police-the-police-are-failing-1-4331213 [Accessed: January 2017].

Third Sector. (2012). *Women Are Underrepresented in Leadership Roles* [Online]. Available from: www.thirdsector.co.uk/women-are-under-represented . . . roles. . . /1131435 [Accessed: 25 May 2015].

Thomas, C., Kidd, D., & Fernández-Aaroz, C. (2007). Are you underutilizing your board? In: *MIT Sloan Management Review* (Winter), pp. 71–78.

Thompson, J. (1967). *Organisations in Action: Social Science Bases of Administrative Theory*. New York: McGraw-Hill.

Tuckett, D. (2011). *Minding the Markets: An Emotional Finance View of Financial Instability*. London: Palgrave Macmillan.

Tuckett, D., & Taffler, R. (2008). Phantastic objects and the financial market's sense of reality: A psychoanalytic contribution to the understanding of stock market instability. *The International Journal of Psychoanalysis*, 89: 389–412.

Ulrich, D. (1996). *Human Resource Champions: The Next Agenda for Adding Value and Delivering Results*. Boston, MA: Harvard Business School Press.

Unwin, J. (2015). *Getting on Board: The Five Ss in Governance* [Online]. Available from: www.gettingonboard.org/news/4585134114/tags/governance [Accessed: 3 December 2018].

Van de Loo, E. (2013). *The Non-Executive Leadership Survey NELS Assessment (Participant Guide)*.

Van der Veer, R. (1996). *The Concept of Culture in Vygotsky's Thinking. Culture and Psychology*, Vol. 2. London, Thousand Oaks, CA, and New Delhi: Sage, pp. 247–263.

Voluntary Sector News (2014). Voluntary Sector Review. [Online]. Available from: www.vssn.org.uk/voluntary-sector-review

Waldrop, M.M. (1992). *Complexity*. New York: Simon & Schuster.

Walker, D. (2009). *A Review of Corporate Governance in UK Banks and Other Financial Industry Entities: Final Recommendations*. London: H.M. Treasury, pp. 139–142.

Weber, M. (1922). The three types of legitimate rule. *Preussische Jahrbücher*, 187: 1–2.

Weber, R.P. (1990). *Basic Content Analysis*, 2nd ed. Beverly Hills, CA: Sage.

Welsh Government (2014). The Well Being of Future Generations (Wales). Act 2015, Welsh Government. Available from: www.gov.wales.

White, R., & Lippit, R. (1953). *Group Dynamics*. White Plains: Rowe and Peterson.

Whitehead, P. (June 5, 2013). Boards are to blame. *Financial Times*.

Wilber, K. (2000). *Integral Psychology: Consciousness, Spirit, Psychology, Therapy*. Boulder, CO: Shambhala.

Winnicott, D.W. (1960). Ego distortions in terms of true and false self. In: *The Maturational Processes and the Facilitating Environment*. In: *The International Psycho-Analytical Library*, 64: 1–276 (1965). London: The Hogarth Press and the Institute of Psycho-Analysis.

Winnicott, D.W. (1965). *The Maturational Processes and the Facilitating Environment*. New York: International Universities Press.

Woods, D. (November 1, 2011). Is a move from HR director to chief executive a bridge too far? *HR Magazine*. Available from: www.hrmagazine.co.uk/article-details/is-a-move-from-hr-director-to-chief-executive-a-bridge-too-far [Accessed: 20 November 2016].

Xpert HR. (2014). What is the gender profile of the UK HR profession in 2014? Available from: www.xperthr.co.uk/blogs/employment-intelligence/2014/01/gender-profile-uk-hr-profession-2014/ [Accessed: 3 December 2016].

Zagier Roberts, V. (1994). The organization of work. In: A. Obholzer & V. Roberts (eds.). *The Unconscious at Work*. London: Routledge, pp. 28–38.

Zenger, J., & Folkman, J. (August 17, 2015). What separates great HR leaders from the rest. *Harvard Business Review*. Available from: https://hbr.org/2015/08/what-separates-great-hr-leaders-from-the-rest [Accessed: 8 December 2016].

Zweig, D. (Winter 2010). The board that couldn't think straight. *The Conference Board Review*, p. 4.

Index

Note: Page numbers in *italics* indicate figures and in **bold** indicate tables on the corresponding pages.